PENGUIN BOOKS

THE ELECTRONIC SWEATSHOP

Barbara Garson is the playwright of *Macbird,* which sold over half a million copies as a book. She is also the author of *All the Livelong Day* and of the plays *Going Co-op, The Department,* and *The Dinosaur Door*. Her articles and stories have appeared in *The New York Times, Los Angeles Times, The Washington Post, The Village Voice, Harper's, McCall's,* and *Mother Jones*. She has received a Guggenheim Fellowship, a National Endowment for the Arts Fellowship, a National Press Club Citation, and an Obie Award.

THE
ELECTRONIC
SWEATSHOP

ooooooooo

How Computers Are
Transforming the
Office of the Future
Into the Factory
of the Past

ooooooooo

BARBARA
GARSON

PENGUIN BOOKS

PENGUIN BOOKS
Published by the Penguin Group
Penguin Books USA Inc.,
375 Hudson Street, New York, New York 10014, U.S.A.
Penguin Books Ltd, 27 Wrights Lane,
London W8 5TZ, England
Penguin Books Australia Ltd, Ringwood,
Victoria, Australia
Penguin Books Canada Ltd, 10 Alcorn Avenue,
Toronto, Ontario, Canada M4V 3B2
Penguin Books (N.Z.) Ltd, 182–190 Wairau Road,
Auckland 10, New Zealand

Penguin Books Ltd, Registered Offices:
Harmondsworth, Middlesex, England

First published in the United States of America by
Simon & Schuster, Inc. 1988
Published in Penguin Books 1989

5 7 9 10 8 6

Portions of this book appeared in a different form in *Mother Jones* magazine.

LIBRARY OF CONGRESS CATALOGING IN PUBLICATION DATA
Garson, Barbara.
The electronic sweatshop: how computers are transforming the
office of the future into the factory of the past/Barbara Garson.
p. cm.
Reprint. Originally published: New York: Simon & Schuster, © 1988.
Bibliography: p.
Includes index.
ISBN 0 14 01.2145 5
1. Office practice—Automation. 2. Business—Data processing.
3. Clerks—Effect of automation on. 4. Professional employees—
Effect of automation on. I. Title.
[HF5548.G37 1989]
331.25—dc20 89–31811

Printed in the United States of America
Set in Galliard
Designed by Beth Tondreau Design

Contents

□ □ □ □ □ □ □ □

Acknowledgments	7
Introduction	9

I. AUTOMATING THE CLERKS — 15

1. McDonald's—We Do It All for You	17
2. With Reservations	40

II. TURNING PROFESSIONALS INTO CLERKS — 71

3. The Automated Social Worker	73
4. The Machine Will See You Now	115
5. The Wall Street Broker: Decline of a Salesman	128
6. Manufactured Advice	155

III. AUTOMATING THE BOSS — 161

7. The Future of Monogamy in the Office	163
8. Electronic Surveillance	205

9. *Piecework Professionals*   225
10. *Command and Control*   237

Conclusion   261
Notes   267
Bibliography   271
Index   275

Acknowledgments

□ □ □ □ □ □ □ □

I'm very grateful to four people who read chapters of *The Electronic Sweatshop* as the book progressed. Del Bowers consistently advised me to let the characters speak for themselves. My editor, Bob Bender, suggested more explanations and persistently pulled them out of me. Erik Wensberg recommended cuts that added elegance of expression. And my agent, Joy Harris, said, "Remember, it's your book."

Warm thanks to members of WOW (Women Office Workers) and everyone else who worked on the play *The Department*.

Thanks to Len for the use of the word processor.

Thanks to Juliet, Frank and my mother.

Finally, thank you to the hundreds of office workers whom I interviewed or worked alongside. They reminded me, by their humanity, that we all deserve something better than the electronic sweatshop.

Introduction

□ □ □ □ □ □ □ □

In the early 1970s I talked to hundreds of people who worked in fish canneries, lumber mills, auto plants and other traditional factories. My book *All the Livelong Day* described the games and gimmicks these workers used to keep from going crazy when their jobs had been reduced to repetitious tasks with no beginning, middle or end.

By the end of the seventies the U.S. work force had tipped from blue to white collar and small computers began to appear on office desks. To professional futurists the office computer heralded a second industrial revolution that would eliminate the routine, monotonous jobs; we would all be transformed into knowledge workers in the postindustrial era.

The first time I used a computer was in 1981 as a data entry clerk. I entered the Office of the Future through a door that led into a windowless basement where dozens of women sat spaced apart, keying with three fingers of one hand. I felt like

Dorothy stepping into Oz, only in this version the movie turned from color to black and white.

There weren't any supervisors in the data room except for one young man in a glass booth who tended the computer and changed our tapes. Yet the women worked nonstop, their fingers flying in a blur as they keyed with one hand and turned little slips of paper with the other. Clearly this work was already as routinized as any assembly line job. But in the factories I'd visited, workers talked, joked, cursed and even yodeled when the supervisor was out of sight. I wondered why my fellow data clerks so rarely stopped to talk or stretch.

Then one night (the data room ran in night and day shifts) the young man in the booth came over to me and said, "If you're going to stay here you'll have to get your productivity up."

I asked what he meant, what my productivity was supposed to be. Sitting at his control panel he played a few "chords" to call up my figures. He could tell, to the second, when I started work, when I took a break to scratch my nose or take a Life Saver, and exactly how many key strokes I'd done all evening. I should have been up to 15,000 keystrokes an hour. I was well below that figure.

In the years since I worked in the basement, I saw office automation rising almost floor by floor to engulf higher and higher strata of white-collar workers. By the mideighties it was clear that the silent, trim executive terminal could track, time and control as relentlessly as the data machine in the basement.

Right now a combination of twentieth-century technology and nineteenth-century scientific management is turning the Office of the Future into the factory of the past. At first this affected clerks and switchboard operators, then secretaries, bank tellers and service workers. The primary targets now are professionals and managers.

The Electronic Sweatshop follows white-collar automation up the occupational ladder from the prototypes—the fast-food burger flipper and the airline reservation clerk—to the stockbroker, the executive and the admiral, as each explains for himself what it feels like when his job is automated. Though this isn't a technical book, the sequence of chapters is designed to clarify general principles of automation.

At McDonald's a tiny computer tells the teenager when to take the potatoes out of the fry vat. At Merrill Lynch an expert system tells the stockbroker exactly how much an individual client should invest in specific securities in order to send three kids through college. (So far the french fry computer is more reliable.) Both these systems were designed to capture the skill and knowledge of the individual griddleman or broker and transfer them to a program. Thereafter the job can be done by workers with less skill and knowledge.

At American Airlines we are able to watch as the two-minute reservation conversation is broken down into a half dozen smaller conversation modules, each of which can be monitored, timed and graded. This helps us to understand what's happening when the more complex interactions of social workers and psychologists are similarly reduced to a series of routine clerical tasks.

In almost all the cases we'll be looking at, the effect is to centralize control and move decision making higher up in the organization.

This was the goal that guided nineteenth-century industrial management. The same principles that transformed craftsmen into factory hands are now being applied to make white-collar workers cheaper to train, easier to replace, less skilled, less expensive and less special.

My aim is to describe this "second industrial revolution" comprehensively, yet I've deliberately eliminated worst cases like the large data entry sweatshops, many of which are now being decentralized or moved overseas. I've tried instead to select locations, industries and automation approaches that are typical of the present and indicative of the future. Procter & Gamble and American Airlines have reputations as decent and concerned employers. Merrill Lynch and McDonald's set the trends in their industries, though they're not wildly experimental. The Defense Advanced Research Projects Agency (DARPA) is in the technological vanguard and influences research nationally. These and the smaller organizations (sometimes unnamed to protect individual employees) suggest what's happening in a broad spectrum of white-collar jobs.

While the companies and job categories were chosen to represent major trends, the individuals I interviewed were largely targets of opportunity. "Hello, your cousin Robin told me you work in a bank." Sometimes I approached strangers on the street as they left work. "I'm writing a book about jobs. Do you work in that office?"

A surprising number agreed to be interviewed with little concern for the consequences. But many others—particularly executives and professionals—were afraid they'd jeopardize their jobs. The policy I adopted was to change the names of everyone I interviewed except for a few very high corporate and government officials who were probably identifiable anyway. After all, what good would it do to say, "John Doe, a former Chairman of the Joint Chiefs of Staff"?

Though their names are changed and some identifying details omitted, and in the case of a Massachusetts social service agency the identity of an individual office has been disguised, the people you're about to meet are not composites. They're real humans speaking in their own words.

□ □ □

I started this research with definite ideas about the industrialization of office work. I was continually surprised, however, at how much further the process had gone than I'd imagined. Extraordinary human ingenuity has been used to eliminate the need for human ingenuity. I can't help but convey admiration for the automaters when I describe the machines and systems they've developed.

I was also repeatedly surprised by the wit and acumen of the people being automated. Of course human intelligence is something I expected to find, but here, too, the details still amazed me.

The one thing I didn't anticipate was the underlying motive. I had assumed that employers automate in order to cut costs. And, indeed, cost cutting is often the result. But I discovered in the course of this research that neither the designers nor the users of the highly centralized technology I was seeing knew much about its costs and benefits, its bottom-line efficiency. The specific form that automation is taking seems to be based less on a rational desire for profit than on an irrational prejudice against people. But this is something I only began to suspect half way through. I'd rather tell the story, beginning at McDonald's, with the hope that if I do it well enough, the reader will understand how these conclusions emerged.

I

□ □ □ □ □ □ □ □

AUTOMATING THE CLERKS

I

□ □ □ □ □ □ □ □

McDonald's—
We Do It All for You

Jason Pratt

"They called us the Green Machine," says Jason Pratt, recently retired McDonald's griddleman, " 'cause the crew had green uniforms then. And that's what it is, a machine. You don't have to know how to cook, you don't have to know how to think. There's a procedure for everything and you just follow the procedures."

"Like?" I asked. I was interviewing Jason in the Pizza Hut across from his old McDonald's.

"Like, uh," the wiry teenager searched for a way to describe the all-encompassing procedures. "O.K., we'll start you off on something simple. You're on the ten-in-one grill, ten patties in a pound. Your basic burger. The guy on the bin calls, 'Six hamburgers.' So you lay your six pieces of meat on the grill and set the timer." Before my eyes Jason conjures up the gleaming, mechanized McDonald's kitchen. "Beep-beep, beep-beep, beep-beep. That's the beeper to sear 'em. It goes off in twenty seconds. Sup, sup, sup, sup, sup, sup." He presses each of the six patties down on the sizzling grill with an imaginary silver disk. "Now you turn off the sear beeper, put the buns in the oven, set the oven timer and then the next beeper is to turn the meat. This one goes beep-beep-beep, beep-beep-beep. So you turn your patties, and then you drop your re-cons on the meat, t-con, t-con, t-con." Here Jason takes two imaginary handfuls of reconstituted onions out of water and sets them out, two blops at a time, on top of the six patties he's arranged in two neat rows on our grill. "Now the bun oven buzzes [there are over a half dozen different timers with distinct beeps and buzzes in a McDonald's kitchen]. "This one turns itself off when you open the oven door so you just take out your crowns, line 'em up and give 'em each a squirt of mustard and a squirt of ketchup." With mustard in his right hand and ketchup in his left, Jason wields the dispensers like a pair of six-shooters up and down the lines of buns. Each dispenser has two triggers. One fires the premeasured squirt for ten-in-ones—the second is set for quarter-pounders.

"Now," says Jason, slowing down, "now you get to put on the pickles. Two if they're regular, three if they're small. That's the creative part. Then the lettuce, then you ask for a cheese count ('cheese on four please'). Finally the last beep goes off and you lay your burger on the crowns."

"On the *crown* of the buns?" I ask, unable to visualize. "On top?"

"Yeah, you dress 'em upside down. Put 'em in the box upside down too. They flip 'em over when they serve 'em."

"Oh, I think I see."

"Then scoop up the heels [the bun bottoms] which are on top of the bun warmer, take the heels with one hand and push the tray out from underneath and they land (plip) one on each burger, right on top of the re-cons, neat and perfect. [The official time allotted by Hamburger Central, the McDonald's headquarters in Oak Brook, Ill, is ninety seconds to prepare and serve a burger.] It's like I told you. The procedures makes the burgers. You don't have to know a thing."

□   □   □

McDonald's employs 500,000 teenagers at any one time. Most don't stay long. About 8 million Americans—7 per cent of our labor force—have worked at McDonald's and moved on.[1] Jason is not a typical ex-employee. In fact, Jason is a legend among the teenagers at the three McDonald's outlets in his suburban area. It seems he was so fast at the griddle (or maybe just fast talking) that he'd been taken back three times by two different managers after quitting.

But Jason became a real legend in his last stint at McDonald's. He'd been sent out the back door with the garbage, but instead of coming back in he got into a car with two friends and just drove away. That's the part the local teenagers love to tell. "No fight with the manager or anything . . . just drove away and never came back. . . . I don't think they'd give him a job again."

□   □   □

"I would never go back to McDonald's," says Jason. "Not even as a manager." Jason is enrolled at the local junior college. "I'd like to run a real restaurant someday, but I'm taking data processing to fall back on." He's had many part-time jobs, the highest-paid at a hospital ($4.00 an hour), but that didn't last, and now dishwashing (at the $3.35 minimum). "Same as McDonald's. But I would never go back there. You're a complete robot."

"It seems like you can improvise a little with the onions," I suggested. "They're not premeasured." Indeed, the reconstituted onion shreds grabbed out of a container by the unscientific-looking wet handful struck me as oddly out of character in the McDonald's kitchen.

"There's supposed to be twelve onion bits per patty," Jason informed me. "They spot check."

"Oh come on."

"You think I'm kiddin'. They lift your heels and they say, 'You got too many onions.' It's portion control."

"Is there any freedom anywhere in the process?" I asked.

"Lettuce. They'll leave you alone as long as it's neat."

"So lettuce is freedom; pickles is judgment?"

"Yeah but you don't have time to play around with your pickles. They're never gonna say just six pickles except on the disk. [Each store has video disks to train the crew for each of about twenty work stations, like fries, register, lobby, quarter-pounder grill.] What you'll hear in real life is 'twelve and six on a turn-lay.' The first number is your hamburgers, the second is your Big Macs. On a turn-lay means you lay the first twelve, then you put down the second batch after you turn the first. So you got twenty-four burgers on the grill, in shifts. It's what they call a production mode. And remember you also got your fillets, your McNuggets. . . ."

"Wait, slow down." By then I was losing track of the patties on our imaginary grill. "I don't understand this turn-lay thing."

"Don't worry, you don't have to understand. You follow the beepers, you follow the buzzers and you turn your meat as fast as you can. It's like I told you, to work at McDonald's you don't need a face, you don't need a brain. You need to have two hands and two legs and move 'em as fast as you can. That's the whole system. I wouldn't go back there again for anything."

June Sanders

McDonald's french fries are deservedly the pride of their menu; uniformly golden brown all across America and in thirty-one other countries. However, it's difficult to standardize the number of fries per serving. The McDonald's fry scoop, perhaps their greatest technological innovation, helps to control this variable. The unique flat funnel holds the bag open while it aligns a limited number of fries so that they fall into the package with a paradoxically free, overflowing cornucopia look.

Despite the scoop, there's still a spread. The acceptable fry yield is 400 to 420 servings per 100 lb. bag of potatoes. It's one of the few areas of McDonald's cookery in which such a range is possible. The fry yield is therefore one important measure of a manager's efficiency. "Fluffy, not stuffy," they remind the young workers when the fry yield is running low.

No such variation is possible in the browning of the fries. Early in McDonald's history Louis Martino, the husband of the secretary of McDonald's founder Ray Kroc, designed a computer to be submerged in the fry vats. In his autobiography, *Grinding It Out,* Kroc explained the importance of this innovation. "We had a .recipe . . . that called for pulling the potatoes out of the oil when they got a certain color and grease bubbles formed in a certain way. It was amazing that we got them as uniform as we did because each kid working the fry vats would have his own interpretation of the proper color and so forth. [The word "kid" was officially replaced by "person" or "crew person" in McDonald's management vocabulary in 1973 in response to union organizing attempts.] Louis's computer took all the guesswork out of it, modifying the frying to suit the balance of water to solids in a given batch of potatoes. He also engineered the dispenser that allowed us to squirt exactly the right amount of catsup and mustard onto our premeasured hamburger patties. . . ."

The fry vat probe is a complex miniature computer. The fry scoop, on the other hand, is as simple and almost as elegant as the wheel. Both eliminate the need for a human being to make "his own interpretation," as Ray Kroc puts it.

Together, these two innovations mean that a new worker can be trained in fifteen minutes and reach maximum efficiency in a half hour. This makes it economically feasible to use a kid for one day and replace him with another kid the next day.

June Sanders worked at McDonald's for one day.

"I needed money, so I went in and the manager told me my hours would be 4 to 10 P.M." This was fine with June, a well-organized black woman in her early twenties who goes to college full time.

"But when I came in the next day the manager said I could work till 10 for that one day. But from then on my hours would be 4 P.M. to 1 A.M. And I really wouldn't get off at 1 because I'd have to stay to clean up after they closed. . . . Yes it was the same manager, a Mr. O'Neil.

"I told him I'd have to check first with my family if I could come home that late. But he told me to put on the uniform and fill out the forms. He would start me out on french fries.

"Then he showed me an orientation film on a TV screen all about fries. . . . No, I still hadn't punched in. This was all in the basement. Then I went upstairs, and *then* I punched in and went to work. . . . No, I was not paid for the training downstairs. Yes, I'm sure."

I asked June if she had had any difficulty with the fries.

"No, it was just like the film. You put the french fries in the grease and you push a button which doesn't go off till the fries are done. Then you take them out and put them in a bin under a light. Then you scoop them into the bags with this thing, this flat, light metal—I can't really describe it—scoop thing that sits right in the package and makes the fries fall in place."

"Did they watch you for a while?" I asked. "Did you need more instruction?"

"Someone leaned over once and showed me how to make

sure the fry scooper was set inside the opening of the bag so the fries would fall in right."

"And then?"

"And then, I stood on my feet from twenty after four till the manager took over my station at 10:35 P.M.

"When I left my legs were aching. I knew it wasn't a job for me. But I probably would have tried to last it out—at least more than a day—if it wasn't for the hours. When I got home I talked it over with my mother and my sister and then I phoned and said I couldn't work there. They weren't angry. They just said to bring back the uniform. . . . The people were nice, even the managers. It's just a rushed system."

"June," I said, "does it make any sense to train you and have you work for one day? Why didn't he tell you the real hours in the first place?"

"They take a chance and see if you're desperate. I have my family to stay with. That's why I didn't go back. But if I really needed the money, like if I had a kid and no family, I'd have to make arrangements to work any hours.

"Anyway, they got a full day's work out of me."

Damita

I waited on line at my neighborhood McDonald's. It was lunch hour and there were four or five customers at each of the five open cash registers. "May I take your order?" a very thin girl said in a flat tone to the man at the head of my line.

"McNuggets, large fries and a Coke," said the man. The cashier punched in the order. "That will be—".

"Big Mac, large fries and a shake," said the next woman on line. The cashier rang it up.

"Two cheeseburgers, large fries and a coffee," said the third customer. The cashier rang it up.

"How much is a large fries?" asked the woman directly in front of me.

The thin cashier twisted her neck around trying to look up at the menu board.

"Sorry," apologized the customer, "I don't have my glasses."

"Large fries is seventy-nine," a round-faced cashier with glasses interjected from the next register.

"Seventy-nine cents," the thin cashier repeated.

"Well how much is a *small* fries?"

As they talked I leaned over the next register. "Say, can I interview you?" I asked the clerk with glasses, whose line was by then empty.

"Huh?"

"I'm writing a story about jobs at fast-food restaurants."

"O.K. I guess so."

"Can I have your phone number?"

"Well . . . I'll meet you when I get off. Should be sometime between 4 and 4:30."

By then it was my turn.

"Just a large fries," I said.

The thin cashier pressed "lge fries." In place of numbers, the keys on a McDonald's cash register say "lge fries," "reg fries," "med coke," big mac," and so on. Some registers have pictures on the key caps. The next time the price of fries goes up (or down) the change will be entered in the store's central computer. But the thin cashier will continue to press the same button. I wondered how long she'd worked there and how many hundreds of "lge fries" she'd served without learning the price.

□ □ □

Damita, the cashier with the glasses, came up from the crew room (a room in the basement with lockers, a table and a video player for studying the training disks) at 4:45. She looked older and more serious without her striped uniform.

"Sorry, but they got busy and, you know, here you get off when they let you."

The expandable schedule was her first complaint. "You give them your availability when you sign on. Mine I said 9 to 4. But they scheduled me for 7 o'clock two or three days a week. And I needed the money. So I got to get up 5 in the morning to get here from Queens by 7. And I don't get off till whoever's supposed to get here gets here to take my place. . . . It's hard to study with all the pressures."

Damita had come to the city from a small town outside of Detroit. She lives with her sister in Queens and takes extension courses in psychology at New York University. Depending on the schedule posted each Friday, her McDonald's paycheck for a five-day week has varied from $80 to $114.

"How long have you worked at McDonald's?" I asked.

"Well, see I only know six people in this city, so my manager from Michigan . . . yeah, I worked for McDonald's in high school . . . my manager from Michigan called this guy Brian who's the second assistant manager here. So I didn't have to fill out an application. Well, I mean the first thing I needed was a job," she seemed to apologize, "and I knew I could always work at McDonald's. I always say I'm gonna look for something else, but I don't get out till 4 and that could be 5 or whenever."

The flexible scheduling at McDonald's only seems to work one way. One day Damita had arrived a half hour late because the E train was running on the R track.

"The assistant manager told me not to clock in at all, just to go home. So I said O.K. and I left."

"What did you do the rest of the day?" I asked.

"I went home and studied, and I went to sleep."

"But how did it make you feel?"

"It's like a humiliating feeling 'cause I wasn't given any chance to justify myself. But when I spoke to the Puerto Rican manager he said it was nothing personal against me. Just it was raining that day, and they were really slow and someone who got here on time, it wouldn't be right to send them home."

"Weren't you annoyed to spend four hours traveling and then lose a day's pay?" I suggested.

"I was mad at first that they didn't let me explain. But afterwards I understood and I tried to explain to my sister: 'Time waits for no man.' "

"Since you signed on for 9 to 4," I asked Damita, "and you're going to school, why can't you say, 'Look, I have to study at night, I need regular hours'?"

"Don't work that way. They make up your schedule every week and if you can't work it, you're responsible to replace yourself. If you can't they can always get someone else."

"But Damita," I tried to argue with her low estimate of her own worth, "anyone can see right away that your line moves fast yet you're helpful to people. I mean, you're a valuable employee. And this manager seems to like you."

"Valuable! $3.35 an hour. And I can be replaced by any [pointing across the room] kid off the street." I hadn't noticed. At a small table under the staircase a manager in a light beige shirt was taking an application from a lanky black teenager.

"But you know the register. You know the routine."

"How long you think it takes to learn the six steps? Step 1. Greet the customer, 'Good morning, can I help you?' Step 2. Take his order. Step 3. Repeat the order. They can have someone off the street working my register in five minutes."

"By the way," I asked, "on those cash registers without numbers, how do you change something after you ring it up? I mean if somebody orders a cheeseburger and then they change it to a hamburger, how do you subtract the slice of cheese?"

"I guess that's why you have step 3, repeat the order. One cheeseburger, two Cokes, three . . ."

"Yeah but if you punched a mistake or they don't want it after you get it together?"

"Like if I have a crazy customer, which I do be gettin' 'specially in this city, and they order hamburger, fries and shake, and it's $2.95 and then they just walk away?"

"I once did that here," I said. "About a week ago when I first started my research. All I ordered was some french fries. And I was so busy watching how the computer works that only after she rang it up I discovered that I'd walked out of my house without my wallet. I didn't have a penny. I was so embarrassed."

"Are you that one the other day? Arnetta, this girl next to me, she said, 'Look at that crazy lady going out. She's lookin' and lookin' at everything and then she didn't have no money for a bag of fries.' I saw you leaving, but I guess I didn't recognize you. [I agreed it was probably me.] O.K., so say this crazy lady comes in and orders french fries and leaves. In Michigan I could just zero it out. I'd wait till I start the next order and press zero and large fries. But here you're supposed to call out 'cancel sale' and the manager comes over and does it with his key.

"But I hate to call the manager every time, 'specially if I got a whole line waiting. So I still zero out myself. They can tell I do it by the computer tape, and they tell me not to. Some of them let me, though, because they know I came from another store. But they don't show the girls here how to zero out. Everybody thinks you need the manager's key to do it."

"Maybe they let you because they can tell you're honest," I said. She smiled, pleased, but let it pass. "That's what I mean that you're valuable to them. You know how to use the register. You're good with customers."

"You know there was a man here," Damita said, a little embarrassed about bragging, "when I was transferred off night he asked my manager, 'What happened to that girl from Michigan?' "

"Did your manager tell you that?"

"No, another girl on the night shift told me. The manager said it to her. They don't tell you nothing nice themselves."

"But, see, you are good with people and he appreciates it."

"In my other McDonald's—not the one where they let me zero out but another one I worked in in Michigan—I was almost fired for my attitude. Which was helping customers who had arthritis to open the little packets. And another bad attitude of mine is that you're supposed to suggest to the customer, 'Would you like a drink with that?' or 'Do you want a pie?'—whatever they're pushing. I don't like to do it. And they can look on my tape after my shift and see I didn't push the suggested sell item."

McDonald's computerized cash registers allow managers to determine immediately not only the dollar volume for the store but the amount of each item that was sold at each register for any given period. Two experienced managers, interviewed separately, both insisted that the new electronic cash registers were in fact slower than the old mechanical registers. Clerks who knew the combinations—hamburger, fries, Coke: $2.45—could ring up the total immediately, take the cash and give change in one operation. On the new registers you have to enter each item and may be slowed down by computer response time. The value of the new registers, or at least their main selling point (McDonald's franchisers can choose from several approved registers), is the increasingly sophisticated tracking systems, which monitor all the activity and report with many different statistical breakdowns.

"Look, there." said Damita as the teenage job applicant left and the manager went behind the counter with the application, "If I was to say I can't come in at 7, they'd cut my hours down to one shift a week, and if I never came back they wouldn't call to find out where I was.

"I worked at a hospital once as an X-ray assistant. There if I didn't come in there were things that had to be done that wouldn't be done. I would call there and say, 'Remember to run the EKGs.' Here, if I called and said, 'I just can't come by 7 no more,' they'd have one of these high school kids off the street half an hour later. And they'd do my job just as good."

Damita was silent for a while and then she made a difficult plea. "This might sound stupid, I don't know," she said, "but I feel like, I came here to study and advance myself but I'm not excelling myself in any way. I'm twenty years old but—this sounds terrible to say—I'm twenty but I'd rather have a babysitting job. At least I could help a kid and take care. But I only know six people in this city. So I don't even know how I'd find a babysitting job."

"I'll keep my ears open," I said. "I don't know where I'd hear of one but . . ."

Damita seemed a little relieved. I suppose she realized there wasn't much chance of babysitting full-time, but at least she now knew seven people in the city.

Jon DeAngelo

Jon DeAngelo, twenty-two, has been a McDonald's manager for three years. He started in the restaurant business at sixteen as a busboy and planned even then to run a restaurant of his own someday. At nineteen, when he was the night manager of a resort kitchen, he was hired away by McOpCo, the McDonald's Operating Company.

Though McDonald's is primarily a franchise system, the company also owns and operates about 30 percent of the stores directly. These McOpCo stores, including some of the busiest units, are managed via a chain of command including regional supervisors, store managers and first and second assistants who can be moved from unit to unit. In addition, there's a network of inspectors from Hamburger Central who make announced and unannounced checks for QSC (quality, service, cleanliness) at both franchise and McOpCo installations.

Jon was hired at $14,000 a year. At the time I spoke with him his annual pay was $21,000—a very good salary at McDonald's. At first he'd been an assistant manager in one of the highest-volume stores in his region. Then he was deliberately transferred to a store with productivity problems.

"I got there and found it was really a great crew. They hated being hassled, but they loved to work. I started them having fun by putting the men on the women's jobs and vice versa. [At most McDonald's the women tend to work on the registers, the men on the grill. But everyone starts at the same pay.] Oh, sure, they hated it at first, the guys that is. But they liked learning all the stations. I also ran a lot of register races."

Since the computer tape in each register indicates sales per hour, per half hour or for any interval requested, the manager can revv the crew up for a real "on your mark, get set, go!" race with a printout ready as they cross the finish line, showing the dollars taken in at each register during the race.

The computer will also print out a breakdown of sales for any particular menu item. The central office can check, therefore, how many Egg McMuffins were sold on Friday from 9 to 9:30 two weeks or two years ago, either in the entire store or at any particular register.

This makes it possible to run a register race limited to Cokes for instance, or Big Macs. Cashiers are instructed to try suggestive selling ("Would you like a drink with that?") at all times. But there are periods when a particular item is being pushed. The manager may then offer a prize for the most danish sold.

A typical prize for either type of cash register race might be a Snoopy mug (if that's the current promotion) or even a $5 cash bonus.

"This crew loved to race as individuals," says Jon of his troubled store, "but even more as a team. They'd love to get on a production mode, like a chicken-pull-drop or a burger-turn-lay and kill themselves for a big rush.

"One Saturday after a rock concert we did a $1,900 hour with ten people on crew. We killed ourselves but when the rush was over everyone said it was the most fun they ever had in a McDonald's."

I asked Jon how managers made up their weekly schedule. How would he decide who and how many to assign?

"It comes out of the computer," Jon explained. "It's a bar graph with the business you're going to do that week already printed in."

"The business you're *going* to do, already printed in?"

"It's based on the last week's sales, like maybe you did a $300 hour on Thursday at 3 P.M. Then it automatically adds a certain percent, say 15 percent, which is the projected annual increase for your particular store. . . . No, the person scheduling doesn't have to do any of this calculation. I just happen to know how it's arrived at. Really, it's simple, it's just a graph with the numbers already in it. $400 hour, $500 hour. According to Hamburger Central you schedule two crew members per $100 hour. So if you're projected for a $600 hour on Friday between 1 and 2, you know you need twelve crew for that lunch hour and the schedule sheet leaves space for their names."

"You mean you just fill in the blanks on the chart?"

"It's pretty automatic except in the case of a special event like the concert. Then you have to guess the dollar volume. Scheduling under could be a problem, but over would be a disaster to your crew labor productivity."

"Crew labor productivity?"

"Everything at McDonald's is based on the numbers. But

crew labor productivity is pretty much *the* number a manager is judged by."

"Crew labor productivity? You have to be an economist."

"It's really simple to calculate. You take the total crew labor dollars paid out, divide that into the total food dollars taken in. That gives you your crew labor productivity. The more food you sell and the less people you use to do it, the better your percentage. It's pretty simple."

Apparently, I still looked confused.

"For example, if you take an $800 hour and you run it with ten crew you get a very high crew labor percent."

"That's good?"

"Yes that's good. Then the manager in the next store hears Jon ran a 12 percent labor this week, I'll run a 10 percent labor. Of course you burn people out that way. But . . ."

"But Jon," I asked, "if the number of crew you need is set in advance and printed by the computer, why do so many managers keep changing hours and putting pressure on kids to work more?"

"They advertise McDonald's as a flexible work schedule for high school and college kids," he said, "but the truth is it's a high-pressure job, and we have so much trouble keeping help, especially in fast stores like my first one (it grossed $1.8 million last year), that 50 percent never make it past two weeks. And a lot walk out within two days.

"When I was a first assistant, scheduling and hiring was my responsibility and I had to fill the spots one way or another. There were so many times I covered the shifts myself. Times I worked 100 hours a week. A manager has to fill the spaces on his chart somehow. So if a crew person is manipulable they manipulate him."

"What do you mean?"

"When you first sign on, you give your availability. Let's say a person's schedule is weeknights, 4 to 10. But after a week the manager schedules him as a closer Friday night.

He calls in upset, 'Hey, my availability isn't Friday night.' The manager says 'Well the schedule is already done. And you know the rule. If you can't work it's up to you to replace yourself.' At that point the person might quit, or he might not show up or he might have a fight with the manager."

"So he's fired?"

"No. You don't fire. You would only fire for cause like drugs or stealing. But what happens is he signed up for thirty hours a week and suddenly he's only scheduled for four. So either he starts being more available or he quits."

"Aren't you worried that the most qualified people will quit?"

"The only qualification to be able to do the job is to be able physically to do the job. I believe it says that in almost those words in my regional manual. And being there is the main part of being physically able to do the job."

"But what about your great crew at the second store? Don't you want to keep a team together?"

"Let me qualify that qualification. It takes a special kind of person to be able to move before he can think. We find people like that and use them till they quit."

"But as a manager don't you look bad if too many people are quitting?"

"As a manager I am judged by the statistical reports which come off the computer. Which basically means my crew labor productivity. What else can I really distinguish myself by? I could have a good fry yield, a low M&R [Maintenance and Repair budget]. But these are minor."

As it happens, Jon is distinguished among McDonald's managers in his area as an expert on the computerized equipment. Other managers call on him for cash register repairs. "They say, 'Jon, could you look at my register? I just can't afford the M&R this month.' So I come and fix it and they'll buy me a beer."

"So keeping M&R low is a real feather in a manager's cap," I deduced.

"O.K., it's true, you can over spend your M&R budget; you can have a low fry yield; you can run a dirty store; you can be fired for bothering the high school girls. But basically, every Coke spigot is monitored. [At most McDonald's, Coke doesn't flow from taps that turn on and off. Instead the clerk pushes the button "sm," "med" or "lge," which then dispenses the premeasured amount into the appropriate-size cup. This makes the syrup yield fairly consistent.] Every ketchup squirt is measured. My costs for every item are set. So my crew labor productivity is my main flexibility."

I was beginning to understand the pressures toward pettiness. I had by then heard many complaints about slight pilferage of time. For instance, as a safety measure no one was allowed to stay in a store alone. There was a common complaint that a closer would be clocked out when he finished cleaning the store for the night, even though he might be required to wait around unpaid till the manager finished his own nightly statistical reports. At other times kids clocked out and then waited hours (unpaid) for a crew chief training course (unpaid).

Overtime is an absolute taboo at McDonald's. Managers practice every kind of scheduling gymnastic to see that no one works over forty hours a week. If a crew member approaching forty hours is needed to close the store, he or she might be asked to check out for a long lunch. I had heard of a couple of occasions when, in desperation, a manager scheduled someone to stay an hour or two over forty hours. Instead of paying time-and-a-half, he compensated at straight time listing the extra hours as miscellaneous and paying through a fund reserved for things like register race bonuses. All of this of course to make his statistics look good.

"There must be some other way to raise your productivity," I suggested, "besides squeezing it out of the kids."

"I try to make it fun," Jon pleaded earnestly. "I know that people like to work on my shifts. I have the highest crew labor productivity in the area. But I get that from burning people out. Look, you can't squeeze a McDonald's hamburger any flatter. If you want to improve your productivity there is nothing for a manager to squeeze but the crew."

"But if it's crew dollars paid out divided by food dollars taken in, maybe you can bring in more dollars instead of using less crew."

"O.K., let me tell you about sausage sandwiches."

"Sausage sandwiches?" (Sounded awful.)

"My crew was crazy about sausage sandwiches. [Crew members are entitled to one meal a day at reduced prices. The meals are deducted from wages through a computerized link to the time clocks.] They made it from a buttered English muffin, a slice of sausage and a slice of cheese. I understand this had actually been a menu item in some parts of the country but never here. But the crew would make it for themselves and then all their friends came in and wanted them.

"So, I decided to go ahead and sell it. It costs about 9¢ to make and I sold it for $1.40. It went like hotcakes. My supervisor even liked the idea because it made so much money. You could see the little dollar signs in his eyes when he first came into the store. And he said nothing. So we kept selling it.

"Then someone came from Oak Brook and they made us stop it.

"Just look how ridiculous that is. A slice of sausage is 60¢ as a regular menu item, and an English muffin is 45¢. So if you come in and ask for a sausage and an English muffin I can still sell them to you today for $1.05. But there's no way I can add the slice of cheese and put it in the box and get that $1.40.

"Basically, I can't be any more creative than a crew person. I can't take any more initiative then the person on the register."

"Speaking of cash registers and initiative," I said . . . and told him about Damita. I explained that she was honest, bright and had learned how to zero out at another store. "Do you let cashiers zero out?" I asked.

"I might let her in this case," Jon said. "The store she learned it at was probably a franchise and they were looser. But basically we don't need people like her. Thinking generally slows this operation down.

"When I first came to McDonald's, I said, 'How mechanical! These kids don't even know how to cook.' But the pace is so fast that if they didn't have all the systems, you couldn't handle it. It takes ninety seconds to cook a hamburger. In those seconds you have to toast the buns, dress it, sear it, turn it, take it off the grill and serve it. Meanwhile you've got maybe twenty-four burgers, plus your chicken, your fish. You haven't got time to pick up a rack of fillet and see if it's done. You have to press the timer, drop the fish and know, without looking, that when it buzzes it's done.

"It's the same thing with management. You have to record the money each night before you close and get it to the bank the next day by 11 A.M. So you have to trust the computer to do a lot of the job. These computers also calculate the payrolls, because they're hooked into the time clocks. My payroll is paid out of a bank in Chicago. The computers also tell you how many people you're going to need each hour. It's so fast that the manager hasn't got time to think about it. He has to follow the procedures like the crew. And if he follows the procedures everything is going to come out more or less as it's supposed to. So basically the computer manages the store."

Listening to Jon made me remember what Ray Kroc had written about his own job (head of the corporation) and computers:

We have a computer in Oak Brook that is designed to make real estate surveys. But those printouts are of no use to me.

After we find a promising location, I drive around it in a car, go into the corner saloon and the neighborhood supermarket. I mingle with the people and observe their comings and goings. That tells me what I need to know about how a McDonald's store would do there."[2]

By combining twentieth-century computer technology with ninetenth-century time-and-motion studies, the McDonald's corporation has broken the jobs of griddleman, waitress, cashier and even manager down into small, simple steps. Historically these have been service jobs involving a lot of flexibility and personal flair. But the corporation has systematically extracted the decision-making elements from filling french fry boxes or scheduling staff. They've siphoned the know-how from the employees into the programs. They relentlessly weed out all variables that might make it necessary to make a decision at the store level, whether on pickles or on cleaning procedures.

It's interesting and understandable that Ray Kroc refused to work that way. The real estate computer may be as reliable as the fry vat probe. But as head of the company Kroc didn't have to surrender to it. He'd let the computer juggle all the demographic variables, but in the end Ray Kroc would decide, intuitively, where to put the next store.

Jon DeAngelo, would like to work that way, too. So would Jason, June and Damita. If they had a chance to use some skill or intuition at their own levels, they'd not only feel more alive, they'd also be treated with more consideration. It's job organization, not malice, that allows (almost requires) McDonald's workers to be handled like paper plates. They feel disposable because they are.

I was beginning to wonder why Jon stayed on at McDonald's. He still yearned to open a restaurant. "The one thing I'd take from McDonald's to a French restaurant of my own is the fry vat computer. It really works." He seemed to have both the diligence and the style to run a personalized restaurant. Of course he may not have had the capital.

"So basically I would tell that girl [bringing me back to Damita] to find a different job. She's thinking too much and it slows things down. The way the system is set up, I don't need that in a register person, and they don't need it in me."

"Jon," I said, trying to be tactful, "I don't exactly know why you stay at McDonald's."

"As a matter of fact, I have already turned in my resignation."

"You mean you're not a McDonald's manager any more?" I was dismayed.

"I quit once before and they asked me to stay."

"I have had such a hard time getting a full-fledged manager to talk to me and now I don't know whether you count."

"They haven't actually accepted my resignation yet. You know I heard of this guy in another region who said he was going to leave and they didn't believe him. They just wouldn't accept his resignation. And you know what he did? One day, at noon, he just emptied the store, walked out, and locked the door behind him."

For a second Jon seemed to drift away on that beautiful image. It was like the kids telling me about Jason, the crewman who just walked out the back door.

"You know what that means to close a McDonald's at noon, to do a zero hour at lunch?"

"Jon," I said. "This has been fantastic. You are fantastic. I don't think anyone could explain the computers to me the way you do. But I want to talk to someone who's happy and moving up in the McDonald's system. Do you think you could introduce me to a manager who . . ."

"You won't be able to."

"How come?"

"First of all, there's the media hotline. If any press comes around or anyone is writing a book I'm supposed to call the regional office immediately and they will provide someone to talk to you. So you can't speak to a real corporation person except by arrangement with the corporation.

"Second, you can't talk to a happy McDonald's manager because 98 percent are miserable.

"Third of all, there is no such thing as a McDonald's manager. The computer manages the store."

2

□ □ □ □ □ □ □ □

With Reservations

Neither the managers nor the griddlemen at McDonald's have to know much about restaurants, bookkeeping or food. The clerks don't have to know the prices or even how to add.

For McDonald's and other fast-food chains, it's the perfect way to use their undereducated, undermotivated high-turnover help. Because no one's going to stay around very long, the company designs a system with little to learn. Since there's little to learn they invest only a few minutes breaking in new help. So there's no need to make the job pleasant or pay much above minimum wage. Of course, that leads to even higher turnover, but the employer is prepared for high turnover because the job is designed to use undereducated, undermotivated, high-turnover . . . etc. It's a vicious circle, eventually producing a labor force fit for McDonald's.

Of course there are still a few people doing extraordinary planning at the center to design a system that requires so little thinking everywhere else. Indeed, it's amazing that Mc-

Donald's was able to devise a kitchen that operates almost as automatically as a factory.

Traditionally the short-order cook was a skilled, sassy, idiosyncratic character—almost the exact opposite of the fast-food stereotype. It was difficult to break his job down into precise, repetitive motions, first because there were so many items on the menu, which could be ordered with so many variations. Second, it was hard to make griddle work as routine as assembly line work because food is more idiosyncratic than bolts. The old-fashioned griddleman had to watch, smell and listen, to know when the burger was sizzling, the steak medium-rare, the hash browns crisp.

McDonald's deliberately set out to eliminate these elements of skill and discretion by making the burger as standard as a bolt. They succeeded. Their uniform patty and pickle chip make it possible to assemble a sandwich in almost the same way you assemble a clock or a toaster.

McDonald's standardized the job by standardizing the raw material. But what happens when the raw material is a conversation? If a french fry is more complicated than a fender, just think how unpredictable a conversation is compared to a fried egg or even a soufflé.

Until recently, airline reservation agents have been high-paid, long-term employees. They were valued because they had to learn all the company's routes, fares and policies. Then they had to apply this knowledge while responding on the telephone to the thousands of turns that even the simplest conversation can take. It seemed that this would always involve a great deal of personal judgment. After all, a two-way conversation isn't made out of interchangeable parts.

But in a feat of standardization even more phenomenal than McDonald's fry vat computer, the airlines have found ways to break down human conversation into predictable modules that can be handled almost as routinely as a bolt or a burger.

This has already downgraded reservation work. And as I

listened to airline reservation agents I slowly realized that something more than their job was being simplified.

I met young people like Kenny at American Airlines, who explained the dozens of ways in which the two-minute reservation conversation was now timed and graded. Kenny, a new and enthusiastic employee, told me that he liked the work, despite its stresses, because he liked being "involved with people." This modern young man seemed to have no idea that involvement had once meant something far more spontaneous than what he now did.

I also met many reservation agents (most of them older) who understood how their own responses were being streamlined, and they resisted. They would have followed company instructions for assembling a car, I believe, but assembling a conversation was somehow different.

Only a few people fear that they will lose their individuality by wearing mass-produced clothing or eating mass-produced food. (Big Macs and Levis may be America's greatest inventions.) But manufactured words are something else. (Somehow, it seems that when they standardize my conversation they standardize the real me.)

Yet the automation of conversation is just an extension of factory or fast-food automation: first the bolt, then the burger, then the word.

In later chapters we'll see far more complex conversations about psychology, finance and welfare similarly reduced to standard interchangeable inputs, with the result that psychologists, financial planners and social workers are reduced from professionals to clerks. I wouldn't have believed it possible if I hadn't seen, in detail, how conversation was automated at the airlines.

Kenny

"6:30?," I said. "Perfect. I'll meet you in the lobby. I'm real short—four-eleven—and I'll wear a pink sweater."

It had taken four weeks to find an airline reservation agent who would talk to me. I think the problem was some union organizing in the industry, which was making people cautious. But then a theatre acquaintance gave me Kenny's number, and he agreed immediately. He even suggested we meet in the company lobby.

□   □   □

I shouldn't have stopped back for my messages before 6:30. "Sorry," said Kenny's voice on the answering machine, "last minute change. Maybe I'll see you the next time you're back in Hartford."

"So, they're on to me here already!" The reservation agents at American Airlines are supposed to check the electronic bulletin board in the computer each day for important messages.

"TO ALL PERSONNEL: [I imagined it flickering on a gray-green screen] ON NO ACCOUNT SPEAK TO A SMALL WOMAN IN A PINK SWEATER."

I wondered if the ban was industrywide.

I decided to show up in the lobby at 6:30 anyway. Perhaps when he sees me . . .

Six-one with curly hair wasn't much to go on. If he had really been avoiding me, he could have walked right past, but he stopped. "Oh, you must be . . . I left you a message." His grandmother was sick. That's why he wouldn't be able to make it for dinner. But, sure, we could reschedule. Why not? "Thursday is my day off this week." He even offered me a lift to make up for the inconvenience.

In the brief ride Kenny told me he'd been working at American for "Let's see, it's a year now. I'm just passing my probation."

"I thought the probation period was six months."

"Yes, but I was laid off shortly after I was hired. They had overestimated their manning need." But Kenny was resilient. "You get used to collecting unemployment when you work in the theater."

And he loved the job. "Reservations is a lot like acting. Eight hours a day you're on with the public. You have to be lively, you have to try to sell, you have to be turned on all day. That's what I really love about it.

"The only thing I don't like is the low pay. I make less here than in the theater."

"Less than in the theater?!"

"It's pretty low."

"I heard about that offer of a full year's severance pay," I said. (Both United and American had offered a full year's pay to anyone with seniority who would quit. Until recently, long-term, loyal employees had been considered desirable. Some of the senior agents made as much as $15 an hour.) "I guess they did it to take new people on at much lower salaries," I sympathized.

"Those older people," Kenny inveighed, "some of them were sitting there just racking up those high hourly salaries, while there's plenty of us out there who truly want to work for an airline."

"What exactly are you making?"

"$5.77 an hour. It's just an entry-level position. If I came in now I'd have to start in telemarketing at $4 an hour. [American had begun to do telephone soliciting for other companies. This $4-an-hour phone job was now the apprenticeship into reservations.] I don't intend to stay in reservations my whole life. I'd like to work at the airport, maybe be a flight attendant. This company has a lot of mobility. I could work anywhere in the country and still work for American."

"And there's the flight benefits," I reminded him.

"Yes." Kenny concurred. "That's definitely one of the main attractions."

We agreed to meet for brunch on Thursday.

□ □ □

"There's AHU, that's After Hang Up time. It's supposed to be fourteen seconds. It just came down to thirteen. But my average is five seconds AHU, because I do most of the work while the customer's still on the phone. There's your talk time, your availability, your occupancy—that's the percent of time you're plugged in, which is supposed to be 98 percent. That's not the same as your availability. There's bookings. You're supposed to book 26 percent of your calls, which is very low. I've averaged 37 percent in the five months I've been here."

Kenny was explaining the computer-collected statistics on which his first raise would be based. Raises currently ranged from 2 to 7 percent. The exact rate depended on how many of the numerical standards, for AHU, talk time, occupancy and so on, you met or exceeded.

"One of the big numbers up to now is conversion rate." I'd never heard of a conversion rate.

"Every call is either action or potential," Kenny explained.

"If someone calls up and says, 'Hi, I want to go to L.A. first class,' that's action. There's nothing I have to do but get the information.

"But the fare shopping! [He held his hands up in horror.] "Where they want to know is it cheaper if I go in the middle of the week or at night or after the holiday."

"You mean like I want to visit my mother in Florida, so I listen to all the rates and then say, 'Thanks, I'll call back after I talk to my mother'?"

"Right. Now if someone were listening in, I would be graded on how I probed for the business."

"O.K.," I said, becoming the customer. "Thank you. I'll

have to call my mother and see what time is most convenient for her."

Kenny played the reservation agent: "And do you think you'll be flying toward the beginning or the middle of the week?"

"Well, uh, I have to be back by the following weekend so I guess the beginning."

"Tuesday we have a flight leaving at 10 and at 4. Which would you prefer? (See, I'm trying to get you to make a tentative booking.) Ten?"

"But I don't really know yet. I'll call back after I . . . ."

"So I give you a sales pitch. 'It costs nothing to save a seat. There's limited seating at the SuperSaver fare.' I could give them every sales pitch in the world and they still say [now he imitates me, repeating like a parrot], 'I have to call my mother, I have to call my mother, I have to call my mother.'

"If we're going round and round and you keep resisting, I move into what we call a close. 'I still have room on the flight leaving at 10 on Tuesday. Let's hold the seat for you tentatively. What's your last name?' And if you say, 'My last name is Garson,' then I know I've booked it. I've converted a potential!"

"Congratulations." I shook his hand across the table.

"But if you still say, 'Dah dah dah dah,' then I could go back to a sales pitch. 'We're coming on the holidays; summer is a hard time to fly; it doesn't cost you anything to hold the booking. Now of the 10 o'clock and the 4 o'clock, which do you prefer?' "

"You're closing again," I said.

"No," he explained, 'Which do you prefer' is called a probe. 'What's your last name' is a close. Now if I come to the close and they don't book I could start around again. I could go around and around for two hours. It's always a pull between keeping your talk time down and getting your conversion rate up. There's no actual rule on it. Generally, I say if you come to close twice and they don't book, let them go."

I stared at Kenny. "That's amazing." I knew, of course, that good salesmen had always analyzed every phase of a contact. But it had never occurred to me that my two-minute reservation conversation could be broken down into opening, sales pitch, probe and close. When Kenny is monitored live, by his supervisor, he'll also be graded for such subjective qualities as tone of voice and effective use of name, as in, "If you like, Mrs. Garson, I can book you on the . . ."

"And you never ask a yes or no question," he cautioned me. "Never say, 'Would you like to book?' It's, 'Which would you prefer, the 10 o'clock or the 4 o'clock?' "

"Kenny, I have to apologize. I always thought I was being a good citizen not to hold seats on SuperSavers. But I realize now I was being a resister. I didn't mean to give you so much trouble. I'll book anything from now on."

"But the system is changing," Kenny informed me, "starting the first of the year. They found out that American was being too pushy on the phone and that the general flying public didn't like our reservation agents. We were down to number 2 instead of number 1. So we're gong to move into a general rating of call effectiveness. When they listen in they'll grade you on how well you used the sales tools: customer's name, tone of voice, all that's the same. But the number that will be important now is the number of passengers boarded under your sign."

" 'Boarded under your sign'?" It sounded like astrology.

Kenny explained. "We each have a number—our sign—which we use when we make a booking in the computer. Your monthlies [monthly computer-generated statistics] contain the number of passengers per hour you worked who actually boarded a plane—that's 'boarded under your sign.'

"So now I shouldn't book unless I mean to fly, is that it?"

"They'll still have the number of bookings on your dailies [the individual statistics that Kenny's supervisor posted near the lockers each day], so you still try to book. But the number boarded ur.der your sign will get the emphasis starting at the beginning of the year."

The new emphasis seemed to suggest a more free-form conversation. But I was mistaken to believe that American Airlines was going to leave things up to the individual agent. Even as I talked with Kenny, supervisors and agents in the four regional offices (Dallas, Los Angeles, Cincinnati and Hartford) were getting time off the phones for retraining.

It reminded me of the way things were said to change in China. One year the Americans were the imperialist hyenas and the Russians the friends of the proletariat. The next year it reversed; and when it reversed it reversed for 800 million people at once.

A study had shown that the emphasis on conversion made American's agents seem too pushy. Now we would enter together into the era of nonpushing, all in the same way on the same day.

"How do you keep yourself tuned in?" I asked Kenny. "How do you keep yourself performing seven-and-a-half hours a day?"

"They provide me with the scenario, the basic script and the props, and I have to keep that alive."

"Are you ever tempted to put someone on hold just to have a minute or two of breathing time?"

"If you put people on hold you're running up your talk time, so it's not a good way to bring your stats up. And at some point you'll be monitored doing it.

"They want you to keep the passenger live on the line. That's where the acting comes in. If you can improvise till you get the answer out of the computer, stay one thought ahead, keep up the patter . . . If anyone was monitoring they'd know I used all the techniques."

"How does the monitoring work?" I asked. "I mean the human monitoring, what does it feel like?"

"We don't know when we're being listened to. You know afterwards because normally you get calls one after another without any let up. Suddenly there's a break, you look around and you see there's calls coming in to the other agents but you're not getting any. Then you hear a voice in your ear, 'Hello.' It's the supervisor from a listening post. Mine is usually on another floor. There are listening posts all over the office.

"You never know when it will happen. I haven't been monitored yet this month so I figure some time this week. It's usually once a month."

"What do they say?"

"Let me try to remember how it was last month. She said, 'Hello, I've been listening to your calls for an hour and you've been doing everything fine. Keep it up.' "

"What would a criticism be like?"

"Usually it's, 'You didn't ask for the business.' 'You should have closed.'

"Sometimes they also listen from the corporate headquarters in Dallas. It's called trunk monitoring. But *they* never come in on the line. You never know about Dallas."

I told Kenny a story I'd heard from a reservation agent in Canada. A woman sat down at the beginning of her shift, plugged in and said to her friend, "The doctor says it's cancer." Then she took her first call. Within an hour she was called into the supervisor's office, who asked sympathetically, "Is there any way we can help about your cancer?" The woman stormed out furious and said to her friend, "How could you have told them!?" The women thought they had to be talking to a customer to be overheard. They didn't know until then that the system picked up their voices as soon as they plugged in.

"Well, here we know it picks up everything," Kenny assured

me. "If you're talking to someone in the office, you cover the microphone tube over." He made a subtle gesture with just one finger, like someone covering the opening of a straw. "But the best thing is to save your sociability for the customers."

"But you really like the job?"

"Except for the pay."

But Kenny fully agreed with the company's wage policy. "They have to be competitive. They have to be able to operate with minimal costs. $5.77 an hour isn't so bad. I don't really have to own a car."

I asked Kenny how he managed on his pay.

"I share a house with two other people, a mechanic and a nurse. In this day and age you have to live communally. It keeps costs down and makes you able to afford a little more extras."

Before we parted I asked Kenny if he knew of anyone else at the office who might talk to me. "Is there someone on your shift?" I suggested.

"Well, see, you start at 7:00 to 3:30, 7:30 to 4:00, 8:00 to 4:30, depending on the manning need. Then there's a whole bunch of people called 'floaters,' which is what I am. Every week you bid for your schedules. I'd have to be there five or six years, I think, before I'd wind up with a Monday to Friday with weekends off.

"Then there's T.L. [Time-card Leave]. You sign a sheet on the table when you come in if you're willing to go home early, and they come around and tell you you can leave if the call volume declines. There's also overtime. You don't have to do it but people who aren't making a lot of money, like me—and Christmas is coming—so I've been working two or three hours over this week. Which is hard. As much as I like the job it's hard to sit there ten hours a day tied to this computer that keeps track of your every move. Your phone line is like your umbilical cord into the computer.

"They also offer you overage leaves—which are without

pay but you keep your seniority and benefits—which I would like to take sometimes to do something in the theater again. But they can't tell you how long a leave it will be till right before, because it depends on the call volume projections.

"You can also take T.L. lunches, which is they'll give you a long lunch if they see a decline in the call volume at your lunch hour. And you can get T.L. before you come in by phoning and then you can start late."

For all these reasons, Kenny didn't really have a shift or a crew he worked with.

"On this job it's not very social. You come in and you plug in and you save your sociability for the customers. But really, that's what I like about it—dealing with the public. No two phone calls are ever the same. You have to start where the ball drops. I like being involved with people."

Jack Burford

Canadian airlines use the same computerized reservation systems as U.S. airlines, and they collect the same statistics on their agents. But they hadn't gone as far in standardizing the reservation conversation. Nor had the shifts become as flexible or the agents as plug-in-able as Kenny. To me, the tone and pace at Air Canada in Toronto seemed slow, polite, almost old fashioned.

In the Air Canada cafeteria in Toronto, the union delegation overwhelmed me with printouts.

"This one's called PASER—How do you like that acronym they picked?—It gives them your number of calls, your percent of bookings, and the dollar value of bookings per agent per hour."

"STAR is more intimate," someone handed me a second sheet of indecipherable figures. "It tallies your number of calls, the average length of calls, the average number of seconds between calls, and your percent of time in line." [STAR and PASER correspond roughly to the dailies and monthlies at American Airlines.]

"Then there's the QAP [Quality Assurance Program]. That's just Bertha in the back taking things down . . ."

"And your supervisor can tape you from any station . . ."

"And they can always listen from the manager's office, and . . ."

"It's like being hooked up to a biofeedback machine!" the union's stress specialist said. "Only it makes you sick instead of well."

On the way from the cafeteria to the union office, I peeked into the reservation room itself. I was surprised by the carpeted calm. There were a large number of mature men and women, well dressed, I thought, for a back-office job. Their phone conversations sounded quiet and unhurried.

"What's that?" I pointed to a bottle of pills on the control desk in the center of the room. "What's EXDOL?"

"Shhh," said the union chairperson, elbowing me toward the exit as I tried to copy the label on an unfamiliar brand of pain reliever. "Shh," she said, "I don't know if you're allowed in here and I didn't ask. Let's get back to the union office."

In the Air Canada stairwell we ran into a middle-aged man with curly hair and a square, smiling face. He nodded and tipped his coffee container at us.

"She's doing a story on the electronic monitoring." Meg, the chairperson, introduced me to Jack Burford. "If you'd like to interview him . . ."

"I see the good and bad in it," said Jack, "so I couldn't really give you the union point of view."

"Terrific!" I said, then apologized to my union hostess. "It makes it a more interesting story to have a lot of points of view."

It was 10 A.M., Jack's lunch break, and he obligingly volunteered to be interviewed. (At Air Canada shifts rotated, three days, three nights, three off, but he swapped with other agents whenever he could to get the 6 A.M. shift. "Sixes are peaceful and I'm up early anyway.")

"Don't you want to get something to eat?" I asked.

"Oh that's all right. I never take anything but coffee," he answered. And he suggested that he bring his coffee into the union office.

Jack Burford was a warm, solid, methodical man who didn't seem particularly rushed. But it made me nervous to know that he had to be plugged back in in exactly twenty-nine minutes. So we got right down to cases while Meg puttered at the file cabinets.

"Now my attitude on this electronic monitoring is, first, it's something you've got to live with, and then it's got its good points in the respect that everyone has to pull his weight."

"What do you mean?"

"I started in reservations five years ago and I'd never typed before so I was obviously very slow." [Jack had requested a transfer from the airport ramp because "I was getting to be of a certain age, and the wife was saying, 'Now you don't want to work outside your whole life.' "]

"When I came off the training I was put next to a couple of girls who would sit talking together for twenty minutes. We were having a seat sale then; the phone lines were jammed up. I was busting my ass but I still couldn't handle it all, and you're sitting next to two people just talking!

"Back then, Air Canada had just installed the electronic monitoring, but the supervisors hadn't learned what information they could get. They didn't know how to come to you and say, 'Look at this eight minutes out of line. [Not plugged in.] What was the reason?' When they did start using it to their advantage, taking people into the office and showing them their statistics, then I found the job easier, because everyone was pulling their weight.

"Of course, there's more pressure too." Jack shifted to consider the other side of the question as if he were literally turning a heavy rock over in his hands. "The original system, you could sit and talk and do anything you wished as long as there was no red light. [No call waiting.] But under STAR and PASER you are plugged in automatically. Say it's a Sunday or a long weekend and it's dead. You can't say, 'Oh well, let's leave one person and the rest, let's have a coffee.' It would show on your STAR that you're out of line. It monitors you in eight-and-a-half hours less the thirty minute lunch and the two fifteen-minute breaks. And they also allow you so many seconds between calls for Clean Up [the equivalent of Kenny's AHU, After Hang Up]."

"Seventeen seconds, isn't it?" I volunteered.

"Or maybe eighteen," said Jack. "I'm not sure."

"Sixteen," Meg piped up. "We lost a second in the last contract." It was down to thirteen at American.

"The point is," said Jack, "not to let it dictate your way of life. I feel you can live with the machine and do your job if you don't let it dictate *how* you do your job.

"Like yesterday I had a customer called from Detroit, wanted to know the fares from Frankfurt, Germany, to Windsor for his son—must have been in the U.S. forces. The fare I quoted the father—he sounded quite elderly—was well over $1000. But I explained that I could halve it by booking from Frankfurt to Toronto and Toronto to Windsor. He was very pleased by that but he couldn't remember it all, so he asked could I jot it down and post it to him, and he'd send it on to his son who'd make the booking from Frankfurt.

" 'We don't normally do that' I said, 'but O.K., I'll do it for you.' So I had to spend time, maybe fifteen minutes, out of line getting the letter out. But I was working and I don't feel at all guilty."

"But, Jack, you were not only monitored out of line by STAR but you don't get any credit for the booking from

PASER." I was beginning to distinguish between the two tracking systems.

"Air Canada will still get the booking down the line," he assured me. "And the customer will remember the service he got and call us the next time.

"If my supervisor tells me, 'you didn't achieve 70 percent yesterday, only 68,' I still know I was doing my job." (The company standard for time in line was 70 percent. The union pointed out that if you deducted the sixteen seconds allowed for Clean Up between calls plus your two fifteen-minute breaks and your half hour lunch, this brought you down to 70 percent of your shift. So to meet the 70 percent, they reasoned, you had to be handling calls 100 percent of your working time.)

"By the way," I asked, "which figure do they really care about, the seats *booked* or actually *flown*? Which is your true bottom line?"

"That's an argument I always have with my supervisor," said Jack. "They want us to start pushing the bookings the way they do in the States.

"For instance the last time I was listened in to I was told, 'There's where you should have zoomed in on the sale.' [He should have closed, in American Airlines terminology.] It was a man who wanted to take the wife and four kids to Calgary in the summer and we didn't have any reduced seats left. They count it as a sale lost because I didn't try to book. But I feel, what's the point of offering a man like that first class? I know he wants the cheapest seats. I know he will continue shopping. So what is the purpose of booking it?

"Personally, if someone calls me for a destination in the States and I can do it with three stopovers that will take him eight hours, I say, 'Call U.S. Air.' "

Meg winced at that name.

"How are your statistics, then?" I asked. I knew that was

like asking a man's income. But Jack gave me a straightfor-ward answer.

"Since I went on the union [became a delegate] my STAR is around 68 percent. Before that I averaged 71."

"Wow."

"It's not hard to achieve, but it requires 100 percent of your time doing your job."

"Don't some people get a few free minutes by jamming?" I suggested. Jamming is the practice of putting a series of calls on hold just long enough to finish a conversation or take that last sip of coffee.

"I would never do a thing like that," Jack replied, truly disturbed. "Sometimes you get a dreadfully angry person on the line and if you take the trouble to find out what's bother-ing him he may have been left on hold. I apologize in those cases and say, 'We've been having a lot of that problem today.' As if it might be a telephone line problem. It's a white lie, but I do it.

"I would never put anyone on hold except to get informa-tion for him. If one adds bad feeling to the world it comes back to one."

"But it is a regular practice, isn't it?" I pushed.

"Such agents are few and far between." Jack insisted. "Per-sonally, I don't believe in any of those gimmicks. I just work at my own pace. If I've got a businessman on the phone and he has rushed out of a meeting to call the airline—say he had a reservation with a car arranged and a hotel booked, and he just wants to change it all for two days later—a lot of people will hold that man on the line while they change all those items. The system allows you sixteen seconds Clean Up time. They do the Clean Up while they're on the phone and they've earned themselves sixteen seconds.

"I personally don't believe in that. As I talk I'm jotting the information down on a pad on the side. I'll let the client get back to his meeting. I tell him, I have the information and if I have any problem I'll call his office. By doing that I'm lowering my STAR. But the other way is a disservice to the client, and he will remember the service he got."

You couldn't call Jack Burford a fanciful man. But he had a way of imagining, or perhaps feeling, the needs of the people on the other end of the line. The elderly gentleman with a son in the army and the rushed businessman were both very real and individual to Jack. And he responded to each of them with a subtlety that went far beyond selecting the appropriate pitch, probe or close. Furthermore, Jack had the flexibility to deal with situations that hadn't been envisaged when the training manual was written.

You would suppose that this subtlety and flexibility is what makes human beings desirable as reservation agents. But apparently not. Both American Airlines and Air Canada had arranged their monitoring and grading systems so that, no matter what your problem, Kenny and Jack got the most credit for asking, "Would you prefer the 10 o'clock or the 4 o'clock?" Under the pressure of dailies, monthlies, PACERS and STARs, the human agent comes to sound annoyingly like a yes/no, on/off, 10 o'clock/4 o'clock digital device.

Perhaps this is a clue to the future of the job. When you hang up muttering, "I might as well be talking to a machine," chances are you soon will be.

At the time I interviewed Jack, Air Canada already had a self-booking machine on the drawing board. Like a bank money machine, it would be operated entirely by the customer. The machine would accept reservations and would also issue tickets, boarding passes and luggage tags. In a sense, the computer-aided clerk is merely a transition toward a machine. Jack Burford wasn't making that transition gracefully. Though empathetic, Jack wasn't a pliant man. The company couldn't easily modernize his concepts of courtesy and decency.

"I feel," Jack declared, "that Air Canada is paying my wages, so I give them the best I can. But on the other hand, I don't let them take over my life or my values."

This brought us to exactly 10:28. Jack got up with a "Good-bye. If I can be of any more help . . ." that didn't sound stressed or hurried. Without compromising his calm manner, his deliberate pace, or his solid values, Jack Burford got back from lunch in time to be monitored in line before the computer's clock moved from 10:30 to 10:31.

□ □ □

The day I arrived in Toronto, the headline in a major tabloid asked, "Are Canadians Boring?"

Before I left Toronto I ran into Jack Burford again.

"Jack," I said, "I now have a half dozen Canadian reservation agents down in these notebooks saying the same thing you said: 'I just work at my own pace.' But how long do you think they can stick to it? I know Canadians are kind of solid . . . no, that's not the word . . . maybe . . . ah . . ."

"Boring?" he suggested.

"Let's say traditional," I found a neutral word. "But still, won't monitoring eventually speed people up and make them handle the customers in a more programmed way?"

"It's the customers that are getting programmed," Jack answered. "They're getting so used to dealing with machines. I got a call from someone the other day that asked, 'Are you live?' I said, 'Well I was when I came in this morning.'"

"And you don't think the agents will eventually become more mechanical?"

"They'll never speed us up like the Americans," Jack assured me. "They will replace us with machines before they can turn us into machines. That's why our union is trying for job security. We know we'll be phased out in the next few years. So we want a contract where we can erode ourselves by retiring and quitting.

"It's a pity, really," he mused. "Everything goes full circle, like that Anne Murray song 'Everything old is new again.' It's really a shame because basically people don't like machines. They find them very impersonal. Then live agents will come back into fashion like something new again."

"But like everything quaint and old fashioned," I said "they'll probably be only for the rich." Air Canada already had a special gold card number where people who paid a fee could speak to less-monitored agents. American Airlines had a similar flagship desk, primarily for travel agents.*

"I do not look forward to the time when talking to a live person is a rich person's privilege," Jack said. "Yes, the new system is coming to Canada, too, but slower."

□   □   □

On the train ride home from Toronto, I had time to wonder why the new systems were coming to Canada slower. Air Canada used the same technology as American Airlines. Why hadn't they scripted and speeded up the reservation conversation as thoroughly?

Was there something about the Canadian personality that resisted? Possibly. It was hard to imagine Jack Burford learning a new sales pitch as quickly as Kenny.

Was it the union? It was certainly because of their unions that Canadian reservation agents had fixed schedules. So far the Canadian airline unions had also resisted the two-tier wage system that had turned reservations into a $5.77-an-hour job for new workers at American. Furthermore, the Canadian unions flatly opposed individual monitoring.

Though they hadn't succeeded in keeping it out, they had

---

* When I returned to the U.S. I discovered that Citibank had proposed to charge a fee for the use of live tellers to anyone with under $5000 in the bank. There was such an outcry over this that the bank gave it up. They achieved almost the same goal by issuing a priority sticker and opening special lines for customers with over $25,000 in the bank.

at least taught their members that monitoring programs can be changed. For instance, Air Canada could collect statistics on the group without a breakdown on each agent. Such statistics would be useful for planning but not for discipline. In the blinking maze of a modern office, computers appear to monitor as automatically as clocks tick. But at Air Canada most of the agents understood that computers don't time you unless they're asked to. So perhaps it was the union's in-depth education that softened the system.

Or maybe Canadian reservation conversations were a little less rigid simply because Canadian airlines were still regulated. Perhaps they'd adapt when they faced harsher competition. Was I observing a national character difference or just a five-year time lag?

□　□　□

By now I began to understand what reservation efficiency entailed. American Airlines had divided the two-minute reservation conversation into segments—opening, sales pitch, probe and close—and provided a set of interchangeable conversation modules for each segment. An acceptable conversation could now be put together like a mix-and-match outfit or a Chinese dinner—one from column A, two from column B.

On one level it's obvious why this is considered efficient. In industry, production is routinely arranged so that the bulk of the work can be done with a minimum of skill. The more an airline can standardize the reservation conversation, the less they need to depend on the agents' experience and judgment. This should make the agents cheaper and more interchangeable.

It's further argued, at least in manufacturing, that this process produces not only a cheaper worker but also a more uniform product. At McDonald's or General Motors, uniformity is considered a positive good. Is a more uniform conversation also a positive good?

As a customer I'd like to reach an agent like Jack Burford who feels free to use his discretion and common sense. But airline systems aim at allowing Jack as little discretion and as little input as possible.

Eventually booking machines may replace reservation agents, but as long as the airlines are still paying human salaries (albeit only $5.77 an hour), why not take advantage of the qualities that make human beings better at communicating? Why spend so much money and effort trying to replicate the perverse inflexibility of a machine?

I went back to Hartford to talk to Kenny's boss at American Airlines.

Charles Zimmerli

Everyone smiled when they mentioned Charles Zimmerli, the Division Reservation Manager at American Airlines. "Charlie is a people person," said a supervisor. "He enjoys people so much."

Regardless of how routine their work might become, Zimmerli seemed able to make 650 reservation agents feel that, to him, they were far from interchangeable. I was glad I'd have a chance to interview a "people person" about the human effects of reservation efficiency.

On my way to Hartford, I stopped on the Lower East Side for hot bagels to bring to our 8 A.M. meeting. But despite fresh bagels and Zimmerli's genuine warmth, our conversation took an unpeople turn at first.

□ □ □

"Good," Mr. Zimmerli welcomed my bagels, "we'll nosh over there." And he guided me to the round table near the window. He was a thin, dark-haired man with a glow of gray and a boyish smile.

"Manning levels," he began before I could even ask a question, "are one of our primary concerns. Let me give you some background. We have an Operations Supervisor who predicts the call level each day. And on that basis we offer something called Time-card Leaves . . ."

"T.L.," I said.

He tipped his head and continued. "One day last week our Operations Supervisor came exactly six calls short of predicting the exact call level. 17,929 calls predicted, 17,935 calls received. Just six calls under."

"Wow," I said. "But what I really wanted to ask you about . . ."

"Yes," he replied with pride. "We mentioned it in today's newsletter." He pointed to the bright-colored one-page news sheet lying on his desk. "We not only get calls from the Eastern Region here but '800' calls from all over the country will get transferred to us if they're undermanned somewhere else. We've established that call length varies from region to region. (We do our business quicker here in the East.) Call length varies with the season, too. We're able to predict for all that. That's how we determine our own manning levels."

"I'm interested," I said, "in the way that the reservation phonecall can be designed to fit into such a . . . ah . . . standard pattern."

"There's what we call an opening to a sales call," he explained.

"I know, and a probe and a sales pitch and a close."

"Exactly. In the training program we have labels for certain types of selling. These become tools that a person is given to use and we expect certain results. We monitor to see that they get certain results from certain tools. You and I can listen now." He pointed to what looked like an ordinary telephone on his desk. "We can listen and say, 'You were very supportive when you asked, "Does you're granddaughter visit you often?" You didn't make use of the name the way we taught you but your tone was good, your use of the probe was good. But, still, the person didn't book.'

"Now we set as a goal that the agent is supposed to convert a certain percent of these calls to bookings."

"What percent, by the way?" I asked.

"It changes, but I would say now about 35 percent."

I wondered if Kenny had been wrong when he told me that the conversion quota was only 26 percent. Had the standard jumped to 35 percent?

"Now, a person may feel depressed," Mr. Zimmerli explained sympathetically, "when he doesn't make his conversion rate. He says, 'I used all the tools but I didn't get the sale. Why are you penalizing me, making me feel bad?' That is why we are moving into a new system."

"A new rating system?"

"Yes, a rating system that talks more about their success in using the tools and less about their success in getting the booking. Of course, we're still concerned about the number of people who board the airplane as a result of their effort. ["Board under your sign," I remembered Kenny's phrase.] We're concerned about the customers not feeling pressured and the agent not feeling penalized. It's the *bookings that hold* that will become the significant number starting with the new year. [Just as Kenny had said.]

"As matter of fact," Mr. Zimmerli continued, pointing through his open door, "we're retraining people out there now for the new system." I looked where he pointed. The Hartford office had once been a K-Mart department store. Now the agents sat at individual cockpitlike workstations dotting the cavernous shell.

"Will there be a new rating sheet for supervisors to grade conversations?"

"The actual sheet will stay the same, but now they will be rated for their effective use of the conversational techniques, not whether they make the conversion."

"Effective use of conversational techniques." It seemed so subjective, like the wet onion slivers in a McDonald's kitchen. "But that doesn't yield a numerical value," I said, surprised.

"Oh yes it does," he reassured me. "You used the probe technique or you didn't use the probe technique, you used the name or you didn't use the name. It's not vague. It can be translated into a numerical determination that everyone can agree on—the salesperson as well as those who are observing."

I decided to express what was troubling me. I didn't take down my own exact words but what I tried to say was:

"Some people like to sell. To them it's a challenge. Other people like to feel they're doing a public service. The fact that your agents were rated as too pushy suggests to me that it's not so easy to come up with an exact conversational scenario that fits all calls and feels comfortable to all agents. You are now changing the system because it wasn't working for everyone. Why design a new system that again tries to anticipate every aspect of a two-way conversation and tries to prescribe a uniform response? Why not let each agent handle it his own way—assuming they all give the same fares and schedules, or course?"

Mr. Zimmerli was very patient.

"Let's go back to the first thing we were discussing—manning. If we're going to be able to predict manning I've got to be able to develop some standards about what's happening to me. This is a public-contact business. Planes get fogged in, people ask unexpected questions. So I've got to systematize it somehow.

"Now if Barbara is handling it in two minutes and getting good sales, [he pointed to me as Barbara, making what I thought was an "effective use of name"] and Charlie meanwhile [he indicated himself] is taking three minutes and getting good sales, I'd rather employ Barbara. Those figures say to me, 'I've got to talk to Charlie. I want him to get like

Barbara. Let's see what she does.' Now I don't want you to stop being Charlie. I want you to bring your Charliness with you, but lets see how we can tighten it. Let's not ask how old is your mother or give them seven possible fares. That's over-servicing."

"But the former standardized phone call scenario", I persisted, "was not the most effective phone call scenario for everyone. The new one may not be either. You hire human reservation agents because they are the only beings, organic or mechanical, that can respond with sufficient flexibility to an open-ended inquiry. Then you try in every possible way to restrict that flexibility."

"But I have to answer the phone 'American Airlines Reservations,' " he said. "I can't say 'Zimmerli's reservation office,' or 'Charlie's reservation office.' Any employer-employee relationship requires a modification of my individualism."

"Look," Mr. Zimmerli picked up one of the bagels I'd brought. "This bagel is created from a recipe in order to guarantee a great uniformity." He paused to make sure I was following. "We are creating a product in reservations. Now you want a certain predictability in the product, don't you?"

I remembered how I'd gone all the way across Manhattan to get fresh bagels. "But I don't want a frozen, packaged bagel."

"But you do want to know what you're going to get. We at American aim at a certain level of standardization."

"And you can manufacture a conversation the same way you manufacture a bagel?"

"It's a matter of degree."

We both agreed to that. But I don't think we agreed what degree of standardization we should aim at, or why.

I thought the reservation conversation should be sufficiently standard so that you always got the current prices and correct flight times.

As a reservations manager, Mr. Zimmerli needed a level of

standardization that would allow him to count, time and grade each phone call. It was more important to have a quantifiable phone call than a flexible agent. Furthermore, Mr. Zimmerli assumed that centrally planned responses would almost always be superior to the decisions agents made on their own.

I told Mr. Zimmerli about Jack at Air Canada, how he'd spent fifteen minutes off the phone writing out rates for an elderly man whose son was going to book from Germany. Yet he didn't even bother to run down all the available rates to the man who wanted to take the wife and kids to Calgary on a summer holiday. "He's overservicing," Mr. Zimmerli objected to the first case. "He's not giving the passenger the full range of services," was the objection to the second.

"Suppose it turns out that in making these two decisions Jack actually maximized Air Canada's bottom line?" I asked. "The first call yielded a big booking in Germany and a loyal transatlantic customer. On the second call Jack was brief and kind to a man who wasn't going to fly Air Canada in the end anyway. Let us just say those were the results."

"But they wouldn't be, not consistently," Mr. Zimmerli insisted.

"But if they were?"

My guess is that American Airlines would prefer a uniform or bagellike conversation, even if it had to be a little stale, to the effective but varied "product" Jack Burford produced by listening and using his own judgment.

Mr. Zimmerli and I kept going around in circles debating whether Jack could possibly be as productive as an American Airlines agent. I'm not sure we were really talking about the same thing. But we both agreed that Jack was one of a disappearing breed.

Before I left, I asked Mr. Zimmerli whether he thought he could do his own job as manager efficiently if he were electronically tracked like the agents. Of course his job was more varied. He sometimes walked among the agents on the floor; other times he met with workers or supervisors in his office. After people left his office he had to decide what to do about their problems. That was his own kind of AHU (After Hang Up time). He wrote reports, he spoke to Dallas on the phone, he attended retirement parties and community functions, he dealt with reporters and he made decisions.

"Not as many decisions as I'd like," he said. For instance, he would have liked to be able to recarpet the whole office but that had to be decided in Dallas.

"Suppose," I said, "the people in Dallas said to you, 'We trust you. We know you managers all work long hours. But some of the reservation offices are consistently more efficient than others. [Since Charlie took over in Hartford, the labor force had gone down from 850 to 650 while handling the same number of calls. I don't know how that compares with the other centers.] We'd like you to record your time by plugging in at each workstation. That way we can tell you how the most efficient manager breaks down his activities. Then you can all follow that model.' Would you personally like to work plugged in that way?" I asked.

"You mean if Mr. _____ [he named the president of the company] could put a speaker in here and listen when we're talking?"

"Yes. Or something like that."

"That wouldn't be appropriate," he said "because my job includes personnel coming in and telling me they have a drug problem and other things that should properly be private."

"Well, O.K." I conceded, "you could turn the speaker off the way the agents put their finger over the mike." I unconsciously made the one-finger movement near my mouth.

"Say, how many people have you talked to here?"

"About a dozen."

"I'm just surprised the way you got that little gesture they all make when they cover the tube."

"Would you work well, and would you like it, if they tracked your different functions?"

"Yes," he said without hesitation. "Yes, if it were explained to me that it was part of the efficiency of the entire company. Most definitely."

It's lucky that Mr. Zimmerli wouldn't mind an executive tracking system, because that's the focus of the most advanced efficiency research.

Toward the end of our interview Mr. Zimmerli's secretary came in, exchanged pleasantries and took the extra bagels for the women outside. He had a nice rapport with his secretary.

As I left, Mr. Zimmerli again pointed to the newsletter on his desk and reminded me about the Operations Supervisor who had come within six calls of predicting the day's call volume.

As he guided me out, our path across the office was accompanied by a tinkle of "Hi, Charlies," each synchronized with a smile and the one finger gesture to cover the mike.

Near the elevator I stopped to listen to a reservation agent answer a customer's question. "The special meal on that flight is a stuffed tomato. The tomato is stuffed with shrimp and crab meat. It's delicious."

"You must have eaten it on a recent flight," I said. "You even know what it's stuffed with."

She pointed to the screen, which described the tomato and its stuffing in big print. "It's all in the computer." When she finished the call she showed me how it scrolled easily to the vegetarian choices, then flipped back to the booking record.

"What beautiful, clear print," I responded enthusiastically.

American Airlines has the most elegantly designed screens in the industry. Finding information is almost as easy as looking it up in a book. This is truly labor-saving design. The basic system for entering a reservation on a computer terminal, the system that makes a booking immediately available all over the country, is also labor saving—and amazing (despite occasional frustration at the airport when the computer's down).

But electronic monitoring isn't labor saving. The monitoring system at American Airlines doesn't make it any faster or easier to say hello. It makes it easier to grade, time and set quotas. It's labor *controlling,* but not labor *saving.*

Now, as I was leaving American Airlines, I wished Mr. Zimmerli and I had spent less time talking about control systems and more about these wonderfully designed screens.

"It's so clear! I'd love to sit down and handle some calls right now," I said. "Only I don't know all the current information."

"That's my problem, too," said Mr. Zimmerli. "I can't work the thing like they can."

The agent smiled at this humble admission with its implied compliment.

Mr. Zimmerli and I finally made it to the elevators amidst more smiles and waves.

I descended to the lobby wondering how they are ever going to standardize what Charlie Zimmerli does to keep the Hartford office humming.

□   □   □

As a reservation agent Jack Burford responds to individual problems with his own common sense and good will. But airline automaters are willing to sacrifice his Jackness (his Jackosity?) in order to get a more uniform conversation.

Charlie Zimmerli also brings a lot of himself to a job that involves resolving problems on a broader scope. It would seem like a great waste of his Charlieness to try to anticipate all the problems and provide him with a set of mix-and-match responses. Yet, as we'll see in later chapters, the methods used to standardize reservation work are also being applied to management jobs. Just as airlines calculate the average AHU, efficiency experts now calculate how long it should take to write the average executive memo and even how long it should take to make the average executive decision.

As this kind of efficiency moves up the occupational ladder, it yields not only diminished jobs but also diminished people.

American Airlines didn't manufacture Kenny, the thirty-year-old who has no plans for a family, no objection to moving, no one expecting him for dinner and yet loves being "involved with people." But he serves their purposes awfully well. American has the computer capability to predict staffing needs by thirty-minute intervals. Kenny has the social capability to plug in and plug out as needed.

But what use is Jack Burford, with a fixed mortgage, a fixed dinnertime, and a fixed philosophy of life? What good is the capacity to reestablish staffing needs on a minute-to-minute basis if the workers insist on getting home when they're expected? What use is the latest survey on the effectiveness of every possible sales pitch when men like Jack are mired down in concepts of courtesy and honesty that they learned as children? How can Air Canada compete with American Airlines if Canadians are stuck with old-fashioned employees like Jack?

My guess is that Charlie Zimmerli would probably find Jack a more sympathetic neighbor then Kenny. They're of the same generation and they have similar feelings about family and loyalty. But I think Mr. Zimmerli will be hiring a lot more Kennys then Jacks. Soon it may be difficult to find many like Jack—even in Canada.

II

□ □ □ □ □ □ □ □

TURNING PROFESSIONALS INTO CLERKS

3

□ □ □ □ □ □ □

The Automated
Social Worker

When I was in college, many people studied social work with the expectation of a civil service job in some do-good agency, the largest of which was Welfare. They knew they'd never get rich as social workers, but, like teaching, it was a respectable profession that paid them for helping others. Besides, it was a secure job—for we have the poor always with us.

The main reward of these jobs was a work style (lifestyle was a later invention) that allowed social workers to interview, visit, fill out forms (alas), make evaluations and decisions and generally function as free human beings while doing worthwhile work.

CPAs deal with numbers. Lawyers deal with contracts. Social workers deal with people. It was the right kind of work for my fellow Berkeley students who pinned IBM registration cards onto their chests to declare *Do not fold, spindle or mutilate*. They demanded to be treated as individuals, not numbers. So they chose to work with individuals, not numbers.

Today I don't meet many undergraduates going into social work. In part this is a matter of fashion. Poor people are out of style. Teaching similarly declines in prestige when children decline in prestige.

But by now social work isn't just a less-prestigious or lower-paid profession; it's hardly a profession at all.

Of course the poor are still with us. So are the welfare centers. But these centers are no longer staffed by autonomous professionals. They're staffed by increasingly regimented clerks. These automated welfare workers have no more chance to deal with people than do airline reservation agents.

How can the "helping professions" be clericalized? How can you eliminate the listening, talking, asking and advising from a job intended to help? It sounds impossible to make social work as physically and mentally constrained as an assembly line job, but that's exactly what's being done.

Up to now, the automation of human services has been slow and messy. In this chapter we're going to look at a welfare system that's been automating fitfully for over ten years.

Industrial automation generally starts with a time-and-motion study. The purpose of such a study is to learn exactly what the job entails and then to break down all the necessary functions into their component tasks or details. This is called "rationalizing" the work. After a job has been rationalized, the workers will usually be given new tools or machines to speed up their now routine tasks. This second stage is called "mechanizing" the work. Owing to policy changes and budget cuts, the Welfare Department was never able to follow through from rationalization to mechanization. Automation hung suspended in midprocess for many years. I arrived just as the federal government stepped in to fund the mechanization stage.

At the individual centers I could still observe the process of studying a job, dividing it into its component parts and returning it to the workers as a series of timed tasks. When rationalization is done "properly," the new jobs should be easy to monitor and require only minor decisions by the workers. When the process is complete, low-paid college graduates will be replaced by lower-paid high school graduates. During the transition—the attrition—older social workers can see their jobs gradually downgraded. Newer workers may not know what the job used to be. Perceptions of movement, up or down, may be relative. But the overall direction is clear. When the process is complete there will be far fewer professional jobs in social work.

□ □ □

It was ten years ago at a party that I met a woman named Catherine, who had quit her job as a social worker in Massachusetts. She'd walked out on the day she was time-studied by outside consultants. "Your classic Charlie Chaplin efficiency men," she recalled, "with watches and clipboards: answer phone, ten seconds; pull case record, thirty seconds; add a baby, six-and-a-half minutes. 'Oh, don't mind us,' she'd mimicked the clipboard men, 'just work at your usual pace.' "

Soon after Catherine quit, a small group of her colleagues were moved out of the welfare center into a special unit to deal with special cases like neglected children. They became part of the new Department of Social Services (DSS) and retained the title of Social Worker. But the vast majority stayed in the Welfare Department, where their titles were changed from Social Worker to Financial Assistance Worker (FAW). At about the same time in other states Social Workers or Case Workers became Income Maintenance Workers or Eligibility Technicians.

In the ten years that followed, welfare departments all over the country began to automate under a federally financed program. Computers could have made Catherine's job a lot easier by simplifying the paperwork. Instead, they were being used as the excuse or opportunity to transform professional social work into clerical tasks.

I wondered what kind of streamlined work routines the early time-and-motion studies had yielded in Massachusetts.

Catherine had no idea. No one she knew still worked in welfare. But by asking everyone who knew anyone I came up with a couple of names of people at, what I was assured, was "not the worst" center. With the usual trepidation, I called my first contact at NTW (Not The Worst) welfare center in Boston.

Eddy Malloy

"What have I got to lose?" said Eddy Malloy, who hadn't the slightest idea what I looked like or what I wanted. "You take the Green Line to _____, walk up _____ St. past a permanent construction site and the third building is us. You'll recognize it by the words 'OVERSEERS OF THE PUBLIC WELFARE' right over the entrance—carved in stone.

"That's some joke," Eddy continued his telephone monologue. "Built as a welfare building, declared a national landmark, can't be torn down. Get the significance of that? Welfare as a way of life, a permanent national system that can't be torn down. ["Good start," I wrote in my notebook, "a social worker who opposes welfare."] "Just go into the lobby, take a seat and watch your purse. ["And doesn't romanticize the clients."] I'll come downstairs and meet you."

"I'm short," I volunteered, "with glasses."

"That's all right, I'll call your name."

"You'll call my name?"

"That's my job. I've got four-and-a-half years' experience calling names of people who want to tell me their troubles. This time I'll tell you mine."

□ □ □

"Erica Williams!"

A middle-aged black social worker looked calmly around the lobby until the skinny teenager sitting next to me rose tentatively from the wooden bench.

"Come this way, Erica," said the welfare worker in a serene contralto. They exited toward the interview room, the teenager carrying a blanket-wrapped package.

". . . answer phone, ten seconds; pull case record, thirty seconds; add a baby, six-and-a-half minutes." That's what must be going on in the interview room, I realized, "add a baby." But the process didn't appear particularly automated.

I noticed a felt-pen sign on the receptionist's counter. It said, "MONTHLY REPORT FORMS." In the left and right margins of the sign were hand-drawn arrows pointing down to a shoe box with a slit cut in the top. As an afterthought, someone had written "Thank you" on the sign in red ink.

A shoe box with a slit doesn't look like a high-tech operation, I thought.

"You must be the writer." Someone startled me as I was copying the sign.

I turned and saw a very young man in rubber-soled shoes and thick-rimmed glasses. Actually Eddy Malloy was twenty-seven. But he reminded me of the *Mad* magazine youths of my high school days. Computer hackers would be the modern equivalent, I suppose.

I learned on the way to lunch that Eddy had graduated from college with a teaching degree but couldn't get a job in Massachusetts, so he subbed for a while in New Hampshire high schools—"Pick-up jobs," he called them scornfully, "professional babysitting." Finally he took a civil service test and wound up in the Welfare Department—"It was supposed to be temporary."

He lived with his mother in a suburb. On the weekends he

supplemented his income (Financial Assistance Workers, "FAWs," then started at somewhat over $14,000 a year) running a booth at a flea market.

"I am," Eddy declared, "the failure of the American dream."

□   □   □

"You mean that for every form you fill out, you have to fill out another form saying you filled out a form?"

"You'll never be able to get this system straight," Eddy expressed his confidence in me. For the entire lunch hour he'd been trying to explain the point system that had evolved from the time studies.

It went roughly like this:

Time standards, in tenths of an hour, had been established for each function that an FAW like Eddy performs. For instance:

Issue food stamp I.D. card _____ .3
  [meaning three-tenths of an hour, or 18 minutes]
Authorize funeral and burial expenses _____ .7
Replace lost or stolen check _____ .4
Complete redetermination _____1.8

The full list contained over sixty functions and was frequently updated.

Each function, like "update medical report" encompassed many "actions," such as going downstairs to see what the client wants, pulling the file, filling out several forms, distributing the forms to supervisors or the Electrical Data Processing center (EDP), returning the case file. The original time studies had identified and assigned time standards for over 1000 actions.

But how did they keep track of it all?

When a worker completed a function—when, for instance, he handed his supervisor the forms necessary to record a change of address or a change of food stamp benefits—he filled out an additional form called a "control slip." At the end of the month the supervisor used these control slips to count the number of points (tenths of hours) each worker had earned.

It was remarkably like the piece-work system in a mink factory I had visited. There, as you finished cleaning each pelt you tore off a tag and tossed it into a cigar box for the supervisor to count. Here, as you finished adding a baby you handed in a control slip. (At the welfare center the control slip was sometimes called a "penny slip," just as it is in a garment shop.)

At the end of the month the supervisor counted the worker's points, his tenths of hours, and calculated how close he came to using 100 percent of his available time. Each worker received a monthly report card with a percentage grade. So far a worker wasn't disciplined unless he fell below 70 percent. That was the system after the time study but before full computerization.

"So these control slips mean you fill out a form for every form you fill out?" I asked incredulously.

"You'll never get it down straight," Eddy assured me. "They keep changing everything anyway."

I'm not sure whether I didn't understand it or I just didn't believe it. Perhaps the system would seem less cumbersome in practice.

□   □   □

"Hi, Opal."

"Is this letter O.K.?" A glamorous blonde handed Eddy an envelope from a temp agency. (We were outside the center returning from lunch.)

"It would be better if they said they terminated you instead of you terminated," he said scanning the letter. "But I'll put it through. It'll qualify your kids. I'll have to ask about you."

"Thanks."

"Will you get credit for that?" I asked as we watched Opal tip down the street on her stilettos.

"If I open her up, I'll get the credit."

"What?"

"Just talking isn't an action," Eddy explained. "Opal earned over 150 percent of her budget the week before last as a Kelly Girl, and the downtown computer automatically threw her off. I spent half an hour this morning telling her how to get back on. I won't get credit for that. And I won't get credit for taking the letter now. But when I make up a T.D. [Turnaround Document] and an MRW [Monthly Report Worksheet] and send it to EDP then I'll get .3"

"I see."

"Opening a case is an action according to the department; talking to people about their status is not. But they'll open her up and there'll be no problem."

□   □   □

The phone rang as we entered Eddy's office. "Sandra O'Malley?" he asked the receptionist downstairs. "What time is it? . . . After 2 I don't cover 'O'." But he went downstairs anyway to help a Hispanic teenager who wanted to register a change of address. She handed Eddy a copy of a rent receipt with her new address. He excused himself to make a photocopy.

While I waited with Sandra, I overheard a welfare worker in the next cubicle appealing, "But I hate to use up your Emergency Assistance for $57. Don't you have a friend you can borrow from?"

Eddy returned with the rent receipt, warned Sandra that her next week's food stamps would still come to the old address and wished her good day.

"An ex-boyfriend maybe?" As we left I caught sight of a heavy, disheveled social worker still pleading, "If you came with a $1000 gas bill I could pay half of it. But this, I can only pay $57 out of the $70 and you use up your emergency assistance for the whole year. If God forbid you have a big emergency, I need something to help you with. If I were you . . ."

"She used to be a welfare mother herself," Eddy explained. "She came up to me yesterday all flustered because she's going on Corrective Action for falling below 70 percent."

"Is that because she gets so involved with the clients?" I asked.

"Mostly she's just a disorganized mess. But I'll get her off. [Eddy handles grievances, though he's at odds with the union on many questions.] I don't know what she gets so upset about. It's her third time on Corrective Action. It's just a game."

Before we left the lobby Eddy picked up a card from one client, had another sign something and told a third to come back with a rent receipt.

"What we run here is a garage," he explained as we walked upstairs. "They come in for air, a valve job, oil. It's a service station, that's all. Only some people don't realize that yet. What happened to Debby [the former welfare mother/social worker I'd overheard] is she spent a lot of time on the phone dealing with some disaster. In this system you don't get points for that and if you don't have the mental capacity to make up the time, you wind up on C.A. [Corrective Action]. But I'll get her off. They just want to give her grief."

It took Eddy over five minutes in the file room to find Sandra O'Malley's old record, bringing him close to the eighteen minutes (.3) allowed for an address change even before he started the paperwork.

"Not that you can't make it up," he said, stopping in the check room. "Remember the woman I got this card from? She picks up her checks at the center because of broken mailboxes. All I have to do is have her sign for the check when I go back down. It's an easy .3—if you're into playing games for points."

Back in his office, before he could write up the O'Malley address change, Eddy was interrupted by a tired-looking woman. She was the third worker so far to ask him about new procedures.

"This," said Eddy, pointing to a box on a form, "tells you to do nothing. The machine has already sent out a letter terminating her. If you want to change it, you'll have to send a form to EDP by 3 o'clock."

It was 2:40. The tired woman sighed.

"Velgumbia?" Eddy said into the phone. He keyed up the name on a terminal that sat on the otherwise empty second desk in his office. (Though the state had compiled an electronic master recipient file, there were very few terminals in the local offices. Eventually the FAWs would enter their paperwork directly onto computers. But for the present it was a one-way terminal, available only for research. Eddy was one of the few workers who used it.)

As the name came up on the screen, Eddy said, "It's her check day. I can pick it up on the way down and have her sign for it."

"Notice what else I'm doing," he said, pointing out his own efficiency. "I'll need the zip code to complete O'Malley's address change. I remember there's another client on the same block so I look her zip code up here [he filled in the form as he spoke] and I save myself a walk down the hall to the zip code book."

I decided not to accompany Eddy downstairs this time. "It's getting to be too many inputs for me," I sighed.

Eddy seemed adroit at following the rules, getting his points and still delivering some kind of useful service. But he had begun only four-and-a-half years ago, when the workers were already called FAWs. I wondered about the long-term workers who had entered the field when the job was called Social Worker and included home visits. Were they able to juggle all these balls in the air at once?

"Are there any long-time workers I could talk to?" I asked Eddy when he returned.

"I've had thirteen supervisors in two-and-a-half years. It's a high-turnover job. Anyway, the end of the month is not a good time to talk to people, because anybody who takes the point system seriously is out there hustling for points."

"What about you? How many points have you gotten since I've been here?"

"Let's see, since lunch I've seen six people and I'll get points for three of them. That's a 50 percent average. Not too bad. For me it's a system to be beaten. I'm dyslexic. I had to beat the school system, too."

"Eddy, you must be brilliant. You handle grievances, you answer my questions, you give clients time you don't get credit for and you're dyslexic. How do you manage to make your points?"

"Want to look at my report card?" He handed me his official Worker Summary (WS-1) for the month of March. After deductions for priority assignments, labor relations and a snow day, Eddy had 119.25 "available hours for standard work" (line 2). In that time his "total earned hours" were 95.3. (line 3). That gave him a "productivity %" (line 2 divided by line 3) of 80 percent with an accuracy rating of 100 percent.

"It was a bad month," he apologized.

"You usually get higher than 80 percent?"

"I aim at 70 percent. I can usually manage to keep it down to 71 or 72. But sometimes when you get close to the end of the month you lose track."

"You're keeping track of keeping your points *down* at the same time as everything else?"

"You want to watch me earn some points since you're worried?" Before my eyes Eddy rapidly completed the address change, which consisted of three documents clipped to the photocopied rent receipt. The top form, the control slip, required nothing but his I.D. number, the name of the procedure and the date. Yet for Eddy that was somehow the last straw. For the first time he dropped his cool, just-playing-their-game tone and became angry. "Look at these control slips. Three copies, three colors, 24¢ each just for the paper. You know what it costs the taxpayer to have me fill out this form each time I do an action? It's asinine!"

Abandoning my interview style I expressed my own guess that the control slip was just a transitional phase; it couldn't possibly be the permanent monitoring system. Of course, it had been the system most of the years Eddy had worked for the Welfare Department. But I assumed that the department would eventually move toward electronic monitoring. Eventually the FAWs would enter their work directly onto the computer, which would tally their points continuously.

Eddy doubted that they'd ever let the FAWs enter information directly onto the master files. He thought it would make it too tempting to create fictional recipients and collect checks. But in any case, he didn't fear computers. After all, the electronic master recipient file was the only development since he'd been there that actually helped him with his paperwork.

"Working directly at a terminal could mean a lot less paperwork," I said. "But at the same time they could program it so you'd be completely controlled every minute. You wouldn't be able to borrow time from checks to talk to Opal. Aren't you worried about a huge speed-up?"

"Speed-up?" He shrugged. "This place is under court order to hire minorities and women. Which means that the standards are always gonna have to be slow enough for . . ."

"Eddy, are you telling me that you are smarter than blacks or women?"

"If I were smart I wouldn't be here, would I?"

Debby Kesselman

"I'm so glad I talked her out of it," said Debby Kesselman, the heavy-set, disheveled worker I'd seen previously. "Actually she needed $70 to keep her going and all I could have given her was $57. I just hated to see her spend her E.A. [Emergency Assistance] on a $57 light bill."

Debby's desk and floors were covered with case files; each one a soap opera of its own.

"I had a pregnant girl who was so messed up, I mean physically, that I told my supervisor I'm taking her to the hospital right now. I didn't ask my supervisor, I told her. She was spewing blood clots from her lungs—this is while I was interviewing her.

"As it turns out, Tammy is twenty years old with the mind and body of a fourteen-year-old. Her baby was born very small. She wanted so much for me to see the new baby, but you have to be a relative to get into intensive care. So we said I was the baby's grandmother. Tammy was delighted; I was proud. It was so silly. Especially since the baby was obviously all black."

Although Debby is white, one of her own four children is black. When they were little, Debby told me, her mother regularly sent three Christmas presents, which Debby sent back with the note, "You have four grandchildren." Perhaps that's what makes her so sensitive about rejected children. And rejected mothers.

"I wish I could have taken her home when she got out of the hospital. Some people have nobody. Just nobody."

"What does your supervisor say when you come back late from the hospital or spend so long downstairs with a client?"

"I have a friend in the unit. We cover for each other's phones, even run down and take each other's clients sometimes."

"But you must be very behind on your paperwork," I said, looking around the room.

"These E.A.s are a legal priority. You have seven days to file the work. I'm twenty to thirty days behind now.

"But you see I have my own priorities. Like never hold a baby. You put that form through right away. Because if there's a medical problem with a newborn I don't want there to be any question about getting it into a hospital."

"But how do you manage to get your points?"

"This point system turns you into a machine instead of a social worker!" she declared. "You don't get any points for keeping a case open by reminding a feeble-minded woman where she's got to go for her baby's Social Security number. It's easier to get your points by letting a case terminate and then reopening it. But who can do that?

"Maybe there are some people who can turn in their points and not care whether they actually took care of any problems. But to me, serving the clients is more important than the points.

"The beginning of this month I said, 'I have a funny feeling I'm gonna go on C.A. and I don't give an F.U.' If you're out there giving service," she said with bravado, "you shouldn't worry whether it's going to take five minutes or an hour."

"How will you feel when they finally get this job on computers?" I asked.

"Well," she sighed, scanning the clutter, "if it gets rid of some of this paperwork . . ."

Kevin Kennedy

Kevin Kennedy is a handsome man in his midthirties. He serves as a kind of senior advisor to the antibureaucratic guerrilla forces still operating at NTW. A young cadre, including Eddy, was planning tactics in his office when I arrived.

Kevin: Look she was closed off on the twenty-fourth; they recertified her on the twenty-seventh; so we can base it on the last thirty days. You follow? Look, what you do . . .

Eddy: I know what I can do and I know what they're gonna say.

Kevin: No, no. Here I've got it.

[He reached up to the shelf behind him for a huge looseleaf procedure manual. Like all good guerrilla commanders he trained his troops to use the enemies' weapons.]

Do you know what a cyclical month is?

Unidentified Female FAW: Whether the case is looked at retrospectively or prospectively they're gonna put her on MR and she's gonna be screwed out of her food stamps.

Kevin: The food stamps have to be looked at prospectively because you don't eat retrospectively. Wait, here, I've got it. . . .

Like Eddy, Kevin takes pride in circumventing the system in order to make it work. But he also enjoys the clients. One of his proudest .3 activities that day was closing the case—"I knew you'd be a success!"—of a nineteen-year-old mother who'd gotten her high school degree and found a job.

"I may be able to get you one more check," Kevin suggested. "You'll have expenses before you get your first paycheck." But it was getting harder to slip in that last welfare check now that W-2s were on computers. Anyway, the young woman was impatient to get off welfare.

In the lobby Kevin was stopped by a teenager who wanted a medical note to excuse her from E.T.

"E.T., like the movie?" I asked.

"Exactly," said Kevin. "Educational Training to prepare you for Extra Terrestrial jobs."

But the bulk of his time was spent untangling confusing communications between the clients and the Welfare Department. "Did you get a letter from me? . . . No that's a redetermination appointment, the other letter. . . . O.K., that's from the computer. Next MR you get I want you to submit this pay stub with it and we'll see if it goes through."

Or the now-familiar Utility Emergency: "You bring in that electric bill and we'll negotiate something with the electric company. . . . You bring in the bill this afternoon, as soon as you can. . . . I'll be here." He repeated it all several times to a blue-eyed, pink-cheeked girl, who seemed peculiarly vague and unconcerned for someone who just had her electricity turned off. Kevin explained to me that she was border-line retarded, "able to live alone, but with little sense of time or urgency. For instance, her electric has already been off for several weeks."

I learned from Kevin that he could in fact get credit for talking to her. When a client comes in on a Utility Emergency Kevin should, according to department procedures, fill out a Notification Form Letter (NFL).

"If I filled out the NFL the client would have four days to appear with the bill and I would have seven days from the initial request to respond. [For filling out the NFL, Kevin would earn .3]

"But I will not do NFLs!" he said emphatically. "First of all, I refuse to fill out three pieces of paper to say I told someone to bring in one piece of paper.

"But mostly I don't do it because if she doesn't get back here in the four days it's a big hassle to get it open again. What's the sense of starting a time clock on a person who couldn't get it together to pay her electric bill on time in the first place? What's the sense of starting procedures that will enmesh a person who isn't good at coping anyway?"

"What's the sense" is a phrase Kevin feels free to use as he applies and manipulates the department's regulations. It makes sense to Kevin to squeeze in one more check for a welfare client starting a job. Without something to tide her over she might bounce right back onto welfare for lack of a babysitter, appropriate clothing or even the carfare to get to work. And to Kevin it makes sense not to fill out an NFL on the Utility Emergency of a feeble-minded client even though it costs him a few points.

But it was becoming harder and harder, even before full computerization, for welfare workers to find these areas of discretion.

It was also getting harder for the welfare workers to know enough to give the clients useful off-the-record advice. The rules on food stamp entitlement are so complicated that it used to take a long calculation, figuring in income, rent, dependents and so on to come up with the allotment for each family. Formerly, the welfare worker made these calculations at his desk and told the client right then what his food stamp grant would be. But now the worker merely takes down the information and sends it upstairs to EDP. There the data processing clerk enters it into the computer, which makes the calculation. The client is informed of his food stamp allotment later.

Every worker I talked to was happy to be relieved of the tedious food stamp calculation. But it left them less useful to the client. Newer workers who'd never done the calculation themselves couldn't estimate for a client that cutting her rent from $200 to $150 a month might in fact make the family poorer.

"I happen to have made a food stamp chart to handle that problem," Kevin told me when I brought up the issue. He pointed proudly to a geometric crayoned design on the wall that I had taken to be a child's artwork.

Kevin's food stamp chart was an ingenious multicolored graphic that indicated at a glance what various budget changes would mean for different-sized families. Actually, it wasn't one chart but a sheaf of papers. "I revise it every time the regulations change. Lots of people Xeroxed this chart," he told me proudly. "They even use it down in Intake."

Despite Kevin's chart, clients were more and more often hearing, "I can't answer that question. The computer will let you know."

I outlined the same scenario to Kevin that I'd tried on Eddy: an automated system with FAWs at terminals entering the data onto electronic forms; eligibility determinations made inside the machine; the computer also programmed to track each worker and calculate productivity automatically.

"Why not have the client enter his data himself?" Kevin suggested, carrying my fantasy one step further. "He comes in and goes to a screen that says 'My problem is *A,* house burned down; *B,* new baby; *C,* change of address.' "

"Why not?" I agreed excitedly. "The customer enters his own data on a bank money machine. It's the obvious next step."

But Kevin was only kidding. "There's too many parts to the job and too many exceptions to ever get it onto a program," he said confidently. "As a matter of fact, there's so much to know that there's only one person in the department who knows it all. That's me. So I'm not worried."

Jo Martin

Before Welfare had been reorganized, with the Department of Social Services (DSS) split off, two black welfare recipients took advantage of a 1960s social program to become welfare employees. They started as clerks, then each went back to school to become a full-fledged social worker. When the split came, one of them, Ellen Jones, was moved up into the DSS to handle foster children. The other, Jo Martin, stayed in welfare where her newly earned title, Social Worker, was changed to FAW.

In my quest for a long-term social worker who'd seen the job change, I phoned Ellen Jones. Ellen felt that her job at

DSS was still basically social work. If I was interested in the changes, she suggested I look up her friend Jo. "I'm embarrassed. I haven't called her in so long. But I'm sure you'll get honest responses from her."

□   □   □

"That's her," said the man, pointing to a desk by the side wall. Josephine Martin didn't look like my imaginary Jane Addams social worker with a grey bun and sturdy walking shoes. She was a tiny woman with flimsy shoes and short, fuzzy hair that you couldn't quite call a natural.

I watched her for a while across the open office. She was pulling pieces of paper out of an overstuffed folder, looking them over and tucking them back in, the way a bird would tuck and smooth the raggedy wisps around her nest. Watching Josephine perched on her chair with one leg curled under her, I realized why all the women in my family sit that way. Our legs are also too short to reach the ground.

When I introduced myself she stood up for a moment and we both smiled broadly, perhaps from the mutual enjoyment of being small. And when we learned that we each had one child, raised alone—"Juliet is sixteen." "Jerome is twenty-six." —we understood the pleasure welling in each other's smiles. "His eight-year-old daughter is living with me now," Jo said, "so I know how much fun you had raising a little girl."

Something about her invited me to say true things.

"People often congratulate me for raising a child alone. But you know," I leaned over to confess, "it's much easier than with two parents."

"I know what you mean," Jo answered with the same freedom. "If my husband hadn't been killed I'd have had two kids to take care of instead of one."

"Oh, I'm sorry," I apologized, "I assumed you were divorced or . . ."

"Oh, that's all right," she comforted me. "I loved my life

with my son. And if my husband had lived," she said cheerfully, "I'd never have been able to go to college or be a social worker."

I made a note to get back to that.

"How are you managing with the point system?" I asked, knowing that Jo was barely making her 70 percent each month.

"It's awful, it's hideous. If I do this whole redetermination," she said, lifting the bulging file on her desk, "all I get is 1.8. But take this WTP," she pulled a form out of the folder, "if I did it alone, it would be .7 just by itself."

"What's a WTP?" I asked.

"It's if a client's kid has turned six and the mother is home, I have to register her for work training."

"I never heard of that one."

"It's like the old WIN program."

"Oh, yes, I remember the WIN program. It decimated my daughter's day-care center."

"Then there's the AP2 and the FSP4 and the EA1 and the . . ." She saw I couldn't get it all down and she backtracked.

"Before we can do the re**dy** [redetermination], we have to take the case, every case, and go through every pocket," she illustrated again with the same tattered file, "find out what has to be done, purge the case—that's pull out any material two years old or older. All that is no points yet. All that is whether they show up or not.

"Then we get maybe two, three hours for a case. Some cases are like that. Just a person with one child. But then come the ones with two, three kids and changing schools and changing grants and do everything else. And that's just forms. That's not interviewing; that's not social work.

"Look at this," she began pulling forms out of her middle drawer. "If the child has turned six you do this one. If the child has not turned six you do that one." As she named each item, she slapped another form down on the desk. "If the child is over sixteen you got to send out an SV1. If there's income you fill out an MR. Then you got to get everybody's Social Security number. Only they haven't got a Social Security number for the baby yet. So you're angry at them because you got your forms to fill out. Then you've got your E.T., grant change, replacement ATP, summary ATP. . . ." She was pulling forms out of the drawer with such accelerating anguish that I felt I had to stop her before she crashed.

"How many forms do you think there are all together? Did you ever count?"

"I don't know. Whenever you start to count you'll always find more. Look, here's one," she said reaching way back into the drawer. "If they were on Blue Cross/Blue Shield at one time but they've stopped working. . . .

"I have to do forty-eight, forty-nine complete reedies a month to make my quota and send out maybe seventy, eighty letters. [Josephine's job at the time was just redeterminations, with no case maintenance.] The way it is now you're not a social worker, you're an FAW. If you take ten minutes out to help one kid in a family you're gonna' fall behind."

"What do you mean?"

"If they say, 'I think my baby is sick. I don't know where to take him' I don't say, 'What's the matter?' I say, 'I can recommend you to Project Good Health.' And I don't even look.

"Now if you is a person with a problem, you don't want to just tell it to everyone. You want to feel it out first. 'This worker, does she have some sensitivity to my problem? Can she hear me?' But I can't hear her. I can't listen to her. I'm just trying to get my points. The whole system is survival. And she goes away feeling as bad or worse than when she came down here.

"See, some people come here, they know the welfare system better than I know it. They just want to get their full grant and leave.

"But some people come here, they are at the end of their rope. They think, 'You is a social worker. That's something. Maybe you can help me.' And they start telling me about a child that is getting out of hand, starting to drink, not coming home.

"If she says, 'Mrs. Martin, he acts up. He really hurtin' himself. But he is a good boy,' and I say, 'I can refer you to the Department of Social Services,' she's gonna say, 'Oh, that's all right.' What she's thinking is, 'They're gonna take my child.'

"You gotta understand," Jo pleaded with me, "these people are up from Alabama with very little education."

"Where are you from, by the way?"

"Alabama. Came up here at sixteen with my husband." But Jo was still concentrating on the other woman's story. "See, she's just afraid they're gonna take her child away."

"And the one with the worst fear is the one least able to help the kid herself," I suggested.

"Right. She's got nobody up here to help her with that kind of problem. Sure, I'm filling out the form trying to get food stamps for her. But they don't want food. It's not that kind of life-and-death. They want to talk to you about a problem.

"I don't like to look off into the distance, cut them off, say, 'Oh, yes, I understand.' You *don't* understand! You can't understand if you can't listen!

"I'm her worker, I'm the one she asked, and I look away. If I say DSS she gonna say, 'Oh, that's all right,' and you won't hear from her again till the problem gets so bad that the child is in jail."

Jo's anguish has been building. Now the knot in her throat seemed to subside a bit. "Before, in the old system, she'd be in here in a week if the child don't want to go to school or starts drinking. Before, when we used to make house calls [here Jo took a little metal file box from the back of her desk], if someone would tell me her daughter was staying out all night I would say, 'Let me come around after school tomorrow and talk to the child by myself.'

"See, I had my box with all my clients arranged in order of the streets." She opened the box lovingly as she named Boston streets. "I learned what streets were next to what and I'd organize my box like that. And some of them would give me phone numbers that weren't for the case records. Just for my box. So I could call to make an appointment. I didn't have to send out letters. And they knew I was coming, and they'd be there, and they'd have all their documentation in the house. Or they'd call and say, 'I can't find the stubs or the rent receipt,' and they'd make another appointment for a different day. So I didn't have to close the case."

"People must have trusted you," I said, "to cooperate so well."

She smiled, "Things went faster when you were doing them over coffee," and continued her reminiscence.

"I could get to five, six people in a day and complete all their cases. I could make time to talk to a child, plan to get there when she came home from school."

Jo's memories of five successful home visits in one afternoon were as shiny with time as her worn-down file box. There must have been days she traipsed around her district and reached no one at all. And surely there were other days she left the center at 2 o'clock and went straight to the movies with little Jerome. (Also socially useful work.) But I was beginning to believe she had a talent for the social work that was no longer a part of her job.

"What might you say to that girl who's started staying out all night?" I asked.

"It's more a matter of listening than what you would tell them," said Josephine. "Some people don't talk to the child about sex, ever. But when they find they can talk to you about it they might ask, 'What he want me to do, Mrs. Martin, is it fair?' "

"My boyfriend wants me to move in with him, Mrs. Martin," I said. [At that time in my life, I needed a social worker too.] "To set up a home together, that is. But he has four teenage children of his own." She was now listening very professionally. Which is to say like a good friend.

"Four?"

"Yes, twelve to seventeen."

"And your daughter has had Mommy all to herself till now?"

"Yes," I nodded. She looked at me and described the scene.

"So his children will come over for weekends . . ."

"It's not weekends. It's joint custody. He feels very strongly about that. Though it isn't worked out yet. It keeps changing."

"His children come to stay for a while and they see their father living full time with this other child. Meantime, your daughter is invaded by four large teenagers. She's screamin', 'Ma, get them out of my room' "

"I don't think she'd ever actually scream like that."

"So she's clenching her fists silently and gritting her teeth at you, 'Why don't you rescue me?' "

"I guess I didn't really train her to be too adjustable."

"Now don't talk 'adjustable.' You and she share a wonderful home together. I can tell by the way you smile. You made a home that was right for you two. You don't want to lose it. And what you and this man have together [I'm omitting some of the little things I'd already told her about Bill] could also be lost in that house."

I nodded. It all sounded true, but . . .

"Your daughter's sixteen, right?"

Once again, I couldn't help smiling that idiotic smile, to think of Juliet, sixteen.

"She gonna go to college, maybe?"

"Probably."

"Now this man, he wants to live with you and make a home for ever and ever?"

"Right. And I'm beginning to think it might work."

"Listen, if this is supposed to be forever, then why can't he wait two more years? Wouldn't that be fair?"

"Why, of course," I said. "Of course." I wondered if the fifteen-year-old girl who was starting to stay out all night would feel as relieved after talking to Jo as I did. Two more years while we both work on our own families, then move in together when we can concentrate more on each other.

"So what you gotta do in the meantime is . . ."

She was interrupted by the phone.

"It's the director. She wants to see me right away in her office." And she left the room.

While Jo was out I thought about how quickly she'd understood my problem. Is that because we'd led similar lives as single mothers? But Jo came up North with her husband at sixteen. When she went back to high school for her equivalency diploma she got out of class at seven minutes to 9. At 9 o'clock she had to be home to put Jerome to bed. And the house had to be spotless, everything cooked and cleaned, or she couldn't go to school. After her husband was killed on a construction job, Jo started college. Was her experience really like mine?

When Jo talked about her clients she assumed their accents —"He hurtin' himself. But he's a good boy."—and their feelings, too. When she listened to me she was hearing a middle-class, New York writer. But I had no doubt she was truly hearing me.

Jo Martin didn't have a bun or wear Red Cross shoes, but she could remember back to the days when a social worker was supposed to help. And she had a true vocation. I guess I'd finally met my old-fashioned social worker who'd seen her profession scaled down to paperwork.

Jo was not good at the paperwork. She faced each client's redetermination the way I face my income tax returns.

Forty-nine rederterminations a month is only a little over two a day. Any monthly quota with welfare recipients as the raw data is bound to be frustrating. There are always so many loose ends hanging out of each folder. But it's not really a high quota. The fact is that Jo Martin is not an efficient FAW. But a human service department that's organized so it can't use her true skill is profoundly inefficient.

"The director asked who you were," Jo said when she returned. "I told her you were doing an interview about my life starting with how I came up from the South. I told her you'd been at DSS, too. Next time you should go to the administration first, she said."

"O.K.," I said. "Maybe I will, next time."

Jo gave me her home phone number and reminded me to give her regards to Ellen. "No," she answered my final question, "I wouldn't take this job the way it is now. But I been here so long and I'm forty-six."

I left, hoping I hadn't gotten her into trouble with the director.

Daniel Sheridan

Several people had described Daniel Sheridan as the fairest and most efficient supervisor at NTW. "Straight arrow" was the phrase that kept coming up.

Daniel's shining, boyish face seemed to fit the description. So did his shiny-clean desk. On a table near the door where the five FAWs he supervised were to place their finished work, Daniel had taped four neatly lettered signs: REDTs, CASE MAIN, PRIORITIES, and REDTs WITH CORRECTIONS. The four spaces were all empty. An FAW popped in as we were leaving for lunch. "Just a quick question. I got a woman here who moved out of her sister's house and she needs her own food stamps." Daniel advised him on the quickest procedure.

As we walked toward the restaurant I took notes on his personal history: twelve years with the Welfare Department; three years as a supervisor; married; two children; a former policeman, who transferred to Welfare when he was injured.

Glancing over my shoulder, I suppose to check my facts, he asked, "Is that your own shorthand?"

"It's my actual handwriting."

"Mine is bad too," he commiserated, "because the nuns made me write with my right hand. They threatened to break my arm if I kept up left-handed."

"Oh dear," I shuddered.

"But still," he said, "I wish there were more Catholic schools, for the discipline."

Good! Catholic-school boy, ex-policeman, pro-discipline: Daniel Sheridan should have a proper management mentality. When we were seated and served, I posed my first question as open-endedly as I could. "What do you think of the time standards and the point system?"

"I blame the union for the way it's operating," Daniel answered concisely.

"You mean because they're sabotaging it?"

"No, because they're not sabotaging it."

"What do you mean?"

"If they followed the rules as the department issued them, this system would have collapsed in three months."

"You want it to collapse?"

"If I were a worker and a union activist," Daniel said, "the first time I did 100 percent in the first three weeks of the month I'd stop work. And if they tried to make me do anything over 100 percent, I'd fill out an overtime form.

"The problem," he declared, "is that all the workers have

developed systems of their own to get the points they need and still deliver a timely service. That's what keeps this place going."

"But why do you, as a supervisor, want the system to collapse?" I asked.

"First of all, because keeping track of points makes more work for me. Second because I am a fellow worker and I see where this system is leading."

"By the way," I asked, "how do you keep track of all those control slips? It seems like you could spend half your time on that alone."

"You could," he said, "but I have my own system. What I do is make a file for each worker for each week and arrange their control slips by the number. All the .3s, all the .2s, all the .1s.

"The workers all claim to be against the system but they don't actively pursue it to the point that the system would collapse.

"What I see them do is go for their 70 percent or their 100 percent or whatever they want and then bank their penny slips for the next month or trade them around. Or help out someone who can't make it.

"The problem is that the union hasn't fully explained to the workers where this system is going."

"What do you mean?"

"I have been told at a training session for supervisors that eventually they won't have to put in the penny slips. Every action the worker does will go directly onto the computer and be counted automatically. Instead of tallying their points I could go over to the computer and it would say this is the fifteenth day of the month, number zero zero zero has earned eighty-six hours of credit.

"At another of the classes I attended, a woman from Washington suggested that eventually welfare will be run like Social Security. You fill out a form and you get your check.

"For the worker that means you don't have to talk to the client. You just take down the information, put it in the computer and the computer makes the decision and gives out the money."

"Or the client can input the information himself," I suggested. "Like you do at the bank money machine."

"This is exactly the philosophy of Monthly Reporting," Daniel responded. "Even now the worker only checks information to transmit it to the computer. He has no determination as to the budget. If the client does what he's supposed to, there is no judgment and no intercession by the worker. There is no real welfare worker.

"But," said Daniel, searching for the brighter side, "the machine doesn't always work. And when the computer makes a mistake it can be by thousands of dollars. For instance, a woman added a new child to the budget and, because of a glitch in the program, every month for the next few months it kept adding a new dependent. She owed us three or four hundred dollars. Also," he said hopefully, "there are frauds whereby a client and a worker, or even a worker alone could . . ."

After a consoling digression on the possibilities of larceny and computer error, Daniel returned to his sober analysis. "Right now the union activists are the most guilty of making this system work. Instead of using their own shortcuts, they should follow all the rules and collect all the points they're entitled to and let the system collapse."

□   □   □

Daniel Sheridan struck me as a profoundly good, courteous and organized man. His natural inclination was to solve problems and to make things work for people. I wondered if he would have the conviction to carry out the policy he advocates were he an FAW. Was he stubborn enough to say, "If they want me to act like a machine, then I will—no matter how much inconvenience it caused for clients and fellow workers? It would be a severe test of his inherent decency.

From what I'd observed, Daniel was correct. The welfare center was working now, in its own peculiar way, because each worker balanced the rules of the point system against his own individual rules of public service and common sense.

Debby and Jo harked back to an earlier era of social work. Many of the services they tried to perform for welfare recipients were now officially eliminated. Kevin and Eddy, younger and brasher, were a product of the current era. They applied their legalistic minds to distributing the entitled benefits rapidly and according to the rules. But the small amount of discretion they were allowed was used to tip the see-saw toward the recipient or at least to head off Kafkaesque entanglements. They took it upon themselves to act as ombudsmen.

Personally, I favor a welfare system with the least possible worker intervention. I think the most efficient plan would be to send every man and woman in the country a $10,000 check each year. This would eliminate all eligibility decisions except alive or dead.

But in the meantime welfare requires each person to tell his story and prove his need. It requires a judgment about each dollar in each case.

One goal of welfare automation is to take every aspect of this overly complex judgment away from the welfare worker and have it made inside the machine—which is to say, at a higher level. The aim is to restrict discretion and intervention (usually pro-client) by workers in the local offices.

But what would happen in those local offices if workers complied by becoming as mechanical and obedient as machines? In Britain unions have shut down the post office and other services through a job action called "work to rule." They merely follow the rules as written, and chaos ensues.

While management works ceaselessly to restrict human

judgment and flexibility, it's also dependent upon them. If any efficiency expert ever perfected a system that repressed these qualities completely, if workers really did just as they were told using no judgment at all, disaster would be immediate. But so far there is no earthly work environment that achieves this management ideal. Even on the most regimented assembly line there's room for discretion. And workers generally use that discretion to keep things moving along. It takes enormous discipline for human beings to withdraw their cooperation and common sense. It's amazing how hard it is to carry out the threat, "If they treat me like a machine, then I'll act like one."

□   □   □

When I left Daniel's office it was 3 o'clock on a Friday afternoon. As I crossed the lobby, Eddy walked past. I gave him my good-bye pronouncement. "Eddy, I'm afraid the next step will be to enter all your work directly onto a computer, which will time everything you do and issue all the grant letters and decisions automatically. And if they could get the client to enter his own data, they'd eliminate you entirely. That's the direction in other services."

"If it's strictly mail and machine," Eddy replied "there'll be riots and destruction of property. It's much cheaper to give them the bodies of social workers to abuse." And he strode off to face his clients.

Maybe Eddy is right. Welfare won't be as easy to automate as banking because the data—welfare clients with their babies and burnouts—isn't as neat to enter into the computer.

Ellen Jones

Ellen Jones had moved up with Jo Martin from welfare mother to clerk to social worker before she was promoted to

the Department of Social Services. I stopped by the DSS to
thank her for putting me in contact with Jo.

"And how is Jo?" Ellen asked as she guided me to her own
office, which was carpeted and air-conditioned. On the way
we passed two women discussing a foster girl and her problems in her new school. "I really should go back and visit the
old center."

"This is the way they work now," I said. And I handed her
the three page list of Work Measurement Standards.

Food stamp change	.5
Address change	.3
Issue food stamp I.D. card	.3
Authorize funeral and burial expenses	.7
Replace lost or stolen check: FCB-1	.4
Issue supplementary over-the-counter ATP	.2
Issue replacement over-the-counter ATP	.6

"Poor Jo," Ellen said, as I explained that the numbers meant
tenths of an hour. "I can remember when we were first asked
to get Social Security numbers on the babies. That was the
beginning, I guess." She shook her head as she scanned the
list. "But it was gradual."

Ellen's officemate, a union activist (Service Employees International Union Local 509 represents both the Welfare Department and the Department of Social Services) pointed out
that the pay slide in the Welfare Department had been gradual
too. "They didn't get a cut in pay when they became Financial
Assistance Workers but they just didn't go up the ladder. So
Social Workers and FAWs kind of . . . ," with her hands she
showed one moving up, the other sliding down, "separated.
But that was gradual too."

□　□　□

Professional futurists have been saying for twenty-five years
that office automation will eliminate the drudge work. The

Office of the Future, they predict, will offer fewer jobs, perhaps, but more skilled ones.

Maybe they mean jobs like Ellen's. Her office deals with foster children, abused children, drug addicts and other special problems. My visit to the Department of Social Services reminded me of one of the frequent patterns in service automation. When a front-line service job, the rank that first meets the customer, is reduced to a clerical function, it's often necessary to create a smaller second rank of better-treated and better-trained workers. These supervisors, ombudsmen or exception workers must be permitted enough discretion to deal with special problems that the lower-level clerks are no longer allowed to handle.

When social workers become FAWs, when telephone operators are monitored, when bank tellers literally become machines, there have to be exception workers to cover cases that weren't coded into the program. (At airline reservation offices special "Flagship" or "Gold Card" phone lines are manned by exception workers, who deal with frequent fliers or travel agents. They're freer to deviate from the script.)

The Department of Social Services was established to handle special problems when welfare became restricted to the routine distribution of checks. The DSS workers have a quiet, carpeted office, a secretary, higher pay and significantly more nonmonitored time than the FAWs. But there are fewer of them, and they see only extreme cases.

So far, computerized service work has necessitated a higher number of exception workers than automaters had hoped. Customers are always demanding to speak to a supervisor. Still, for every Ellen in DSS there are dozens of Kevins and Jos about to become computer-aided clerks. Contrary to expert predictions, the majority of jobs are being downgraded. Fewer service workers are free to use human discretion.

By now you have to be a special good customer to see a

human banker. Or a special bad customer to see a human welfare worker.

□ □ □

Ellen handed me back the list of sixty-eight functions. "Nobody knew it would end like this."

"I don't think this is the end," I said, folding away the contraband document.

"Poor Jo. What a different head."

Gene DeLucia

Two weeks later I arranged a telephone interview with Gene DeLucia. DeLucia was head of the systems unit of the Department of Public Welfare and Special Assistant to the Commissioner for Systems. Many of the members of his systems group were on loan to the Department of Welfare from high-tech firms that also consult for the Defense Department, where systems analysis was developed. After automating welfare in other states, they were now in Massachusetts to oversee a three-year, federally funded project called MPACS—Massachusetts Public Assistance Control System. Though automation had proceeded piecemeal for ten years, it seemed it would finally go all the way under MPACS. DeLucia was the perfect spokesman, then, for "where it's at and where it's going in welfare." And that's just what I asked him.

□ □ □

"Basically I am trying, or rather the systems group is trying, to transfer as much computer power as we possibly can to the end user. The goal is to get as close as possible to a paperless office.

"What I envisage is that the client comes in and the Financial Assistance Worker turns to a terminal. If this is a new client the machine will prompt the questions to be asked. The Financial Assistance Worker just fills in the answers as stated by the client. At that point the eligibility for all categories of welfare aid from the state of Massachusetts will be automatically determined. Are they eligible for a grant and in what amount? Are they eligible for medical benefits? Are they eligible for food stamps and in what amount?

"There will be no turn-around document, because the material goes right into the computer. At that point we can give the client a statement saying, 'Here are your benefits and this is the information they're based upon.' Which he can check right there."

"Could the clients eventually input the information themselves?" I asked.

"I would like nothing better than to see a bank of terminals in the lobby for the clients to do the preliminary input. But that will not happen within the next three years. Our first goal is to make our own workers computer literate."

"What about measuring workers' productivity?" I asked. "Will there be a computerized version of the control slips?"

"What we want to do is put the head office in a position to measure the workers' productivity directly. We want to know how many redeterminations did they do, how many clients did they interview and with what level of accuracy, not only for the local office but for the individual operator. [I wasn't surprised to hear that the head office would be able to bypass local directors and supervisors and peer directly into the screen of each welfare worker in the state. But I was surprised to hear Mr. DeLucia already referring to the FAWs as "operators".] With computers we should be able to do this for each operator automatically."

"What will be the standard of productivity?" I asked.

"What I'd like to do and what I'll be able to do are not necessarily the same thing. It will depend on the outcome of other factors including union negotiations. But if it were my role to plan the terminals, I would want to be able to access, for each operator, how many clients they saw on a daily or hourly basis and with what level of accuracy."

"Would there still be productivity standards or quotas by the tenth of the hour?" I asked.

"No. With the computerized system the goals can be dynamically set. I can trap all the information to measure how people are meeting the standards across the state at any given moment. That way I can tell on an ongoing basis if the standards need to be higher or lower." ("Trap all the information . . . across the state at any given moment." I began to understand the allure of omnipotence.)

DeLucia explained the priority that guided the MPACS project and the similar PACS studies in other states. "The federal government has funded these studies to achieve a certain level of consistency. That means that if there are sixty local offices in a state they want to know that there will be consistency in the application of the welfare guidelines. In addition, the government wants more management information available. But consistency is the main thing."

"Does that mean," I asked, trying not to sound hostile, "that there will be significantly less discretion for the welfare workers?" I thought I was asking a negative question and feared that it might prompt a defensive answer. But Mr. DeLucia and I were oriented so differently to the concept of workers' discretion that he wheeled around to defend the opposite flank.

"There will definitely be much less discretion," he assured me stoutly. "However," he admitted, "if the worker is so inclined he can still shade the information going into the computer." This was said as an admission that no system is perfect.

Like many consultants who apply the systems method, Gene Delucia has a tendency to speak abstractly. This is natural, since the theory of systems analysis asserts that the method is equally applicable to almost any endeavor from moving troops, to match-making, to disposing of garbage.[1]

Though he seemed remote from the daily workings of a welfare center, DeLucia gave me a well-stated summary of what I know to be state-of-the-art thinking among systems analysts automating public service. From his description, it seems that social workers will wind up half-way between receptionists and airline reservation agents.

A Hole in the Floor

Welfare was in one way a fortunate service profession to study at this time. Budget cuts and a general lack of purpose had left automation dangling for almost ten years. That meant that without any trick photography we were able to watch, in slow motion, a process that normally goes too fast to see.

In order to automate any job, white-collar or industrial, all its functions have to be broken out. When Henry Ford designed his automobile assembly line, he had to make sure he included every step from *weld motor* to *attach running board*. He couldn't afford to say afterwards, "Oh, we forgot the door handles." Similarly, welfare automaters have to include every operation from *add baby* to *issue funeral allowance*.

But normally with computer automation, there'd be no extended period of keeping track of every function on paper. The decade of control slips and constantly amended time standards at the Welfare Department is obviously absurd. Add a baby, .3; issue burial expenses, .7. It looks like a parody of the systems approach to human services.

In most cases, from the appearance of the first clipboard men to the installation of the fully automated system, there's little time to do much more than worry about who'll keep their jobs.

When a skilled job is routinized, some people move up to become supervisors or exception workers. The rest are usually fired, transferred or disappear through a process of accelerated attrition.

It's hard, then, to show through interviews that a professional job has been downgraded, because the professional is usually gone. There's "a hole in the floor," a phrase I first heard at an insurance company where it was used to describe the void created by eliminating a position as opposed to just laying off a person. The person now doing the major part of the job may have started as a clerk. And the new clerical job may be an upgraded position. Even now, while the welfare system is still in transition, FAWs no longer need college degrees and they're paid less than social workers.

Because Welfare has been automating piecemeal and because it's a civil service job, more employees stay on. Therefore, we're able for once to watch some individuals move down steadily, step by step, from autonomous professionals to skilled clerks.

I left Boston wondering which of the social workers I met at NTW would still be there when they finally reached the level DeLucia referred to as "operators."

□ □ □

Fourteen months later, most people at NTW had at least heard the acronym MPACS. A gaggle of social workers were gathered in the hallway the day I dropped in again.

"That MPACS thing, it's definitely going through."

"Nah, they called it off again."

"Look, there's no way they can start it up till . . ."

"It's rescheduled for February," Daniel Sheridan cut through the confusion. "They're asking for volunteers." Daniel passed around a letter requesting six supervisors to staff a model MPACS unit. A suburban welfare office had been selected for the test site.

"So it's not till February."

"Way out there?"

"Volunteers, huh?"

"Yeah, lateral transfers."

"So they don't want a typical unit. They want to pick all antiunion people."

"No, I think it just means . . ."

No one was sure what it meant except Eddy Malloy, the FAW who loved computers.

"Everything we do is gonna be done from our desks now," Eddy began one of his frenetic monologues. "They give you an I.D. number. When you turn it on in the morning, you're on. When you turn it off in the evening, you're gone. It's a total control system. Look, I've got . . ."

The FAWs dispersed, unable to absorb Eddy's Cassandra-like vision.

In the months since my last visit, Eddy had changed more than anything else at NTW. He was still a somewhat awkward youth but he'd grown his hair long, moved into his own apartment and become the union's official automation expert.

"I've got copies of the proposed screens." We were in his office now and he was pulling papers out of shopping bags. "Got myself a slot on the committee: I'm in with this guy who's writing the GSD [General Systems Design]. This company that got the contract to computerize us [shoving more papers at me], they've already done Georgia, they're in the process of doing New Mexico. Twenty-three states are already . . ."

"What about the monitoring programs?" I asked.

"That's what they won't tell us. There's a state Right-to-Know law. I think I could force them to disclose . . ."

Eddy's phone rang. "Belmont?" he hopped over to his old one-way terminal and scanned the screen. "Yes, Lavone Belmont is active in that she has two children, Cherisa and Shawn. . . . Right."

"A hospital," Eddy explained when he got off the phone, "for the medical billing. Previously I would have had to find the T.D., then check the master file down the hall, which comes out once a month. With the computer, if you open a person today, they're open. It's still a terrific tool."

"So why doesn't the union say, O.K., we'll take the computers but without the monitoring programs?" I asked. "*No Monitoring*. Before they get you on line, before you become so tied to the machine that you can't even . . ."

As soon as I suggested a confrontation on electronic monitoring Eddy did an understandable about face and began explaining why there wasn't any rush.

"The better people will train the others at first. While it's still training there'll still be some physical freedom."

"O.K., so you personally will be able to walk around for the first few months," I conceded. "But you just told me yourself, it's a total control system. Once they switch you on . . ."

"It's not gonna go in for at least a year and a half. They'd never put it in before an election year. Anyway, a third of these welfare buildings aren't usable as is," Eddy continued reassuring himself. "They'll have to Mickey Mouse it around to fit in all their computers. Too many terminals generate too much heat in these tiny old rooms. I got the health and safety regulations here . . . We're gonna fight them every step on . . ."

"So you're gonna fight them on how many terminals they can put in each room?" I shook my head. "You're gonna nitpick, slow 'em down. That's the whole plan?"

"Listen," Eddy told me conspiratorially. "I can bring down this machine, and every machine in the building due to a hardware flaw. The Welfare Department is so incompetent, they gave the contract to a company that sells a machine that I can crash just by . . ."

"By everybody pressing the same button at the same time," I cut him off.

"All it takes is *two* people," he protested.

"Oh, Eddy, don't you think they can fix that? Besides, you love the computer. It's a wonderful tool."

"Yeah, but once they put in the monitoring we're done, we're gone, we're EDP operators."

We'd come full circle.

I continued educating poor Eddy: "The welfare workers in Sweden said they wouldn't use computers unless all the time they saved on paperwork was used to do real social work." Eddy was pacing fast and shaking his head, but I continued. "The Canadian Postal Workers Union got an actual clause in their contract that says no monitoring on groups less than ten. The Blue Cross/Blue Shield workers in California are asking for . . ." There were pitifully few examples I could cite.

"We'd lose the point if we said no individual monitoring," he insisted.

"Call it a matter of health and safety," I kept at it. "Monitored clerical workers have the highest rate of stress diseases: heart attacks, high blood pressure, muscle strain." Eddy was by now pacing faster and banging his fists against his thighs. "Or call it privacy," I wouldn't stop. "Several unions in Europe have been able to . . ."

Eddy's despair turned to anger. "The system is called MPACS," he hissed at me. "Massachusetts Public Assistance *Control* System. 'Control' is the operative adjective. How can I tell them to take out the control? Control is what the system is about!"

□　□　□

All the way home I felt bad about asking twenty-eight-year-old Eddy Malloy to raise a quixotic banner against the entire second industrial revolution. He was right. Control is what the system is about. He'd be asking management to give up the most powerful control tool ever invented.

The state Welfare Department, supported by federal grants,

had brought in a high-powered team of systems analysts. Their techniques had been perfected at Lockheed, the RAND Corporation, Aerojet-General and so on, with limitless Pentagon funds.

Who did Eddy have on his side? Ironically, Eddy was the only one who liked computers well enough to take a close look at the proposed screens. How could he convey the numbing detail of the electronic sweatshop to Debby, Kenny, Jo and the others?

For the last ten years, welfare had been evolving from a social work profession to a clerical job. This was policy with or without computers. The bureaucratic blizzard in which every paper generated another piece of paper was distressing to all the welfare workers. But it had led the conscientious workers to believe that they'd always be able to get around the system; they'd always be able to pinch time from the paperwork to do their social work.

Even now, as the federal government looms over them with MPACS, the social workers at NTW still can't imagine that they will ever sit at a terminal dispensing welfare the way other workers dole out phone reservations or Big Macs.

4

□ □ □ □ □ □ □ □

The Machine Will See You Now

By now you have some idea why you can't expect flexible conversation from a fast-food counterman or an airline reservation agent. If you want individual attention you'll have to go to a slow-food restaurant or a travel agent.

Spontaneous human contact is minimized when customer service is automated. But even before automation, these weren't essentially relationship jobs. Conversation was necessary, of course, in order for the waiter or the reservation clerk to find out what you wanted and to transmit your order. But human contact was only a by-product of these services, not the product itself. It's not as if McDonald's has automated love, motherhood or psychotherapy. Nor did the Welfare Department truly automate social work.

No one in the Massachusetts Welfare Department would claim that today's welfare clerk provides the same kind of human services as the old-fashioned social worker. She's not supposed to. When the department changed the title of its front-line employee from Social Worker to Financial Assistance Worker, it had decided to get rid of whatever was left of the diagnosing, counseling and comforting functions. In this sense the social work hasn't been automated, it's been eliminated.

But outside of welfare, more ambitious planners are determined to automate human services in a more profound sense. They're developing programs that can "listen" to your problems, "mull over" possibilities and deliver the kind of advice you'd expect from a personal counselor.

These programs are in the category called "expert systems." They're the first commercial products of the field of computer science called "artificial intelligence."

Interestingly, the first and still most famous computerized counselor was designed by a man who had no intention of replacing human beings. In his book *Computer Power and Human Reason* [1] this unusual computer scientist pleaded with his colleagues to understand that human intelligence was almost divinely different from anything they could simulate. Yet he inadvertently created the computer therapist that inspired a generation of automaters to believe that they could replace human sympathy with something cheaper.

Joseph Weizenbaum and ELIZA

In 1966 Joseph Weizenbaum of MIT demonstrated a language-processing program that could play (or in Weizenbaum's word, "parody") the role of a Rogerian therapist. "The Rogerian therapist is relatively easy to imitate," Weizenbaum explained, "because much of his technique consists of drawing his patient out by reflecting the patient's statements back to him."

Weizenbaum named the program ELIZA, after Eliza Doolittle, because, in a very limited sense, he would be teaching it to talk.

To test the program, he invited students and staff at MIT to type patientlike statements into the computer. ELIZA answered in print.

Here's an example of a conversation generated between a young woman (roman type) and ELIZA (*italics*).

Men are all alike.
In what way
They're always bugging us about something or other.
Can you think of a specific example
Well, my boyfriend made me come here.
Your boyfriend made you come here
He says I'm depressed much of the time.
I am sorry to hear you are depressed
It's true, I am unhappy.
Do you think coming here will help you not to be unhappy
I need some help. That much seems certain.
What would it mean if you could get some help
Perhaps I could learn to get along with my mother.
Tell me more about your family
My mother takes care of me.
Who else in your family takes care of you
My father.
Your father
You are like my father in some ways.
What resemblance do you see
You are not very aggressive but I think you don't want me to
    notice that.
What makes you think I am not very aggressive
You don't argue with me.
Why do you think I don't argue with you
You are afraid of me.
Does it please you to believe I am afraid of you
My father is afraid of everybody.

What else comes to your mind when you think of your father
Bullies.
*Does that have anything to do with the fact that your boyfriend
made you come here*

ELIZA was the ancestor of today's expert systems. It supplied its responses by using the vocabulary and syntax rules Weizenbaum provided. But, as Joseph Weizenbaum passionately insisted, ELIZA neither converses, analyzes nor understands human feelings. It merely juggles words.

Because he understood these limitations, Weizenbaum was amazed by the way people responded to ELIZA. Some became so engrossed in their therapy that they asked him to leave the room so they could carry on their session in private.

More disturbing was the response from professionals. Carl Sagan, the astrophysicist, wrote[2]:

> . . . I can imagine the development of a network of computer psychotherapeutic terminals, something like arrays of large telephone booths, in which, for a few dollars a session, we would be able to talk with an attentive, tested, and largely nondirective psychotherapist.

In an article in *The Journal of Nervous and Mental Disease*,[3] ELIZA was hailed by therapists as "a therapeutic tool which can be made widely available to mental hospitals and psychiatric centers." The same article suggested that "several hundred patients an hour could be handled by a computer system designed for this purpose," and it explained that a real therapist isn't much more than a sophisticated program anyway:

> A human therapist can be viewed as an information processor and decision maker. . . . He is guided in these decisions by rough empirical rules telling him what is appropriate to say and not to say in certain contexts.

To Joseph Weizenbaum, ELIZA's programmer, psychiatry was one human being helping another. "What can the psychiatrist's image of his patient be," Weizenbaum asked, "when he sees himself not as an engaged human being acting as a healer, but as an information processor following rules?"

The most disturbing response that Weizenbaum dealt with was among his colleagues. Computer scientists hailed ELIZA as an example of artificial intelligence. To Weizenbaum it was clear that his computer "understood" only in the weakest possible sense. It could follow grammatical rules. But it couldn't understand what people felt or meant. It could never understand, for instance, "just what kind of emotional impact touching another person's hand will have both on the other person and on himself. . . . The knowledge involved is in part kinesthetic, its acquisition involves having a hand, to say the very least. There are, in other words," wrote Weizenbaum, "some things humans know by virtue of having a human body."

As the pursuit of artificial intelligence expanded at MIT and most other universities, Weizenbaum, a seminal computer scientist, became more and more isolated by his insistence that computers could never exhibit human intelligence.

Doctor, Lawyer, Military Chief

In the twenty years since Joseph Weizenbaum first showed his little ELIZA around MIT, research in expert systems has been funded primarily by the military. The military developed automatic pilots and expert command systems for sea and air battles. (See Chapter 10, "Command and Control," for more on military expert systems.)

Slowly, expert systems began to be used in the civilian world. They appeared first in industrial settings, where they replicated scarce expertise in fields like oil-well drilling and telephone-line maintenance. Then they began to be consulted for medical diagnosis. Now they're creeping up into the less precise areas of social, psychological and financial expertise.

Periodically interest was aroused anew in the idea of a computer therapist, but no one followed through with a commercial ELIZA. Maybe there was no market. People who can afford psychiatry expect personal attention. For poor people, even mass-produced therapy was still too expensive; costly machines were needed for expert systems.

But in the past twenty years computer hardward has steadily improved so that expert systems similar in principle to ELIZA are now much easier to program and can be run on small computers.

What's most distinctive about expert systems is not the computer hardware or even the programming, but the class of workers—doctors, lawyers and military commanders—whose decision making these systems are designed to replicate. The intention behind these systems—to transfer knowledge, skill and decision making from the employee to the employer—is certainly not a new management goal. In fact, the way expert systems are created sounds exactly like the turn-of-the-century time-and-motion studies conducted by men like Frederick Taylor and Frank Gilbreth. As I listened to the enthusiastic "knowledge engineers" who build expert systems, I couldn't help imagining them in derby hats with stop watches in their vest pockets.

The much-hated stop-watch men stood right behind the laborer and broke his job down into its elementary units: grasp, bend, release load, stand up. The modern knowledge engineer performs similar detailed studies, only he anatomizes decision making rather than bricklaying. So the time-and-motion study has become a time-and-thought study. The most novel thing about building an expert system is the science-fiction-sounding vocabulary used to describe the process.

To build an expert system, a living expert is debriefed and

then cloned by a knowledge engineer. That is to say, an expert is interviewed, typically for weeks or months. The knowledge engineer watches the expert work on sample problems and asks exactly what factors the expert considered in making his apparently intuitive decisions.

Eventually hundreds or thousands of rules of thumb are fed into the computer. The result is a program that can "make decisions" or "draw conclusions" heuristically instead of merely calculating with equations. Like a real expert, a sophisticated expert system should be able to draw inferences from "iffy" or incomplete data that seems to suggest or tends to rule out. In other words it uses (or replaces) judgment.

Can we really automate the expertise of professionals like doctors, lawyers and military commanders? Don't they use intuition as well as rules? Don't they have to look at each case? It's tempting to say that expert systems just won't work. But skilled bakers, tailors and blacksmiths also laughed at the idea of automating jobs that required so much experience and judgment. Perhaps it would be better to ask whether it will work after we've looked at some expert systems more closely.

It's both tricky and tedious to try to capture all of an expert's expertise. I got a sense of this neo–stop-watch procedure when I talked to an estate planning expert who had been cloned into a financial planning expert system.

Natalie Choate

Natalie Choate is the world's first successfully cloned estate planner. Miss Choate, a Harvard Law School graduate (1970), is the partner in charge of pension and estate planning at a prestigious Boston law firm. Over the course of a year, including four months of intensive sessions three or four times a week, she contributed her expertise in estate and retirement planning to PlanPower, a financial planning expert system developed by Applied Expert Systems Inc. (APEX) with the backing of The Travelers Insurance Company. Other experts were debriefed in tax planning, investment planning, and related fields.

PlanPower was the first white-collar expert system I'd heard of that was available on the open market—cost: $70,000. Until then most office expert systems had been developed by corporations or other institutions for their own internal use.

□   □   □

"Did you enjoy being cloned?" I asked Miss Choate in her office.

"It was great fun . . . gave me a chance to think about what I really do in my practice. . . . The most difficult thing to capture was the things that were intuitive for me. The judgments you make when you look at the client and start to talk."

"For instance?" I asked

"For instance, I would say to Bruce, [Bruce Henderson, APEX executive and knowledge engineer] that I would never recommend a particular kind of trust for a young couple. And he would say, 'How young is a young couple?' I'd say. 'Well, in their twenties.' "

In order to convey the difficulty of transforming intuitive judgments into rules, Natalie brought out her notes and recreated some of the debriefing conversations that went on between her and Bruce, for hours, days and months.

> Bruce: You mean the husband is in his twenties or the wife is in her twenties?
>
> Natalie: I guess the husband is in his twenties.
>
> Bruce: So we should make a rule, if the husband is thirty years of age or over we recommend this trust. If the husband is twenty-nine years of age or younger we recommend the other trust.

"Hearing it that way I'd say, 'Well he may be thirty-one and be too young or he may be twenty-nine and old enough.'

"Eventually Bruce's questions made me realize that my judgment wasn't based just on age. Wealth might be a factor. So we'd pare it down till we'd get to a rule that balanced age and wealth. But of course the first client who walked into the office might be the exception to that rule.

"Or there would be a case where we would say, this estate plan is for someone with assets of $750,000 or more. But again the first person to walk into the office with $749,000 might be a good customer. And a person with $800,000 might be wrong because you think it's going to shrink, not grow. So you have to account for that intuitive feeling with rules for determining if this is a shrinking or growing situation. We'd be hours and hours working out all the possibilities till we came up with a rule that was good: a rule that encompassed what I actually did in practice. . . .

"I remember once, a month later, I looked at a rule we had developed and it didn't make any sense to me. So I said let's change it. But we checked it out and found that it was surprising but right."

" 'Right' means?" I asked

" 'Right' means it maximized the estate."

I asked Miss Choate if she would use the expert system in her own office.

"In my own practice? No. I might use it as a check for my own consistency. If I came up with something different from the system I'd check again to make sure I was at my best that day. But in the case of a real difference . . ." Natalie gestured dismissively, confident that she was the real expert.

"How do you feel now that the first few PlanPowers are being shipped out?" I asked. "Right this minute someone in another state may be unpacking or consulting you."

"I love it, it gives me a feeling of . . . You see, as an estate lawyer in a private practice, I draw up X dozen wills a year or X number of plans. But with the APEX project I feel I will do millions of estate trusts. It gives me a feeling of . . . immortality.

"There are people, I'm told, experts, who get upset by the thought that they could be replaced by a system. But the way I feel, if it ever gets to the point where it's as good as I am— let it. I'll go do something else."

□   □   □

Expert systems don't usually replace the expert who's been cloned. Like Natalie Choate, he or she was selected because he's among the leaders in his field. He'll probably go on to acquire new expertise. The program is created to capture some of his knowledge, experience and judgment so that it can be used by other workers who won't ever have to acquire the same level of expertise. In a sense, it's future experts who are being displaced since fewer Natalie Choates will be needed.

As Bruce Henderson, Miss Choate's personal knowledge engineer, explained:

"You and I are not financial planners but with this system we could be. You see, half the job is customer relations. . . . One way our system can be used, the relationship person [salesman, broker or whoever deals with the customer] can sit down and do 'what-ifs' with a mouse. Talk to it like it's a financial planning assistant. . . . Another scenario, the relationship person can take down the data and there's a back office where a low-level staff person can do the work of running the plan. The system saves a great deal of training or retraining and brings some very advanced thinking to everyone."

If the financial planning expert system works according to Bruce Henderson's second scenario, a salesman/clerk ("relationship person") can take down information from the client. A data-input clerk ("low-level staff person") can run the program in the back office. The APEX system will automatically print out a sixty- to eighty-page personal financial plan in good English with specific advice like: "The summer home could be remortgaged to finance . . ." or "John's IRA should be invested in. . . ."

Natalie Choate's estate planning expertise can be doled out in large quantities by people who never have to learn planning themselves.

□ □ □

What if I could learn geometry or a foreign language, then take the disk out of my brain and drop it into your brain? I wonder why humans don't have slots in their heads for disks. As it stands now, each of us learns everything the slow, painful way. Little children practice hours a day for years before they can speak their native tongue. Why are we such inefficient learning machines?

In order to learn, each human being goes through an active process that makes the material his own. Each person who learns a language changes it.

When my daughter was a year and a half old, I would bend over her and say, "Here's your orange juice." And she would repeat "Orange juice." Or I would say, "Here's you're apple juice." And she would say "Appoo juice." (I unconsciously mouthed the words with her, "appoo juice," "orange juice," as though I were somehow drawing them out of her soul.)

Then one day I said, "Juliet, here's your orange juice," and she said, "No, I want appoo juice!"

Where had that sentence come from? She'd never heard anyone say "No, I want apple juice."

It was marvelous. It was frightening. (It was also the beginning of the terrible twos.) I had created something that was not my creation. My own daughter would go on to say the most extraordinary things ever uttered in the English language. Long after I die, she'll be saying things I never could dream of. What greater gratification could there be for a parent?

But most employers aren't looking for that kind of gratification. They'd just as soon the salesman go on saying "apple juice" as long as that's the company's line and switch to "orange juice" when company policy changes.

Active learning leads to constant modification. Everyone who learns how to speak can say not only what he was taught but many new and unpredictable things.

But expert systems, like almost all the other management systems we've looked at, will discourage change and diversity. Like the programming at McDonald's or American Airlines, the standard application of expert systems assumes that there is a best way. It also assumes that that best way is best determined by those in charge.

An expert system can be updated, of course. With a sophisticated program like PlanPower, it's easy to add new products, new prices, new tax rules. But the majority of people who use the program will never be qualified to reprogram it. It's no longer essential that they learn in the normal human sense. When the company changes its line, a new disk can be dropped into their slots. Instead of a continuous and evolutionary process, change becomes periodic, abrupt and top-down.

If expert systems worked ideally, there would soon be fewer experts left on earth who could actually exercise and modify important skills. Maybe that doesn't matter with personal financial planning. (I don't really care if there are only six estate planners in the world. I don't even care if they're all wrong.)

But it has mattered over the centuries that not hundreds but hundreds of millions of people have contributed to the evolution of our sciences, languages, arts and crafts. Every human being who learned how to speak has contributed to the way our languages are now spoken. Everyone who ever hummed a tune has changed musical history.

It's dangerous to confine our species' expertise to a few. Especially to the few who grab for it.

But this is a philosophical issue. Office expert systems don't work that well yet. PlanPower, as I mentioned, was one of the first white-collar expert systems on the market. Its MIT entrepreneurial promoters were pleased to tell a reporter how it was supposed to work. But there was no way I could see it in operation.

So instead I looked at financial planning expert systems developed in-house at Merrill Lynch and Shearson Lehman Brothers. Both firms had decided to build less sophisticated or less comprehensive expert systems than PlanPower. Which certainly doesn't mean that they're less sophisticated companies. Indeed, there's no better way to find out how the technology will actually be used in the financial industry than to look at the two innovative giants, Shearson Lehman Brothers and Merrill Lynch.

5

□ □ □ □ □ □ □

The Wall Street Broker:
Decline of a Salesman

"There was a time," a retired stockbroker said nostalgically, "when the brokers at your large wire houses were like independent professionals doing business under the Lehman Brothers or Paine Webber umbrella. But by the time I retired, you were more like an employee. The customer belonged to the firm."

Their traditional independence may be declining, but it's still common for stockbrokers to change firms every few years, taking their big customers with them.

Quite naturally, brokerage management doesn't like to lose customers, nor does it enjoy bargaining over commissions with employees who can simply walk away with the clients.

A major goal of brokerage management is to bind clients to the firm rather than to the individual broker. The goal of the broker, meanwhile, is to become the client's trusted personal advisor.

It seemed logical that the ongoing battle for client loyalty would somehow be expressed in brokerage computing. Yet I couldn't imagine how any technology could daunt the free-wheeling Wall Street broker.

□   □   □

The financial industry was in a small whirl in 1986 when I happened to look. Perhaps it always is. From a distance there seemed to be only one kind of movement during the long bull market of the 1980s, represented by a solid, black line streaking up. But when I came closer I noticed the small whirls and spirals. The particular whirl of 1986, accelerated by deregulation and tax-deferred retirement accounts (IRAs and Keoghs), was rapidly transforming banks, insurance companies and brokerage houses into competing financial supermarkets. All three types of financial institutions were now advertising insurance, stocks, bonds, mutual funds, tax shelters, retirement plans and so on. To tie their many products together, Merrill Lynch had invented the CMA (Cash Management Account).

Formerly, brokerage firms had earned their money primarily through fees or commissions on securities transactions. But now, like banks, they make a great deal of money by using or lending clients' money. But first they had to get hold of it. That's called "asset gathering."

At seemingly the same moment, many financial institutions realized that one way to attract a customer's total assets was to offer a total financial plan.

To that end the brokers at Merrill Lynch, Shearson Lehman Brothers, Prudential-Bache, and other large houses were to become financial planners. The "personalized" plans they offered would suggest ways in which all the client's assets could be gathered into the firm's many new products and accounts.

But stockbrokers don't make commissions on consulting or asset gathering. They've traditionally made their money buying and selling stocks and bonds. That's what they're paid for and that's what they know how to do.

To promote the new approach, both Shearson and Merrill Lynch changed the title of their basic broker to Financial Consultant (F.C.). But what's in a name? How do you change a broker into a consultant? How can the old-fashioned broker (or "stock jockey," as I heard him derisively described by brokerage executives) suddenly become an experienced consultant on everything from college planning and estate planning to insurance and real estate?

How can an organization like Merrill Lynch, with over 10,000 brokers, see that their new Financial Consultants practice the art with some uniformity? (After all, the firm can be sued if its advisors give wildly unprofessional advice.)

And how can the brokerage bind the new financial planning customers to the firm instead of to the individual consultant?

Expert systems held the promise of a mechanical answer to these questions. Both Shearson and Merrill Lynch had developed computerized Financial Planners. Shearson's PRO (Personal Review Outline) was intended to be given free to every customer. Merrill's PathFinder was a more elaborate report designed to be sold for $250.

But the first problem wasn't selling the public, it was selling the salesmen.

□   □   □

A systems designer at Shearson talked candidly about his new product and his difficulties getting brokers to use it.

"Here's the PRO." Kevin Bernstein showed me a four page questionnaire that asked about assets, dependents and attitudes toward risk. " 'Just a few questions, would you like to fill it in?' That's what the broker says. Then we keypunch it— no one reads it—and it produces this document." He showed me a sample plan, a well-written, twelve-page report. Kevin had no doubt that the PRO was a terrific product. His problem was promoting it internally.

"We do a roll-out for our sales force, division by division.

In each area we rent a hotel room, do a road show. We show them how it will help them leverage their time, help increase their commissions, but we can't send out orders.

"Wait, let me tell you how it starts, let me back up. First a company like Shearson goes out and decides what business they're in. We've made a conscious decision that we want to be in the financial service business. And we want to convey our goods through people we call Financial Consultants. (I hope you'll note that Merrill started calling them Financial Consultants *after* Shearson.) . . .

"Now many of our brokers were always doing some kind of financial consulting. But a lot of them are still back there in the dinosaur age: buy the stock, make the commission, sell the stock, make the commission. Dialing for dollars I call it. They get on the phone, 'If I could double your money in two years would you invest $10,000?' If he says yes, you say 'What about $20,000 dollars?'

"But that way all you get is his play money, the $20,000 he can afford to lose. But what about the $200,000 he's got in C.D.s and the money market? As his Financial Consultant, you'd be playing with a bigger pool so you don't have to make a commission on every transaction. . . .

"You know how I designed the PRO?" Kevin asked me. "I drew up the questionnaire first, very short, very simple. I threw it on the table and I said, 'This is your mother. She says "Kevin, I sent you to college, you got an MBA, now tell me what should I do with my money, and don't use any big words and don't give me a million options." '

"That's the discipline I enforced on my staff: confine yourself to the information you can get off this form, write the letter you'd write to your own mother. . . .

"The important thing about a PRO is that it doesn't tell the broker exactly what to sell, but it makes the client familiar with our products. And, maybe more important, it gets some of the newer products out on the table for the broker to look at too. So it's educational for the broker, but it doesn't replace him.

"This is not a stand-alone product," the PRO designer emphasized. "When I rolled it out at these road shows I said to these brokers, 'If I'm smart enough to build a piece of software to make you obsolete, I'm smart enough not to try it. Because there are 5000 of you and you have the customers.'

"So the PRO is not designed to come up with the right answer or to be the salesperson. . . . Shearson can't put an ad in *The New York Times:* 'Fill out this form; we'll mail you a complete financial plan.' No, we send the plan back to the broker. He's the first person who reads it. We tell the broker to customize it. Take a red pencil and circle things. Say, 'In your case there might be a better product than a real estate trust.' You say to them, 'This is good general advice but the computer didn't meet you. I did.'

"Remember," Kevin philosophized, "there's an old saying, 'People don't care how much you know, unless they know how much you care.' And I'll add to that, 'You can't *tell* them you care, you've got to *show* them.' So before you send it out mark it up, show you spent time. Say, 'I thought about you because I know you.'

"This shows the investor that this guy is not just a stock jockey. He gets to see that our brokers are doing business the Shearson way, as Financial Consultants. Also, the PRO gets the right questions on the table. . . .

"One of the things I do at those roll-outs, I offer a $25 bonus to each broker who sends in ten PROs by the end of the month. It amazes me what a salesman will do for $25. (Well, that's why they're salesman, I guess. They're competitive.)

"But I can't order them to use the PRO. . . . My problem is not that PRO will be good or bad but that it will be irrelevant. There's quite a few tools for brokers that sit there on the shelf.

That's the worst thing that can happen to a system; it isn't used."

□ □ □

I didn't meet anyone at Merrill Lynch who expressed Kevin's doubts about getting the brokers to adopt the new approach. At Merrill Lynch Advanced Office Systems, [ML/AOS] a senior executive invited a junior systems man to sit in while he explained a range of computerized aids for brokers.

"Some of these systems can be categorized as information systems rather than expert systems. . . . For instance, a system that shows me all my clients who make over $50,000, shows me all my clients who hold IBM, shows me all my clients who have expressed an interest in IBM—they give you the ability to access and manipulate information. . . .

"One of the things that we at ML/AOS have to worry about is information overload. The F.C. gets on his desk each morning enough information to paper his room. So we do information retrieval systems. For that we have to know how do you file things; what's your daily routine?· If you look at enough individuals you begin to see patterns. And it's the patterns we're automating, not the exceptions."

The junior man, who hadn't spoken much, said, "We like to watch what the good brokers do. Oops, I keep saying 'brokers.' "

"You actually go out and watch the brokers work?" I asked.

"We watch like a bug on the wall."

"Like a time-and-motion study?"

"Well, no, that's an industrial phrase," the junior man explained. "Just if a guy's good, if he's got a new angle you go see if it's something unique to him or something you can make a uniform Merrill product."

I asked if some salesmen weren't reluctant to pass along information.

"What we're finding," explained the senior systems man, "is that in order to get a sales individual to put something on a piece of paper or into a terminal he's got to see some benefits from it. You have to bring them into the process. The goal is to in-gather information about the client and his assets. Now that brings us to financial planning."

He explained PathFinder and the new expert systems CollegeBuilder and HomeBuilder. All three would enable the broker to provide a uniform style of financial consulting and thereby become more effective at asset gathering.

Before I left, I asked the same question I'd asked Kevin at Shearson, "Are salesmen worried about using new products or sending in too much information because they don't want their clients to become the company's clients?"

Kevin had answered, "Sure, but I don't know if they have a choice. . . . The business is changing."

At Merrill, the senior systems man replied, "Some brokers may be paranoid. Of course, the company does have an interest in holding on to their clients, but a company can't be paranoid."

The junior systems man seemed genuinely hurt at the idea of brokers holding back information. "If they don't want to input their client's data, then they don't have to use our cross posting or CollegeBuilder or any of the other systems that save them. . . ."

They reminded me before I left that PathFinder was rated highest among the computerized Financial Planners. They never expressed Kevin's anxieties about getting the brokers to use it.

In fact, though, it was very difficult to find any broker at Shearson or Merrill using either expert system.

Heidi Farrell: An Ambitious Alice in Wonderland

"I have an appointment with Miss Farrell," I said. Heidi Farrell had left Merrill Lynch and moved on to another large, prestigious brokerage firm.

I waited near the receptionist's desk, expecting to hear the staccato heels of a dressed-for-success woman. Instead, I was greeted by a young girl in a long, dark skirt and high necked, ruffled blouse. Her hair was pinned back like Alice in Wonderland.

Heidi was the perfect mix of efficiency and concern as she took my coat, seated me at her half-walled workstation and brought a cup of tea. The Quotron on her desk—the standard broker's terminal—swiveled to serve the young man in the adjoining cubby.

"Why did you leave Merrill Lynch?" I asked

"At Merrill it was all rules and forms. Every situation fit into one of their procedures. But to me everything in this business is idiosyncratic. Besides, I felt that many of the forms were to the disadvantage of the clients and the brokers. Here, [at her new firm] you fill out the name, address, Social Security number."

"But don't you need a certain amount of personal information to do financial planning for your clients?" I asked.

"As a matter of fact, me and my partner," she pointed to a young man a few desks away, "are developing our own program to do financial planning. Let's face it, it takes a long time to do all that math by hand. But our program will have nothing to do with the firm. This will be our own private program.

"At Merrill the point of financial planning was to collect all the client's information and then sell him Merrill products. You learned how to tie the client into a knot, a knot where the client belonged to the company."

"I guess you never used PathFinder then?" I asked.

"Actually, PathFinder was pretty good for the $250. And you're not obliged to use Merrill products. But no, I never used it."

"Do you know any broker who did?"

She couldn't remember any.

"But I did use the CMA [Cash Management Account] account. It seemed like a useful account [the CMA included a credit card and automatically swept interest or any other loose cash into a money market fund] until I had to transfer a few of my clients out of CMAs. Then I saw why the older brokers kept everything in stocks and bonds."

The phone rang.

"I'm sorry to hear that," Heidi said, sounding professional. Then surprisingly, "Maybe we can go to the movies. O.K., I'll be here till 9."

"My sister," she explained. "She has no heat. She lives way over in a tenement on West _____ Street. Well, you get what you pay for." Heidi lives on the East Side, within walking distance of the office.

"Was there any pressure on you to open CMA accounts?" I asked.

"Oh yes. In fact there was this big broker at Merrill. He was about sixty, an incredible salesperson. No, it goes beyond that. A great professional. [She paused for a moment to honor him.] At sales meetings they would discuss the advantages of CMAs. How you can gather all the client's assets, how eventally you will end up with more commissions. But this big broker never used CMAs. He had everything in cash, everything in ready assets. And they would be on him in meetings. 'Come on, Joe, make those CMAs!'

"He could resist because he was big. They didn't want him to leave and take his clients with him. But I was one of the smaller people. I'd write up CMAs all the time. And really," she admitted, "I felt then that they were for my own benefit.

I respected salesmen like Joe but I also thought—well, you see, the company put down the older people, somewhat for resisting change—so I thought, well, CMAs weren't in existence when he started. He doesn't want to call up all his clients —he had thousands of clients—and tell them all to come on in and sign these papers, fill out all these forms. That may have been one reason. But the other reason was, with straight stocks and bonds he could pick up his book at any time and leave.

"CMAs made my paperwork a lot simpler while I was there, but when I moved, to get those goddamn accounts out of there, it was murder. It took months. I jeopardized my relationship with my clients. The only people who came with me, they had to really like me personally. People who came with me had to deal with all that paperwork and back-and-forths.

"Poor Sally," I said. [My friend Sally, a novelist, was Heidi's client.]

"She didn't feel the worst of it," Heidi assured me. "They tried the hardest to hold the ones that had real money. Well, that's the game. [Heidi softened toward her former employer.] The more liquid assets you control, the better the game player you are. After all, the goal of the money game is money."

"What is your goal?" I asked. "Would you like to be an independent broker some day?"

"Oh definitely! In the meantime I'm building my client base. Most of the people in my book have made money in real estate. Now they've sold their houses and they're looking for an investment that's as safe and appreciates the same way. I'm not a trader. The traders live in front of their Quotrons. You burn out. I specialize in real estate. My clients are speculators too, but in the long term. I have a small real estate investment myself so I understand the situations my clients face."

"How old are you?" I asked. I was beginning to be impressed or perhaps dismayed by this little girl in barrettes who invested in real estate, lived on the Upper East Side and planned to build her book of loyal clients and then walk out with them.

"Twenty-eight," she answered.

Heidi had graduated from a respectable college. Her older sister, the one without heat, had dropped or drifted out of a more prestigious college.

"She's on the ten-year plan, you might say. My sister is the creative one," said Heidi. "But what good is creativity if you don't sit down and actually create something?"

Heidi summarized her philosophy as a broker. "I try to make money for my clients, myself and my firm, in that order. If my clients make money, I'll make money myself in the long run."

She began organizing her lists for the evening's cold calling.

"It doesn't bother you to call strangers and ask them to invest?"

"What's the worst thing that can happen?" she asked. "If they hang up, are you worse off than you were before you called?"

"I guess that's true," I answered. "But I always imagine how busy people are. I was even afraid to call you."

"I'll try to find you someone who used PathFinder," she promised and she added a note to her "to do" pile.

Len Deusenberg: An Aggressive Trader

I phoned Len Deusenberg, a Senior Vice President at a prestigious brokerage house, to ask if it was really so difficult to transfer clients out of Merrill and Shearson brokerage accounts.

"Let me tell you about my own personal IRA," the broker volunteered, though he'd never spoken to me before. "When

I moved from Shearson, my own IRA dropped from $20,000 down to $13,000 and I couldn't get my hands on it, couldn't do a transaction. Four months without a trade! Me! I'm an aggressive trader. And I couldn't do a thing about it.

"Think how upsetting that would be to a client. I'm supposed to be serving the customer and I can't even find out what's in his account."

In his eight years "on the street" Len had worked at five different brokerage houses. He's a Senior V.P. at his present firm by virtue of the fact that he brings in over $750,000 a year in commissions. The average broker does about $150,000 a year.

"The biggest producers," Len assured me, "are the brokers who specialize—stocks, bonds, options. Not the financial planning guy. But the firms may not care about that anymore. They may be happier with a large number of average brokers who have no leverage. Guys they can replace and keep the customers.

"Right now, the industry is trying very hard to make the broker less powerful over the customer's bottom line. As they come to have more control they can give the broker a smaller percent. Typically, the highest you can get at a major house now is 45 percent. They may add a bonus, contests, profit sharing. You might be able to cut a deal for 50 at one of the majors. But 35 is typical.

"But the thing I find incredible," Len slowed down for emphasis, "Merrill has started a system of salaried brokers for small accounts. Noncommissioned brokers! That's an affront to people like me."

[Dan Donahue, the manager of Merrill Lynch's Fifth Avenue office, with 250 brokers, confirmed for me that his company now uses noncommissioned brokers for small or inactive accounts. The five salaried brokers in his branch happen to be women. "They're licensed brokers, yes, but they're not Financial Consultants and they don't want to be," Mr. Donahue assured me. "They don't want the pressure of 'Buy 10,000 shares of XYZ. Sell 10,000 of. . . .' They're former secretarial types. What we call account assistants here. . . . Yes, I'd say there's going to be a lot more of them."]

"Salaried brokers!" Len was outraged. "That's the direction management is pushing. Even here, fewer and fewer of the trainees that go through our program are really stockbrokers. They go through a training and it's like cookbooks: mutual funds, C.D.s. They're money raisers for the firms. But what do you get on a mutual fund? A one shot commission and . . ."

"Say Len," I interrupted, "can I interview you in person?"

"Why don't you come in around 4 o'clock when the market closes."

□   □   □

I arrived early so I could watch a big trader at work.

Deusenberg had a private office rather than a desk or work-station on the open floor.

"I'll be a little rude for the next fifteen minutes," he told me turning to his Quotron.

Len was a pudgy fellow, in his early thirties with rolled-up sleeves and striped suspenders. He cultivated his old-fash-ioned trader image, enjoying the work and the effect.

"Thought you'd like to know," he said into the phone, "Am Tech just reached 13 and it's been . . . Well, it's a start, you're no longer at a loss. Did you take a look at Datanet?* [Some of Len's clients follow the market on their home or office computers.]

"Are you following Datanet?" he asked on the next call. "On the charts it looks like rock bottom and there's another reason . . .

* The names of all the stocks and commodities mentioned in Len Deusenberg's office have been changed.

"This is Charlie Van Weisel," Len introduced me to the dapper man who had just entered the office, "our top securities analyst. [Back into the phone] And another reason: Noonan said if it traded in the midteens there'll be a company buyback. And he's always been a man of his word. [Away from the phone.] She's writing a book on the industry and computers." Len completed the introduction and turned back to his phone call.

Seeing a reporter, the analyst whipped out a copy of his weekly investment column. "Haven't watched a news program in years," he began an unprovoked monologue. "Never buy *The Wall Street Journal* . . . separate the wheat from the chaff . . . into the long-term trends. . . . You hear all this talk about oil prices going down. [He paused so I could take down his predictions.] After six months they're going to be up. They say interest rates are going to stay down. They're not. For the last four years I said up: they went up. I avoid the media so I can concentrate on the long-term trends."

"I'm looking at trends in the relationship between the broker and the firm," I said. "When I interviewed systems people at other houses, they were quite conscious of using computers to collect more customer information and to make the broker more dependent on . . ."

"I been in this business twenty-nine years," Van Weisel announced. "It's a trend."

"Wall Street is the last frontier," Len interjected while waiting for a connection. "The days of the free-wheeling, free-enterprising broker are . . . Hello, yeah, I can hold . . . the firms are trying to intervene between the broker and the client. . . . Hi, Barry, you been following Datanet?"

"There's something to that," Van Weisel said, "but they also want to know where the client is invested so they can get him out if there's a problem." Van Weisel is a partner in Len's firm.

"There's another side to that, though." Len continued conducting both conversations at once. "They want to get a wedge in between the client and the broker so that the client becomes the firm's client."

"Well, there's something to that too," said the analyst, not really conceding the point. "If that call comes for me, I'll be down the hall." He took back his columns and gave me the benefit of a parting piece of advice. "Look ahead: see what the long term trends are. Write what people are going to want to read two years from now." And he left.

"Hey, Barry, congratulations! ["They just made him Chairman of the Board," Len signed to me.] Does that mean you'll be so busy I'll have to handle your account on a discretionary basis? . . . Just kidding."

Len listened to Barry's stockmarket forays while making pedagogical comments, "Good . . . excellent . . . I'm proud of you holding onto the Dynamix, but you still have a tendency to pull out too short-term on the options. . . . Look, it's hard learning, but for six months you're doing . . . Oh my God, you had that much passive income! . . . No," he chided, "you won't buy the Datanet. You'll wait till it starts rising because you're so anxious not to buy it till it stops falling."

Charlie Van Weisel returned while Len was still on the phone. He called Len's attention to an item which would be disseminated over the Quotron system the next morning as part of his daily report to the firm's brokers.

"Hey, Charlie," Len called to the departing analyst, "Don't announce it to the troops till I have time to act on it. [Then back into the phone.] Yeah that was Van Weisel. . . . Yeah, he and I go back a long way. . . . Well, listen, congratulations again. . . . And you just keep an eye on Datanet."

"You see what I was doing?" Len asked when he got off the phone. "I was giving him leadership. And he also had the benefit of hearing Charlie Van Weisel right here. (We made a lot of money last year in tobacco shares and platinum with Charlie's research.)"

"Now that client," Len continued, "happens to be a veteran engineer, just made chairman of the board, thirty-five years old, he's a genius. And I'm his broker. Of course he can go to a discount broker—which I'm sure he does sometimes. But he relies on me for the leadership.

"There's a big push to make us so general that we become clerks in a financial supermarket. Merrill Lynch, Paine Webber, Bache, Shearson are all selling insurance, real estate, financial planning. But the way I conduct my business is still 90 percent as an old-fashioned trader."

"Is there a lot of pressure on you to do financial planning," I asked, "or to sell the company's new products?"

"The pressure is intense. Eventually even the older brokers give in and do the company line. I still have some clout because of my production, but you'd be surprised how little that means."

"What is the pressure like?" I asked. "I know it's subtle but if you could put your finger on . . ."

"The subtle pressures?" Len enumerated facilely, "Losing secretarial support, having your phone ripped out, being fired. It graduates. There are carrots and sticks."

[One of the sweetest carrots at a brokerage is the kind of immediate access that Len Deusenberg has to analysts like Van Weisel. A common complaint of smaller or out-of-favor brokers is that they can't get hold of research reports and can't contact the analysts before making an important trade.]

"You see, they have a lot of information on you. Everything that's in here [tapping the computer] they know. Generally there's been a high regard in this industry for the specialists and aggressive traders. They're the big producers. But now the companies have a *grid of information* to analyze exactly where each commission dollar is coming from."

Len showed me a copy of his weekly commission statement. According to the printout, he'd brought in tens of thousands of dollars in commissions in several categories. But there were double zeros in the month-to-date column next to mutual funds and the company's cash management fund.

"They can do all kinds of breakdowns, what I did last month, last year, last week. How I did it, with what products. Just this morning I got a printout with my top twenty for the quarter."

"Top twenty what?" I asked.

"That's, let's see, [he examined the printout he'd tossed aside earlier in the day] seems to be the top 20 percent, which individual clients generated the most commissions. I also get statements of which clients don't have_____[his firm's version of the cash management account]. Now some of this information is useful. But it's all to sell stuff.

"With computers the company can calculate not only how much business you're doing, but exactly how much money they'll make on each piece of business. By now a firm like Merrill may be making more from interest than commissions. So now the pressure on the broker is not only to do more business but to do it exactly 'our' way.

"But what happens when things change?" Len asked rhetorically. "Stocks can go bad, bonds can go bad, commodities can go bad, financial planning can fizzle."

"The healthy way is to encourage a diversity of brokers so the house can survive in changing climates. But they've got their grid telling them the one right way. Frankly, I'm not sure they even know the most profitable way. Sometimes it seems we're under pressure just to do volume."

"But you don't do it their way?" I asked. "You still don't do financial planning?"

"My niche is bringing stock ideas to the attention of people willing to incur a businessman's risk. The customer who'll call me back and say, 'Len, that idea you gave me about Datanet, I like it. Buy me 1000.'

"My clients want me to bring them ideas that they're not going to hear advertised or read about in the paper. They can read a book on financial planning. Oh, I'll do some of that for anyone who needs help. But most of the people in my book have taken care of that sort of thing a long time ago. Now they're looking for the opportunity to make money and they understand the skill required. Of course anybody can look smart in a bull market, but my clients know the difference. They enjoy being partners with me in an activity that involves skill and risk. The moment I become less than a trusted advisor to the client, the easier it is to replace me."

As I was leaving Len asked if I knew anyone who could help him design a customized computer program. He wasn't sure that the firm would let him run his own program on the company's computers. "It's a political matter." But he wanted something speedier. "With their system I can only find out what's in the client's account as of the time the market closed yesterday. I want something that will update their accounts, real time, as I trade."

"You really love this business," I remarked. "The money, the speed, the trading real time."

"You know how I got into it? This is funny. I was in college and I saw an advertisement for a summer job: 'Sales Assistant, Lehman Brothers.' I thought it was a clothing store. I thought I was going to be getting shoe boxes out of the back room. But I took to it immediately.

"That's still the great thing about this business. Just about anyone can give it a try, from all socioeconomic backgrounds. Wall Street is still the Wild West. Even with all the regulation it's one of the last areas of entrepreneurialism."

"So personally you're not that worried about expert systems or grids of information? You're never going to become a bank clerk or a salaried broker?"

"The salaried broker is the next step. You can see it coming. But I'll stay ahead of it because I have clients who know the difference."

I asked Len about his long-range plans. Did he hope to go independent with his largest clients?

"You can never build your book to that point. People die, people go elsewhere. You're always looking for new clients.

"My ulterior motive is to get so good at trading with other people's money that I can do it with my own money and then retire."

□   □   □

Len Deusenberg used the phrase "grid of information" to convey something that he felt closing in around the professional broker. Many data clerks, telephone operators, fast-food managers and airline reservation agents grope for that same concept as they find themselves hemmed in by multiple numerical ratings.

Till now, most workers could only be measured by a couple of numbers at once: usually how fast or how many, plus some calculation of error rate. But computers can monitor more than just quantity and quality. They can measure performance on many scales at once.

For the airline clerk, the hamburger flipper, the McDonald's manager—and now the stockbroker—there are vertical factors (How many reservations, How many burgers, Dollar volume per hour); there are horizontal factors (After Hang Up time, Fry yield, Crew labor productivity). In most cases, there are also what I call "diagonal factors," subjective factors like tone of voice or McDonald's QSC (Quality, Service, Cleanliness). Even a factor like friendliness is reducible to a number.

Dozens of vectors cutting vertically, horizontally and diagonally across a small work area result in a grid bisected so many ways that each person has only the tiniest space within which he can maneuver. As the number of numbers increases, the grid closes in around you. Eventually each square becomes so small that there's only one possible way to move your arm or your head. Only one way to do the job.

For managers and salesmen the grid of information hasn't yet created the kind of physical constraint that it has produced for data entry clerks. A broker can still stand up, sit down or make a phone call. The computer isn't timing his bathroom or coffee breaks. But as Len Deusenberg pointed out, "With computers the company can calculate not only how much business you're doing, but exactly how much money they'll make on each piece of business. . . . So now the pressure on the broker is not only to do more business but to do it exactly 'our' way."

The grid is tightening. But Deusenberg feels confident that he can keep ahead of it. So did the other well-established brokers I interviewed. As long as they had a book full of clients who trusted them, most brokers felt that they could ignore the pressures or pep talks urging them to do business the new financial planning way.

□   □   □

There's a wide range of "risk tolerance" among brokers. Each successful broker attracts clients who roughly share his investment aesthetic.

As it happens, most of the brokers I interviewed were conservatives. Or at least they considered themselves the opposite of an aggressive trader like Len Deusenberg. Yet to a man and woman, they echoed Len's conclusion: "The moment I become less than a trusted advisor to the client, the easier it is to replace me."

Many of these successful brokers had always provided some form of financial consulting. They didn't object to the financial planning approach as long as *they* remained the trusted source of advice, rather than the firm or the firm's computer program.

For that reason it was difficult to find an established broker at Merrill Lynch or Shearson who used PathFinder, PRO or CollegeBuilder. I had to look among newer, less-confident employees until I happened on a broker using one of the computerized financial planning tools.

Michael and Jeff: An Average and Less-Than-Average Broker

"Row six, turn right, the desks are numbered." The receptionist directed me to a statistically typical broker. He'd been with Merrill Lynch three years and did $150,000 in commissions.

My aunt had never met him. She'd been told on the phone that he was replacing her former Financial Consultant, whom she'd never met either. Still, she volunteered to call "her broker" for me and reported back that he sounded like an amiable man.

"I try to do whatever the customer wants," Michael said. Which may explain why he agreed to an interview. "My book runs from hundred dollar accounts to a million dollar account. I try to do what each customer wants."

"Do you act as their Financial Consultant," I asked, "now that you're officially an F.C.?"

"Well, in terms of evaluating their priorities [he thought it over], yeah. But in terms of taking over the person's total picture and trying to map it out, no. Most people tend to know what they want—or have an idea."

"Have you ever used PathFinder?"

"It's not the sort of thing you go out and actively solicit. You're not from the company, are you?"

I explained again about the book I was writing and reassured him that all the brokers I interviewed would be anonymous. "So you've never had any experience with Path-Finder?"

"Actually a doctor called and asked about PathFinder, so I sent him the form and I understand he's returned it. . . . Yes, completed. I guess they'll send his report to me and then . . . I'm not sure of the procedure."

I asked about CollegeBuilder, a newer Merrill Lynch expert system.

"No, I never . . . wait. [He skimmed through the papers on his desk.] I think I just got one of those back. It went out to all my clients as a statement stuffer." [One way to reach over the broker's head and go directly to the client is through the advertisements enclosed in their monthly statements. That month Merrill had inserted an application for the College-Builder program.]

Michael searched his desk. "It's a computer program but I don't know how to work it. Jeff," he addressed a bulky young man sitting at the desk next to him, "do you know if that CollegeBuilder thing is up and running?"

"You have to be here before 8 in the morning or after 6 to run it," Jeff explained. "I'll do it for you tomorrow morning," he reached good-naturedly for the form. Michael pulled back just perceptibly.

"Funny," said Michael, "the newer you are the more knowledgeable you are about the computer systems."

Jeff, the new broker, was as large, floppy and eager as Michael was slim and contained.

"See how it works," he leaned across Michael's desk to show me the CollegeBuilder form. "They fill in name, address, phone number and then the names of their kids, grade in school and where they're gonna go, like MIT, Yale or they can just fill in Public, Private, Ivy."

The questionnaire also identified the client as parent or grandparent, asked his age, current federal tax bracket and demanded:

Your Estimate of the Annual Inflation Rate of College Costs: (circle one)
4% 5% 6% 7% 8% 9% 10% or _____ %

"You use *their* estimate of inflation?" I was surprised.

"If they don't fill it in we use 7 percent. And if they don't fill in a tax bracket we say 25 percent."

Jeff showed me a CollegeBuilder plan. This particular print-out, many times longer than the original questionnaire, anticipated costs of over $300,000 to send three specific children to three specific universities in the years from 1998 to 2009.[*] CollegeBuilder calculated the annual savings necessary to pay the projected college bills if the parents began investing right now in TIGRs (pronounced "tigers," the acronym for Treasury Investment Growth Receipts) to be held in tax-saving custodial accounts for each child. The numbers were specific and staggering. For Andrew, $5,760 a year; $3,475 a year for Stephen; and $3,862 for little Patrick, born just that year.

"You use *their* estimate of inflation and *your* guess at their tax bracket? ["GIGO," I wrote in my notebook. That's the professionals' acronym for "Garbage In/Garbage Out."] And this really works?"

"It's like offering cocaine to an addict," Jeff answered enthusiastically. "There's two things that make up the American dream. One is to put your kids through college, the other is to own your home. But putting the kids through college is the more difficult. If you buy a $150,000 house you have thirty years to pay it off. But the college, you have four years to do it."

A good point, I thought. Later I read the same thing in the CollegeBuilder brochure, but there it was a $90,000 house. So Jeff had "customized" the example for our part of the country.

"Now, supposing the kid's good enough for grad school, that's three more years, or you think he's going to be a doctor.

---

[*] Numbers, and dates have been slightly muddled to disguise the particular broker and client.

Let's say you have one child that wants to go to Brown in the year 2004, that's $188,000. . . . And the other MIT or Notre Dame, and [Jeff rolled on unstoppable with horrifying numbers: $70,560, $94,600, $42,720 a year.] And the check is due September 1 of the year 2000."

"Have you actually gotten any new clients this way?" I asked. "Have you sold any TIGRs through CollegeBuilder?"

"I called a lady today and she said to call her back."

"Do you make a commission on TIGRs?" I asked Michael.

"You make $3.80 to $5 on a TIGR—meaning on each $1000 in TIGRs."

"Each thousand at maturity," Jeff interjected.

"Is that good?"

"No," Michael answered. "Besides, if you sell stocks and bonds you can expect to resell them in six months. Whereas TIGRs tend to be held for ten to eighteen years. So it's only a one-time . . ."

"If you have your own client you do what you want," said Jeff. "But when you're a newcomer you sell whatever you can. . . . See, I could buy her Telephone, which I think will triple in ten years. But will it definitely? With CollegeBuilder . . ."

Frankly, Jeff didn't seem to me like the kind of person who'd make it as a broker (though, remember, I'd known him only a few minutes). His big puppylike enthusiasm and his very acceptance of all the new Merrill Lynch systems suggested that he wasn't sharp or cool enough for Merrill Lynch. But maybe Merrill doesn't need such sharp brokers anymore. Like the medieval church that discovered it could distribute holy sacraments through corrupt vessels, perhaps Merrill Lynch can now distribute shrewd advice through Jeff.

After all, if their expert systems actually work, then a Merrill broker doesn't have to know much more about investments than a McDonald's cook has to know about food. The company still needs to hire some top-notch financial brains to formulate basic investment plans, but the bulk of the brokers out in the field merely need to customize these plans. There's no reason to pay enormous fees like 45 percent of total commissions to an ordinary salesman or "relationship man."

I left Jeff customizing a CollegeBuilder for the lady who'd asked him to call back.

"What's the hardest part of being a broker?" I asked Michael, expecting to hear about cold calling or paperwork.

"Telling people about losses," he answered simply. "Fortunately, I haven't had many losses of consequence, but there's one client, an account I opened my first month in business. We'd done a covered call with options. It was going to be a quick transaction—in and out. But it got into trouble right away and it has never recovered."

"Was it the client's idea?" I suggested.

"No." There was a long pause and no excuses. "It was my recommendation. It was also a first-time investor. I lost a lot of sleep over that. Most clients don't object to losses as long as you keep them informed. But now I have to call her and finally take the loss."

I had completely forgotten about losses. Every broker I'd interviewed had such a convincing system, such solid information that even conflicting strategies all seemed sound to me, at least while I sat in their offices.

Expert systems, even the less sophisticated ones, can protect against losses caused by inexperience. With an expert system, no one has to take advice from the firm's new brokers. The advice comes instead from the firm's homogenized "expert." It's as if every client sat down with the same planner on the same day. Of course, many investors have lost money following the firm's daily recommendations. The blue plate special may not be any fresher than the waiter's personal choice.

An expert system doesn't guarantee good advice or even cautious advice. But it guarantees standard advice. The system passes along whatever strategy the company adopts at the moment.

But so far, no one at Merrill Lynch or Shearson is confined to giving out only the "expert's" advice. An established broker might use the system to do some quick calculations or to try some what-ifs. Or he might ignore it. He doesn't automatically become a salaried broker doling out machine-made advice just because there's a new program in his computer.

Brokerage houses will have to do a lot more reorganization and a lot more education (or de-education) before they reduce the majority of brokers to the salaried status that Deusenberg foresees. The process is under way, but the resistance is strong.

I was told repeatedly and semitautologically that brokers resist computers because they're "resistant to change." But very few professionals resist systems that bring them timely information. In fact, several of the brokers I met were buying or designing additional programs to keep ahead of other brokers. What they resist are computer programs that take information or autonomy away from them. The problem for the systems designers isn't how to get brokers to use computers but how to embed the "in-gathering" or intrusive functions into programs that brokers want.

I was amazed how selectively established brokers "resisted" (or ignored) programs and products that tied the client closer to the firm. They were remarkably clear about their own interests.

Stockbrokers may be the most class conscious of all American workers. Perhaps this is because they aren't really workers. They're owners. But the thing they own is intangible. It's the thing Willy Loman tried to describe to his brother, Ben[1]:

It's contacts, Ben, contacts! . . . when he walks into a business office his name will sound out like a bell and all the doors will open to him! I've seen it, Ben, I've seen it a thousand times! You can't feel it with your hand like timber, but it's there!

Willy Loman's intangible is the asset that brokers own; it's the property they take with them from firm to firm; it's the basis of their independence. If the broker didn't partially own his clients and contacts, the company wouldn't have to cajole or bribe him to use their new financial planning approaches and their new computer aids. They could simply order him, the way they would order any other employee.

The tug-of-war over the customer has been going on long before computers entered the scene. Computers are only tools with many uses. But the battle for control turns tools into weapons.

6

□ □ □ □ □ □ □

Manufactured
Advice

As I write, brokers are just beginning to sense the career slide that's been going on for two decades in social work. If I waited just a year or two longer, I could have set my broker-age story in a branch bank or the actuarial department of an insurance company. Knowledge engineers are busy cloning bank loan officers and actuaries now.

Of course, this white-collar slide wasn't caused by the computer or by the expert system. The same downward shift is being implemented in many different offices using many different tools.

The discretion of Federal probation officers and Workers' Compensation judges is being limited without the use of expert systems. New sentencing grids in probation and automatic award schedules in Workers' Compensation minimize decision making by these professionals. But grids and schedules aren't "systems," they're merely pieces of paper.

The important element isn't the computer program but the

management determination to centralize decision making. However it's implemented, the result is more clerks, whatever their titles, and fewer full-fledged professionals.

Does this mean that expert systems work, that clerk-plus-ELIZA equals doctor, that clerk-plus-PathFinder equals broker?

Consumer Union rated PRO, PathFinder and similar planners as being more like sales gimmicks than professional consultants. I'd be surprised if any of the specific expert systems we looked at are still in operation by the time this book is published. And, so far, the original ELIZA is still a parody rather than a functioning therapist.

I have, however, seen an ELIZAlike program in operation. Frankly, this one seems more like a farce than a parody. But I'm going to describe it because só many similar systems are now being tried, and I'm certain they'll be improved.

PSYCH SCAN

In New York State, methadone maintenance clinics are required to have a psychological and social history (a "psychesocial") in each patient's file. Since the understaffed clinics have no time for personal interviews, a company called Auto Assess, Inc., provides a battery of fill-in-the-blank "PSYCH SCANS," "carefully prepared," says the company's brochure, "to accommodate the limited attention span of clients and patients under stress."

So the addict, seated or nodding out in the waiting room, self-administers his Auto Assess PSYCH SCAN. His responses are keyed into computers by data clerks at The Creative Socio-Medics Corp. (I didn't make up any of these names.) Like PathFinder, PlanPower, or PRO, the computer program generates a narrative report. The report arrives back in the center within a week, clean, typed and ready to be filed away, without anyone's having interviewed the patient or even having read his responses. In most cases this service is paid for by Medicaid.

Many of the counselors I met at methadone clinics made fun of the computerized reports. "Very interesting, I see you had three to seven siblings." They were not exaggerating. A sample in the Auto Assess training manual reads, "Since the age of 18 the client has been arrested four or more times."

Needless to say, this is rather impersonal compared to the few handmade psyche-socials I found in centers that still hired psychologists to conduct interviews. But even if the machine-made and the handmade reports were equally valid (or equally useless), a self-administered questionnaire means less human contact for someone who may desperately need it. Imagine being handed a multiple-choice questionnaire on the day you finally decide to break the drug habit and get back into society.

The Auto Assess questionnaire is another example of the Help Yourself approach to automating services. Just as bank customers enter their own data at money machines and airline passengers will soon enter the data to book and ticket themselves, psychological subjects can be asked to administer their own tests. It may seem ridiculous to serve addicts this way, but, since most of them aren't paying, they're in no position to demand a custom-made product. Right now, computerized human services are primarily distributed to the poor.

When mass-produced clothing first appeared, it was also meant for the poor. Wealthy people saw it as a parody of tailormade clothing. Sleeves and collars fit the individual about as well as a PSYCH SCAN fits the individual. But even disdainful aristocrats had to admit that it did cover the body, and cheaply. (And even I have to admit that a PSYCH SCAN does cover the facts, and cheaply.) In time (in fact, quickly), mass-produced clothing got better and even cheaper. Eventually some manufacturers began to offer more expensive "custommade" lines.

If a PSYCH SCAN sounds like a joke, remember that we're at the beginning of the automation of human services. Standing at this point in history, it seems obvious to me that a human doctor or a human financial counselor who talks to you personally will always be able to make a better diagnosis or give more fitting advice than an expert system. But 150 years ago it must have seemed equally obvious, even to a clothing manufacturer, that a real tailor who measured the individual body could make better-fitting garments than any mass production system. This is still true. Yet today it's hard to find that good tailor. And it costs a great deal to buy his services. But it's easy to find good, or good enough, mass-produced clothing. Over the years mass production was developed and improved while skilled craftsmen grew scarce.

I'm certain that mass production of human services will also be improved. That's not because manufacturing advice is a good or an obvious idea. We've seen how hard it is to make an expert system with anything like human sophistication, even in a relatively cut-and-dried, dollars-and-cents area like estate planning. But this hasn't deterred the creation of expert systems on bargaining strategy for corporate negotiators, on dinner-party seating for hostesses, on style and vocabulary for writers and even on employee and child discipline.

Even if these systems work, in their own rigid way, it may be basically wrong-headed to eliminate so much personal contact in the advice business. Perhaps human service shouldn't be so efficient. But the idea will surely be developed, not because it promises a superior product, but because it promises an inferior worker.

After all, Merrill Lynch doesn't want to hire 10,000 investment experts, each of whom does business his own way and has his own loyal clients. Most employers would prefer to distribute their products through cheap, easily trainable and easily replaceable employees. Perhaps even more important, they want to control what their hired professionals are saying and doing. This is why expert systems will be perfected.

The name "expert system" may disappear as the technique for making the systems becomes simpler. But whatever the programs are called, most of us will eventually take advice and receive services from centralized experts, spread around thinly. That means that more people in the advice or human service business will be employed as the disseminators, rather than the originators, of this advice. In some offices this may be implemented by promoting clerks, in others by demoting professionals. But overall it means less skill, less autonomy and fewer good jobs.

No, PathFinder-plus-clerk doesn't equal broker; PSYCH SCAN-plus-clerk doesn't equal counselor. As a matter of fact, assembly-line-plus-assembler never really equaled tailor or carpenter. But it equaled clothing and furniture that was good enough. Just as most of us buy assembled automobiles, most of us will wind up taking off-the-shelf advice.

In one sense it's amazing that anyone should think of selling mass-produced personal advice. In another sense, it's amazing that service corporations waited so long to automate their primary workers.

III

□ □ □ □ □ □ □ □

AUTOMATING
THE BOSS

7

□ □ □ □ □ □ □ □

The Future of Monogamy in the Office

People will adapt nicely to office systems if their arms are broken. We're in the twisting stage now.

> William F. Laughlin
> Vice President, IBM, 1975 [1]

If you think a secretary without a boss is sad, you should see a boss without a secretary.

> Mary L. ———
> Typist, Procter & Gamble, 1985 [2]

I just read about a new computer program called Productivity Map that will, according to *InfoWorld* magazine, "help track the performance of managers the way other programs track inventory and sales." [3] Apparently, Productivity Map juggles numerical ratings for productivity factors in difficult-to-measure departments like Finance, Research, Personnel and Engineering and comes up with a single number that says how the department is doing at any moment.

It sounds not only dreadful but also silly. How can a manager ever reorganize or experiment if his superiors can look at the computer at any moment and say, "All last week you were running at a 12, but you fell to 9.5 after lunch today"?

Productivity Map's development was funded by a consortium that included 3M, Westinghouse, GTE, Northern Telecom, Nabisco Brands and the U.S. General Accounting Office. I couldn't see the program in operation because it was still in its test phase. To get a better idea of how it worked, I phoned Allison Kleebatt, an executive in Organization and Manpower Planning for GTE's Human Resources staff.

"Can it really come up with a single number a 'How'm I doin'?' for managers?" I asked.

"You got the medium and the message mixed up there," Ms. Kleebatt informed me. She explained that the measuring system, called OM (Objective Matrix) has been around for a long time. Productivity Map was just a way of running it on a small computer.

"Now OM is a useful and flexible system. You can use it to measure productivity for any kind of white-collar worker."

"Even creative workers like programmers?" I asked.

"Programmers? Hah! There's a mystique they try to keep up, but programming is production work. [Her tone said '*mere* production work.'] That's been known for a long time."

"Even Human Resources," Kleebatt democratically attacked her own department, "filling open positions, processing paper; it's already known to be production work. And the things people like to think of as being more 'creative' like designing salary plans, designing promotion plans; it's production work. That's already known."

"So you feel that OM could apply to departments like Engineering?" I asked.

"Oh engineers! They're the worst. They don't want to think

they can be measured. But if there's an output it can be measured; if there *isn't* an output, then what do they hold the job for?"

Many planners share Ms. Kleebatt's confidence that no job is too creative to monitor, no output too intangible to count. But it's unusual to hear anyone express such glee—at least over the telephone to a stranger—about finally measuring those creatives who think they're too special to be reduced to numbers.

Monitoring, measuring and routinizing are usually justified as means of reducing labor costs. The fact that they reduce people is supposedly incidental. When I started this research I myself believed that efficiency—often miscalculated—was the motive behind the degradation I was seeing. This corresponded with what I knew, or thought I knew, about the first industrial revolution.

□   □   □

At the turn of the century Frederick Taylor, the original time-study man in the steel industry, summarized the basic precepts of industrial automation in his influential books *Shop Management* (1904) and *The Principles of Scientific Management* (1911).

> The managers assume . . . the burden of gathering together all of the traditional knowledge which in the past has been possessed by the workman and then of classifying, tabulating and reducing the knowledge to rules, laws and formulae. . . .
>
> All possible brain work should be removed from the shop and concentrated in the planning or laying out department. . . .
>
> The full possibilities [of this system] will not have been realized until almost all of the machines in the shop are run by men who are of smaller caliber and attainments and who are therefore cheaper than those required under the old system.[4]

The same principles were pithily restated for the computer age by a systems analyst at AT&T, Paul Smythe, in 1977.

> The work must be carefully organized in the programming department so that the great bulk of it can be done by $3.00 an hour clerks with virtually no training.

So the first industrial revolution aimed at turning manual workers into "men who are of smaller caliber and attainments." The second industrial revolution aims to turn the rest of us into "$3.00 an hour clerks."

This certainly sounds like the processes I had seen at McDonald's and American Airlines, where "all possible brain work" was removed from the shop and concentrated in the planning (or programming) department. It also sounds like the principle underlying expert systems. There, too, the brain work, the decision making, is centralized.

For the majority of us, the nonplanners, the Taylor system limits decision making, restricts autonomy and reduces skills. As Taylor himself foresaw, it turns us into interchangeable hourly workers.

These are not nice ideas. They mean that office, service and professional work are deliberately being arranged like factory work in order to make people cheap and disposable. When we're reduced to a dime a dozen, we feel like a dime a dozen. To me that's the worst part of this production system; it makes people feel bad.

Nineteenth-century Taylorism wasn't practiced for the purpose of making people feel bad. It was all done in the name of efficiency. The theory is that you get a better, more consistent product by standardizing production; you get a cheaper product by cutting labor costs. So you make a cheaper, higher-quality product by using a cheaper, lower-quality worker.

But where are these higher-quality, cheaper products? Go into today's most automated offices and try to buy a better, cheaper service. In some cases you may be able to. But I don't see any indication that most office automation is being planned for the sake of efficiency, in the old-fashioned "build a better mousetrap" sense.

Instead of calculating how to make a cheaper product, offices seem to be automating automatically. The new equipment is then used as much for its labor-controlling abilities like monitoring and measuring, as for its labor-saving abilities like computing and typing. All the traditional Taylorist cost-cutting procedures are applied with very little attempt to find out if they actually cut costs. For instance, despite all the monitoring, measuring and keystroke counting in modern offices, I can't find any study indicating that word processing has ever cut the cost of getting out a letter. Even less is known about electronic mail or electronic calendaring.

Of course, executive offices are different from factories. Even if we did have some cost-benefit studies on word processing, we still wouldn't know very much about front-office efficiency. Measuring memos and counting keystrokes can't tell you anything unless you know what all that communication is about. What does the office do? Does it do it better with more memos and letters or with fewer memos and letters? I should think that office efficiency depends, at least a little, on what all those drafts and final copies say.

A hand scrawled "yes" on the bottom of a one-page proposal can be efficient if it hastens the production of some useful item. But what does a favor-currying memo contribute to productivity? What do reams of legal-sized documents about a takeover contribute to a company's profit (or the world's well being)?

It may be efficient to put blinders on a horse, tighten the reins and lash him every so-many feet. But not if the carriage is racing in the wrong direction. So in the large sense, office automation has nothing to do with efficiency.

Certainly, the billions invested in artificial intelligence can't be justified on the basis that expert systems make decisions more cheaply than humans. Most research in artificial intelligence is done by the military or began in the military, and military expenditures don't have to be justified in terms of ordinary efficiency. The exigencies of war (or war games) demand systems that can react faster than humans and can function where humans can't easily be placed, for instance on missiles or out in space. Cost is a minor consideration.

But here on earth the crude decisions made by expert systems aren't better or cheaper than human decisions. They are acceptable not because they're efficient but because they offer top management a way to control or eliminate autonomous humans at lower levels. The desire to get rid of decision-making humans or to reduce them to numbers—to make them production workers in Allison Kleebatt's sense—has become a goal in itself. It simply can't be explained in terms of cutting costs. This is clearest in the older industries.

Relatively labor-intensive Toyota and Honda auto factories are operating profitably in the U.S. using American workers. Yet, to compete with the Japanese, General Motors invested billions in the highly automated, totally integrated and disaster-prone Saturn plant, built in 1984, which was designed to use as little human labor as possible. Faced with their own inefficiencies, American manufacturers repeatedly respond by looking for ever-more-extreme ways to control and eliminate production workers. Yet production workers are a surprisingly small part of their costs.

John Simpson, Director of Manufacturing Engineering for the National Bureau of Standards, Washington, D.C., estimates that in metalworking direct labor is 10 percent of the total cost. Yet, as of 1982, Management and Engineering were expending 75 percent of their cost-cutting efforts on that 10 percent.

No such statistics are available for offices, but judging by observation I'd say that automaters happily spend twenty salaries to get rid of four secretaries. At first this surprised me. But as I proceeded with the research for this book, I came gradually to realize that the old-fashioned capitalist motives of efficiency, profit and greed were merely the rational covers for a far-crueler philosophy.

The goal of modern management—to dictate exactly how a worker does his job and to make him accountable for every minute of the working day—is irrational. It can sometimes be defended in terms of efficiency or productivity, but its only consistent objective is control for the sake of control. That's why any large group of workers who can be automated eventually will be.

As neo-Taylorists turn their eyes higher up the occupational ladder, the irrational quest for control merges with a primitive struggle for survival. "Automate or be automated" seems to be the motto as managers and executives turn upon themselves.

Front-office Automation

During the most dynamic phases of the industrial revolution, vast enterprises were managed by their owners with the help of one or two clerks. In Victorian fiction "clerk," "book-keeper" or "chief clerk" was the position to which a poor but diligent factory lad might rise—and then, of course, marry the boss's daughter.

In the small, family-style offices of that period, prudent supervision might simply mean watching over the clerk's shoulder from time to time. Standardization could be achieved by saying "Here, do it my way." While factory workers were rigidly controlled, office workers were still basically independent or autonomous within their own spheres of responsibility.

But by the late nineteenth century, operations like payroll

and billing had come to employ a significant amount of labor in manufacturing companies. Furthermore, there were now large institutions like banks and insurance companies whose entire function was keeping track of money and whose entire staff was clerical.

Eventually separate departments were created to handle the routine, repetitious tasks connected with payroll, billing, shipping, inventory control and so on. Staffed mostly by women whose status became more like that of clerks in the modern sense, these units were large enough to attract efficiency experts in earnest. Turn-of-the-century time-and-motion studies calculated by the tenth of a second how long it took to open envelopes, how long it took to close file drawers and even how long it took ink to dry. Office typewriters came equipped with mechanical meters that counted keystrokes. (Smart typists soon learned to raise their keystroke count by indenting paragraphs with five strokes of the space bar rather than one stroke of the tab key.)

Usually, these bookkeeping or operations departments were located in the back of the office, away from visitors and windows. Eventually, they became separate back offices with supervisors and managers of their own.

But the real managers, the real bosses, stayed in what became known as the front office—later called the corporate, executive or administrative office. The front office is the place where company policy is made and disseminated to all the other departments. It's the place where receptionists and secretaries interact with executives. It's the generic office my mother envisaged when she told me that a young lady should work in an office, not a factory.

By the time computers were introduced, the back office was thoroughly industrialized (and, in my opinion, one of the worst places to work).[5] Computers may have added physical discomforts—at first the noise of keypunch machines, later the glare of screens—but they didn't suddenly transform an office into a factory. In the back office, computers merely mechanized work that was already organized on the factory model.

Computers came to the front office, however, at the very moment that executives were (and are) beginning to be industrialized. Frankly, I'm surprised it took this long to begin industrializing the front office. Administrative offices had become enormous before corporations got serious about standardizing the work of managers and executives. But some time in the seventies it began to happen. As Harry Braverman noted in 1974 in his book *Labor and Monopoly Capital,* "There is ample evidence . . . that management is now nerving itself for major surgery upon its own lower limbs."[6]

Because this is happening at the same time that computers are being introduced, front-office automation is bound to look confusing. It's even more confusing because its most important goals are deliberately obscured.

When computers are set down in the front office, their valuable word- and number-juggling features are used to camouflage their monitoring functions. Nonspecific communication needs are used to justify reorganizations that undermine old social relationships and impose new controls. The artifice or caution used to introduce these changes suggests that top managers still feel a bit squeamish about operating "on their own lower limbs."

Nevertheless, the operation has begun. If word processing were merely about processing words, its introduction wouldn't be much more complicated than the introduction of electric typewriters. What we're about to see goes far beyond the installation of a new machine.

Elizabeth Anderson

A systems man guided me around one floor of the corporate loan department he had just automated for one of the largest banks in the world. The outer walls—an entire city block—were lined with the one-window cubicles of bright young loan officers.

The inner space was dotted with the new "clusters," consisting of one or two word-processing terminals operated by women in their twenties. Each cluster was administered by an older woman, usually a former personal secretary, who had elected to stay on with the firm. "We never fire anyone due to automation," my guide explained. "Everything is done by attrition."

In one particular cluster I noticed an older woman sitting at one of the new Wang word processors. She was bright-eyed, gray-haired and primly dressed except for a pair of red earmuffs.

After work I caught her at the elevator and asked if she'd mind talking to me about her job.

"You picked me out because I was the only old lady on the new typewriters," she guessed.

"Well, yes," I admitted. "And the earmuffs."

"Oh gosh," she put her hands up to her ears where the muffs had been. "I'm still looking for comfortable ear plugs. Not that it's so noisy, but the printing out is so steady; it gets to you more than a whole room of old-fashioned typewriters."

She agreed to be interviewed at home, if I didn't mind making a few quick stops—the cleaners and a stationery store for ink. "My hobby is calligraphy."

Elizabeth Anderson has worked in offices for more than thirty years, eighteen with the bank, twelve with her last boss.

" 'No straight typing.' That's what I learned to say by my second job after high school. So you might say my life has been one big circle, since I'm back at straight typing.

"But it's what I chose. I chose to learn the word processor and I love it.

"Before this new system I would say I had a pretty cozy relationship with my boss. He might send me uptown to return a blouse that didn't fit his wife, so he couldn't very well tell me not to make personal calls. Not that I stayed on the phone all day. My job was to get his work out, which included staying late if I had to. It also included making corrections and sometimes writing his letters myself. I was familiar with all his correspondence. He appreciated me and I expected to stay with him till I retired.

"Then the consultants started coming around. First a lot of talking, then a lot of measuring but 'nothing to worry about.' Then one day I was given my two choices. I could learn the word processor or I could stay on as the administrative assistant in a cluster. Sounds real sweet, doesn't it? Like a chocolate peanut cluster.

"Actually, there was a third choice. I could quit. Which is what quite a few wound up doing, one way and another.

"How did I decide on the word processor? Well, for the first time in my entire working life, I actually sat down and thought about my career goals. And I realized that I had exactly one career goal: to last out four years and collect my pension. Believe me, I saw quite a few forced out with less than four years to go—'attrition.'

"Since they kept adding new men to each administrator's cluster, I saw which way the wind was blowing. In the end there won't be any real secretaries. 'But typists ye have always with you.' [Elizabeth was a religious woman and her walls were decorated with her beautifully calligraphed biblical quotes.]

"And I'm very glad I learned the word processor. If only I could have had it while I was a secretary. When I think," she sighed with longing and regret, "when I think of those years of correction tapes, white-off, retyping. Yes, I love this word processor. And I want you to copy that down. *I love my Wang.* [She waited while I printed it clearly in my notebook.] It's not the machine that gave me the shaft," she added.

"What's the shaft?" I asked.

"Straight typing seven hours a day. That's the shaft. The worst thing is when work comes by me with wrong spelling, wrong information. Sometimes I think I should correct it. I did at first. But that's not how they judge me. You know the first screen on all the documents don't you?"

"Yes," I nodded. The systems man had shown me proudly how the computer automatically creates an identifying screen, which includes the identity of the typist, the time spent and the total number of keystrokes, recalculated for each revision. "It's a standard program."

"Then you know what I'm judged by—the number of keystrokes. So why should I take time to correct their work? And why should I stay two minutes past lunch if they're timing me that way?"

"Why should you, indeed," I agreed.

"Well the worst part of the thing is that I do. Oh, sometimes I let mistakes go by and I feel so stupid. Sometimes I correct them and I feel even stupider! I don't know what to do!

"But maybe you shouldn't talk to me. Go back to the office. Look around. Those young women don't complain. They're working on a new machine. It pays much better than regular typist. They think they've made it up to secretary. They don't know what a secretary was."

She smiled. "Oh gosh. Now I'm really sounding like an old lady." She imitated herself as an old codger with a quavery voice. "In *my* day we had real snowstorms. In *my* day we had real tomatoes. In *my* day a secretary was a real secretary; a job was a real job.

"But tell me the truth," she leaned over to me confidentially, "didn't the tomatoes used to taste different?"

□ □ □

It's a basic business principle that each task should be done by the least-skilled, or at any rate the lowest-paid employee possible. Accordingly, it's wasteful for an executive to spend his high-priced time typing letters, opening mail or dialing the telephone when these jobs can be done by a secretary who may be paid anywhere from a half to a fiftieth of her boss's salary.

Because executives like to think of their own time as so extraordinarily valuable, secretaries proliferate both as a convenience and as a sign of prestige. So each manager and then each assistant manager becomes the supervisor of a staff of one. In the old fashioned office this supervision was usually informal. Elizabeth Anderson took her boss's wife's blouses back to the store and stayed late when a report was due, so he couldn't very well object if she made personal calls or left early once in a while. In the Office of the Past, the manager and his secretary constituted an autonomous team whose job was to get his work out—one way or another. But what was his work?

Management is one of the most mysterious business functions. No matter what a company sells, whether it's a service or a manufactured product, management doesn't produce the item. Management produces coordination or control over all the other activities of the business. Coordination is hard to measure; control is hard to control.

Management is not only mysterious, it's also expensive. In the sixties American companies realized that office costs were increasing much faster than manufacturing costs. Managers, with their salaries and perks, often consumed over 50 percent of these escalating office costs. By the early seventies magazines like *Administrative Management* began to use the phrase "the social office" to describe the expensive and unregulated environment in which the mystery of management took place.

Efficiency experts realized that they had to break into that private, almost domestic, setting in order to begin monitoring and regulating middle management. But how do you measure a manager's output? It would be difficult and perhaps even a little embarrassing to hook managers up to bells, buzzers or keyboards. Anyway traditional measuring devices wouldn't tell much about managerial efficiency, because the manager's product is intangible.

But a manager, whose job is deciding and coordinating, has a shadow who translates these mental activities into concrete, measurable items like phone calls and memos. If the secretaries' tasks could be enumerated and monitored, then the company could begin to study—and standardize—the mysterious job of managing. This was impossible while secretaries remained the personal employees of each boss. The core of the social office and the heart of the mystery was the relationship between boss and secretary. Automaters realized that they could never control the front office until they separated the boss from the secretary.

So in the seventies, while Weathermen talked of smashing monogamy, IBM talked of smashing office monogamy by breaking the one-to-one relationship between secretary and boss. To accomplish this radical aim, IBM took a machine that would have been a valuable tool for an old-fashioned secretary like Elizabeth Anderson and linked its use to a scheme that would separate her from her boss and make her a supervised employee of the company.

Following the IBM word processing plan, companies at first automated by replacing private secretaries with distant pools of communalized clerks. But it often took three days to get a simple letter out of these early word processing centers. This was a blatantly ridiculous way to use a machine on which a secretary could correct and retype a letter in minutes. By the end of the seventies many firms were shifting to smaller pools, or clusters, like the one Elizabeth Anderson worked in.

Changes in the size and physical location of work centers, however, didn't mean that IBM had abandoned its militant stand against the one-to-one relationship.

"In the office of 1985," went a research corporation's 1978 prediction, based on the IBM word processing plan, "there are no secretaries. You receive services from a pool shared by several managers in your group; we call this pool the Administrative Support Center. Within the Support Center, there are Administrative Support Specialists, Information Storage/Retrieval Specialists and Word Processing Specialists."[7]

In this polygamous utopia all the needs of each "principal" or "word originator" are filled by "specialists" in shared work centers. The secretary is freed, then, from the whims of an individual dictator; the executive loses his office wife but gains access to an automated harem. Most important to the IBM plan, the one-to-one relationship is severed.

At first the need to separate the boss and the private secretary was explained in terms of the size and cost of the new machine. Since a typical personal secretary types only 20 percent of the time, it could be argued that it wasn't feasible to install an expensive machine and let it sit unused 80 percent of each day. It made more sense to establish a work center, where the word processor and its trained operator—also called a word processor—could be employed full time typing for many executives.[*]

But when word processors became almost as small and cheap as electric typewriters it was still considered poor policy to simply place a terminal on each secretary's desk. Of course the machine would save typing time but what would the old-fashioned boss/secretary team do with that saved time? Would

---

[*] When typewriters were first introduced, their operators were also called "type-writers." Later they became typists. So far in the electronic office, both the machine and the operator are still called by the same name—word processors.

the company really gain anything by making them more efficient?

In the separate work center, the word processor became not only an efficient way to type but a way to gain control over front-office anarchy. In a work center upper management could begin to identify, count and time the productive secretarial functions such as typing, filing, taking messages and making travel reservations, and eliminate whatever else was going on. Then, with or without the added efficiency of electronic word processing, they could reduce the ratio of "support staff" to "principals," that is, eliminate secretaries. Most important, through work centers the firm could begin to figure out what the principals, the managers themselves, were actually doing.

In 1976, officials at both Xerox and IBM told the German radio-documentary maker Hans Helms that middle management was the chief target of office automation.

"They told me in PARC [Xerox's prestigious research center in Palo Alto]," said Dr. Helms, "that the real goal of office automation is not so much to get rid of the typist at the base but this very expensive middle-management layer. One of them even drew me a figure, a Marilyn Monroe hour glass.

"He said, 'The employment chart of the future would move from the pyramid shape to the Mae West. The goal right now is to pull in the middle.'

"At IBM in Dallas," Dr. Helms continued, "they told me almost the same things. There they stressed that the most resistance is expected from the middle managers who feel their jobs threatened."[8]

Though managers may have been the main targets of office automation, resistance, or at least loud cries of pain, seemed to come first from secretaries. But each secretary had a boss who had gone through the separation with her. And he too had a story to tell.

In 1981 I wrote an article that was published in *Mother Jones* magazine about office automation and got the following response from Lucille Schmidt in Cincinnati.

Lucille Schmidt

Your article ["The Electronic Sweatshop"] was very power-ful and, unfortunately, very true.

I have been employed with The Procter & Gamble Company for 13 years now. Four years ago I was promoted from secretary to manager. About that time, our Division brought in Word Processing equipment. All the secretaries and quite a few of us managers were very interested in the new technology and eager to utilize it to streamline the work. But then something very strange happened.

There was a reorganization. . . . all secretaries and clerks now became part of an organization called Administrative Services. . . .

One of the first visible signs that Administrative Services had arrived was the removal of the Executive Secretaries from the offices they had shared with their male bosses. No longer would there be 1:1 relationships as this did not "meet the needs of the business." All secretaries regardless of status, experience or rank were now "equal" and shared an office or "work center" with two or three others. They were given new job descriptions. Women whose typing was considered excellent became Information Processors and typed eight hours a day. Others were Support Secretaries. They were told they must learn to work as a team. . . . If there were conflicts involving workload or personality, they were given "feedback" in their Performance Evaluation that they didn't understand the team concept. . . .

Secretaries were transferred from one job to another, from one location to another, with little warning and no prior discussion. This was called career planning. Questions were not tolerated: those who questioned any aspect of the system were "resistant to change."

A monthly newsletter extolled the virtues of the new system. "Production reports" displayed the weekly output—pages typed. There were team meetings, not to discuss the work or how to effectively get it done, but to learn the "team concept." . . . Administrative Services was the office of the future . . . improving productivity for managers and providing a challenging and rewarding work life for the secretaries and clerks.

Absenteeism and tardiness skyrocketed . . . There were disabilities, "stress related," as indicated on the medical reports. Many resigned. There were some early retirements. Requests for transfers to another Division were refused. They were told to "make the system work."

. . . Cost reduction reports "proved" the many thousands of dollars being saved.

[Lucille Schmidt was asked repeatedly to become a manager in Administrative Services, the new bureaucracy that provided clerical support for almost 3,000 engineers. But Lucille was already a manager. She didn't think of supervising secretaries as a step up.]

"After all, my position as Personnel Manager provided regular interaction with the Paper hierarchy." [At Procter & Gamble there's a soup hierarchy, a soap hierarchy, a cosmetics hierarchy and so on.] "I represented our division at various meetings at Corporate headquarters, I was respected for my technical and interpersonal skills and had well-established credibility. . . . For two years I was able to resist a transfer to Administrative Services. Then I was told it's this or the front door —there was no option.

I am now an Administrative Supervisor.

I am to take attendance (I forego the "bedcheck"), report any absence or overtime and arrange for LOs [Temps are called Low Overheads at Procter & Gamble] to cover any planned or unplanned absences. I am to provide a "joining up" plan for personnel new to my area. I am to give written performance evaluations and provide action steps for further "growth." I

am to hand out the 3 × 5 cards notifying of a salary increase.
I am to call meetings to share (read) organizational announce-
ments . . .

Of course I know why I was transferred here. . . . Few positions in Personnel carry much responsibility and much authority. I held such a position but I am female, a former
secretary, and my father's collar is blue. Now I am a leader of
secretaries, all female, in an organization of female secretaries.
Now I am "back" in my proper "place" and I can grow and
progress all the hell I want. . . .

[Despite excellent benefits and seniority at Procter & Gamble, Lucille was thinking about leaving the company.]

I will probably have to relocate to another part of the U.S.,
but I'm angry and scared and starting to get bitter here and
that's not healthy. . . .

Your article showed only the tip of an ever-growing ice-
berg. . . .

Four years later I phoned Lucille in Cincinnati. By then
she'd left Procter & Gamble, taking a $10,000 pay cut—
"Though I'm almost up to my old salary again"—to run the
office of a small investment company.

Over the phone I didn't sense that knot of anguish in the
throat that I could practically hear in her letter. "For a while
there," she acknowledged, "I was getting to be the kind of
person I don't like to be around. But now I work with three
intelligent men, they respect me, they let me learn everything
I can about the business. In fact, I'm going out later to shop
for a word processing system to put on my own desk.

"At Procter, they give you a new machine and this somehow makes you 'a different kind of resource.' . . . Oh, Barbara,
it's such a waste—such a waste of people. The way they put
in word processing there, you had a lot of smart women getting dumb very fast."

At Procter & Gamble the Division Heads had been free to

make certain choices about office automation. The system Lucille described was established in the Engineering Division in 1978 after the Director of Engineering read about word processing on an airplane and decided right then, "60,000 feet in the air" so the story goes, to try it out at once. Engineering, located on the outskirts of town a good distance from the new corporate headquarters, was known as a technically experimental and bureaucratically informal part of the company.

An automation team was formed. The team visited an IBM center and selected the IBM OS6 to be used in small work centers. (Later the IBMs were gradually replaced with Wangs. But the system remained the same.)

Lucille encouraged me to visit Cincinnati and see what the six-year experiment with word processing had wrought.

"Matter of fact, I've got a luncheon date this week with a couple of secretaries I used to supervise. I bet they'd love to talk to you. And I'll get you the extensions of some managers —some ADs and Ds (Associate Directors and Directors)— and a Section Head in Soup."

"In the soup department?" I tried to get it straight.

"No," Lucille corrected me, "not the Soup Division, Soup Engineering. Anyway, he's now in the Management Systems Division. I know it's confusing. I'll print up a road map of the company hierarchy. You'll need it to get around. . . ."

□ □ □

Procter & Gamble is among the top 50 of the *"Fortune* 500" and the largest advertiser in the world. The company was formed in 1837 when two brothers-in-law, James Gamble, a soap maker, and William Procter, a candlemaker, merged their businesses. By the Civil War they were the largest firm in Cincinnati. They supplied soap and candles to the Union army.

Though the presidency went out of the family in 1930,

Procter & Gamble still has a family or paternal atmosphere. The company has a reputation as a decent employer. Among reporters, the company has a reputation for being secretive. It's difficult to interview anyone at P&G. The company prefers to get its messages across through paid advertising and well prepared public relations releases.

But Lucille knew many employees, and I arrived in Cincinnati with a few contacts of my own. Procter & Gamble employs over 20,000 people in Cincinnati, over 60,000 worldwide. So almost everyone who ever lived in the city of seven hills has a cousin or a high school sweetheart who still works for P&G.

Lucille found that quite a few of the secretaries she knew had quit or been given outplacement in the two years since she herself left. I wasn't surprised, since one goal of the IBM system is to reduce the ratio of support staff to principals. But I soon found that a surprising number of principals in the Engineering Division were gone too. Many of the men I called from both my own list and Lucille's were "no longer employed."

Those I managed to reach were either too busy to be interviewed or not sure they should be. But everyone had time for a caustic laugh when I mentioned that my subject was Administrative Services. Some of the men referred me to former associates who, they suspected, "might have more time to talk" now that they weren't with the company. One of those was Tom Oppdahl.

Tom Oppdahl

Tom Oppdahl had supervised a unit of over 100 engineers before his "early retirement." His fellow managers liked him and were gratified to tell me that he now had a good job— maybe even a better one—in Dayton.

I arranged to meet Oppdahl in Dayton, at the end of his work day. I could interview him in his car on the way home. (His new job entailed a long commute.) I felt embarrassed about questioning a fifty-five-year-old displaced engineer, a man who had commanded a group of 100 professionals at P&G and now worked in a small job shop over a clothing store.

But in Dayton I found Oppdahl well ensconced as Vice President for Engineering of a small but long-established job shop that even did a little design work for Procter & Gamble. "That didn't come through me," Tom made clear. "They had the contract already."

Tom's chief concern was modernizing the shop, which meant finding and training employees to use computer-aided design (CAD) systems. He was glad to answer my questions about CAD and good at explaining it.

It was harder for him to talk about his early retirement from Procter & Gamble. It's not that he was ashamed of being displaced. It's more that he was uncomfortable expressing anything that sounded like a personal feeling or a complaint. It's as if he wasn't entitled. But eventually I got the story from Tom, his wife and his daughter.

Oppdahl had been overseeing an engineering project in California when rumors drifted West about accelerated attrition in the home office. Then, after more than twenty two years, Tom got his first less-than-superior rating..He was surprised and hurt, but he accepted it as a normal evaluation. It took his wife to point out that Procter might be preparing the ground for firing him. A poor rating could help protect the firm from an age discrimination suit. Tom confronted the company directly (he was proud of that) and learned that they were only waiting for his fifty-fifth birthday. For the sake of the early retirement benefits (there were still two more boys to put through college), he stuck it out for a year and a half while looking for a new job.

"That must have been a difficult year and a half," I said.

"A couple of my friends died in the process. Fortunately I had already had my heart attack."

Tom had been the head of a section that published P&G's internal engineering manuals, built industrial models of their manufacturing plants and designed the thermal systems— boilers, air conditioning and sprinklers—for all P&G plants worldwide.

"I had three key subordinates, each of them had about thirty, thirty-five engineers. But I was stretched too darn far. I had more going on than I could keep track of.

"Then, before Administrative Services, I got a young secretary, right out of high school. She was a darn smart and agressive person. She and I sat down and made an outline of the things that had to be done and I said, 'Erin, I want you to take all the administrative tasks that you can and let me focus on the engineering.'

"It was fabulous. . . . She handled reports, sending them out wherever they needed to go; personnel, if a person needed to move from this building to that she'd handle the paperwork, get all the corporate approvals; travel arrangements, you just tell her where you wanted to go, what meetings you needed to attend, she'd work out the flights, the hotels. It didn't take long before I could describe the intent of a non-technical letter and she could compose and sign it herself or prepare it for my signature.

"The bottom line is that our team approach increased my productivity at least 50 percent, possibly doubled it. She was so good that I lost her. She got promoted to another organization in P&G. I think she's still classified as a secretary over there but with a level of pay I couldn't command.

"After Erin left, I was loaned out by P&G to another corporation to supervise an engineering project. So I didn't experience the first six months of Administrative Services. I was 'off campus,' so to speak, the day it was announced. I missed the day when your personal secretary couldn't talk to you any more.

"Actually, there was never a time when a secretary couldn't talk to her former boss. But there were secretaries who chose not to talk to their former bosses, the kind of bosses who had abused them. There were also some secretaries who I did not then, nor do I now, respect, who used Administrative Services as an excuse to say 'I can't do that,' or 'I don't take dictation; use the telephone,' or 'You have to fill out the form before I can get your airplane tickets.' There were two causes for that type of behavior, either she was lazy or she resented the bastard."

"But no," I rushed to defend the women, "they were not supposed to serve as personal secretaries anymore. One typist told me about lectures from the head of Admin. Services, like sermons she said, 'The one-to-one relationship is the office of the past: in the office of the future we will move forward into. . . .' "

"True," Tom stopped me, "but some of them took it to the extreme."

"Did you feel personally demoted," I asked, "when a typist said, 'You'll have to fill out a form,' or 'I'm sorry but I don't take dictation'?"

"Demoted?" He played thoughtfully with the concept. "No, I did not feel demoted. I felt that I had lost a quality of service and I resented that.

"Well . . . ," he thought some more, "in one respect I was demoted. I was demoted in that I had to do more things for myself.

"A letter had to be transcribed by a voice telephone and done by a pool of people you didn't see. Everything was in order of the queue. If it was an emergency you handed it in Monday, it went into the queue and you would get it back Wednesday. And if you needed a correction it would go back in the queue. To make changes or small corrections was extremely time consuming."

And the whole beauty of the word processor is the quick way you can make little changes, I thought. How profoundly perverse—it hadn't hit me this clearly before—to take the miraculous typewriter that could make changes in an instant and set it up so an executive has to fill out a form and wait hours (or even days) for the new version to come back from the pool. Just filling out the form takes longer than making most corrections.

The second great advantage of a word processor is that it specifically eliminates routine retyping. This should leave people freer to do more varied work. Yet the work center system creates a huge caste of people who do nothing but type.

So a rigid, regulating schema had negated the two main advantages of this wonderful, flexible machine.

"Travel arrangements," Tom continued. "You'd have to fill out a form saying when you wanted to leave. They even had on it, 'What flight do you want to take and what hotel?' So you had to go to the travel guide and look that up yourself. If you didn't fill in those details, you couldn't predict the arrangements you'd get back. Like you could have a plane that left at an inconvenient time. Or you could get a plane that left Florida just when you asked, but it terminated in Atlanta and you'd catch the next leg the next day. Your hotel could be an hour from where you had to work. Common sense and judgment seemed to disappear."

"What did you do if you had to get a report out fast?" I asked.

"Sometimes it didn't get out. Really your performance depended on the friendships you could make and how much you could get done unofficially. You'd try to use the system and not abuse friendships. But where you had a critical situation, friendship was the only thing that made it happen."

"If it depended on friendship," I suggested "there must have been some men who could never get anything done."

"Yup," he laughed, "and they deserved it. There is some justice.

"But if you were on good terms with a secretary you could walk over and hand something to her and say, 'Could you make those changes? I need it today.' And you'd have it promptly. But if it was one of the malingerers she'd cover up with all the bureaucratic answers why it couldn't be done and how you couldn't get it till 2 o'clock and if you don't like it, go talk to my boss."

"Weren't the supervisors supposed to keep the manager away from the typist?" I asked. "I'm surprised they let you go directly to her desk."

"Early on, some supervisors tried to say, 'You can't come in here and talk to her.' But then what happened was *they* became the mailman. The support secretary had twenty or more people to support. So they'd let you deliver your own.

"The real way they kept the principal away from the typist was to put your typist down four floors and in a corner. You'd ask someone for a change and she'd say, 'Gee I don't have that document on my Wang. It's on a different system.'

"Eventually I got proficient on the word processor myself. That's how I finally got the best out of the system. What I'd do was make a rough draft of my letters on the terminal as quickly as I could have dictated them. Then I'd use the Administrative Services secretary to call up the document, format it, correct the spelling and tell me when she was finished. After that I'd call it up on my terminal, do the editing and instruct her when it was to be printed. Writing directly on the computer like that was the best system, better than dictating on tape or telephone, better than hand-written copy. I was the only manager I know that had a terminal in my office."

"How'd you get it?" I asked.

"A little bit of pulling strings, a little bit of authority."

"And how did you get the typist to call up your document quickly? Didn't she still say it had to go in the queue?"

"I was sharing her workload by typing the first draft, so she was more cooperative. And even though it was via machine, she would know who she was doing it for. It was personal. I could thank her."

"You see," Tom explained, "in theory you can be more efficient if you just handle the mail, or you just make reservations, or you just type. But they made the typists do just one thing and then took away the accountability. They weren't working for anyone."

"They were accountable to Administrative Services," I said.

"Their bosses in Administrative Services had them accountable by how many pages they did but not what pages or how well. I'd rather have a letter on time with a couple of typos that can be corrected with Wite-Out than a perfect letter two days late. They were judged by errors per page or typeovers per line, not on responsiveness to the needs of the business.

"Under Administrative Services," Oppdahl summed up, "I went from 150 percent efficiency down to less than 100 percent because I was doing secretarial functions just to get things done. It's inefficient. You had $30,000–$40,000 engineers doing what a $15,000 secretary could do better if she had the motivation or the permission to do it. It was just inefficient."

"But Ivan [the head of Administrative Services] told me," I said, becoming devil's advocate, "that Administrative Services cut the ratio of support staff to principals by 30 to 40 percent where there was no resistance."

"IBM and Wang and idiots like Ivan are selling the computer, so they redesign the office to match the machine instead of vice versa."

"They say their system offers a countable and a predictable output," I continued.

"What's countable may not be what counts. The bean

counters can count the keystrokes but the intangibles get lost. I take that back; it's not only intangibles they miss. They measure the easily measurable things, but they can't even differentiate between a typo and a mistake that makes the letter nonsense.

"The department was bloated, so yes," Tom declared, "there was a need for efficiency. But they answered the need with a corrupt system. They needed transportation, so they went out and bought a camel."

Sophia Crandall

The majority of Procter & Gamble secretaries felt demoted or exiled when they were moved into work centers. But to Sophia Crandall, the separation of the secretary and the boss promised a kind of liberation.

Mrs. Crandall had been a certified executive secretary when word processing was first considered in the Engineering Department. She was part of the original team that visited the IBM center and selected the IBM OS6.

With the start-up of Administrative Services she became a Group Leader. In the P&G hierarchy that was only one rank below Tom Oppdahl. She outranked most of the men that her group of clericals supported.

Even the engineers who most resented Administrative Services respected Sophia Crandall's skill and honesty. "She'd probably be willing to talk to you," I was advised by an executive who declined to be interviewed himself, "because she doesn't owe her position to any clique at Procter."

Sophia was a tall woman of sixty with tight gray ringlets. She had a large jaw and thick-rimmed glasses. But bubbles of wit rising to the surface kept threatening to subvert her severe demeanor. She looked like Lily Tomlin playing my second-grade teacher.

At her home after work she gave me a formal history of Administrative Services.

"In the beginning," she acknowledged, "there was a lot of trauma for the managers. We started out with a survey trying to get them to write down what they did over a month's time. We asked them what support work they needed. We didn't realize that a lot of managers don't know what a secretary does. They have no idea what reports flow through their office.

"Some of them could understand the benefits to them of the increased productivity in word processing. But there were other needs. I call them the ego needs. The people who think of their secretary as a fixture or a perk to do personal-type things. Those were the people who tried to undermine the system. Those were the ones who would fuss or complain about any minor thing. And who tried to get the support staff to do personal-type things without the other managers knowing about it."

"What kind of personal things?"

"To run and get stamps if they brought their bills in to be mailed. To run from one building to another for a personal stamp. Or to make tennis appointments. One manager had this large tennis club and used secretarial support to line up the tennis games and to type up the league's schedule. A lot of personal letters, too.

"One man," Sophia remembered "his secretary had always baked a birthday cake for him. He bragged about her baking skills to the other managers. But his secretary had been transferred into a work center. As a part of our survey of support needs we never took down his birthday or arranged a cake. When it came to the birthday he kept coming out of the office looking, but there was no cake. (He wasn't the kind of man you'd bake a cake for unless he was your boss.) That was the kind of issue."

"But weren't there real trade-offs under the old system?" I

asked. "I mean, you typed his personal letters and he let you make personal phone calls; you typed his kid's term paper, he let you leave early on a school holiday."

"But the trade-off was never money."

I'd never heard it stated that simply.

"He could brag that his secretary was the best baker, but the number of times you took things back to the store, or the number of personal letters you typed or the number of cups of coffee won't get you a raise in a large company. A secretary may be quite appreciated by her boss, but when it comes to advancement . . ."

"What about praise?" I asked. "That's not money, but I talked to one Information Processor who complained about typing all day and then, she said, 'You do a big project with complicated charts, lots of tabs, you type all day then the support secretary carries it back and gets the credit. You don't hear anyone say, 'That's a good job.' '"

"That is accurate," Sophia said. "And that is one of the things that made us evolve the system back to combined roles [the sharing of administrative support work and word processing]. The information processor didn't get to hear the praise.

"But for a lot of people," Sophia said disapprovingly, "the problem of praise is still the separation from the man. If I tell them, as a woman, they've done a good job, it's not received as much. Really, it depends on the level of their own confidence. The best secretaries, they knew themselves when they'd done a good job. They knew how to recognize it. A few still had to go back and hear it from a man." She brooded over these weak sisters.

"Wasn't that another problem?" I asked. "Didn't the secretaries keep running back to their old bosses, and the bosses to their old secretaries?"

"More the managers," she said, "the older managers. A lot of secretaries wanted change.

"There was a problem at first because we had not done much assertiveness training to help them deal better with the managers hanging around their desks expecting them to do this or find that."

"Assertiveness training?"

"Oh yes. We had a number of formal assertiveness training sessions to help them explain to the men that their work load does not allow them to go get stamps. We practiced with role playing."

I pressed for examples.

"If he stands over you, 'Just make this change please,' you say, 'You make me nervous standing there. I'll be glad to make your change and return it to you.' The women had to practice to be able to say 'The work will get done in order. You won't get it any faster by standing there.' "

"One man claimed," I said to Sophia, "that some women were just waiting for the chance to say no to the men, especially the ones who had had abusive bosses before."

"For some, " she acknowledged, "as they did the role playing they got a new . . . uh . . . perspective and they would be anxious to go back and put it into practice. It really all hinged on the male-female dynamics.

"One manager came into my office storming because a woman had told him she couldn't do something. He said, 'I have never been told no by any woman!' I thought, 'At your age it's about time some woman told you no.'

"We had one male information processor and he never had near the same problem with managers trying their games on him. He did not need assertiveness training . . . .

"A lot of the complaints about Administrative Services," Sophia drew herself up to make a controversial point, "a lot of the complaints was because a female organization held a bit of power for once.

"One of the things certain managers did to test us at the beginning was to put everything in as rush to see what the system could handle. That was one of their underhanded ways of doing it."

Sophia had to recapitulate the history of Administrative Services' monitoring attempts in order to explain the method that evolved to counter these artificial rushes.

"At start-up we had the operators fill out daily production reports. Most of the information they could take right off the machine. The computer would tell them how many pages they typed. There was a systems manager at the beginning," she remembered, "who was pushing for us to count everything. He wanted us to measure the lines of type with a special ruler. Some areas did it but I said, 'No, I won't do that.' I refused. But in regard to the rushes, we did ask the women to keep sheets on. . . ."

"Why did you refuse to measure lines?" I interrupted her train of thought.

"I always felt strongly, it's one of P&G's beliefs, that the human resource is a valuable asset of the company. Our staff were very honest. I was not going to measure what they did with a ruler.

"But they were asked to keep a sheet on the rushed pages and the author of those rush documents. If you found a manager who had 75 percent rush work, then you asked some questions about it. 'Does this say that you're not so organized as you need to be? We could help you with that.' "

Sophia Crandall had refused to make the typists measure their own lines but she insisted on keeping track of the managers' production, at least in regard to rushed pages.

"Could anything else on these clerical productivity reports be used to evaluate the managers?" I asked. "Did *their* superiors ever ask to see them?"

"If someone is going to write a document and he has to keep revising it ten, eleven times before you can send it out, then yes, someone at the higher level could ask for that kind of information. Our daily productivity report included the number of rushes, the number of draft pages, the number of revisions and whether the revisions were due to managers' changes or our errors. Yes, some of the higher executives did feel we could give them some information on their staff, that we could have an input on the communications skills of the managers and how they interfaced with the organization."

"Were there any typists," I asked, "who always looked for their old boss's tapes or continued to give them special service?"

"A few secretaries that would take care of their old boss's work ahead of other people would be moved further away. If the team concept is to work, if we are to move forward to the idea of supporting the larger group in total, it is essential to break the one-to-one relationship between the secretary and the principal. Most of the women had no trouble with that."

"You are really some feminist," I said.

"My husband used to kid that I was a woman's libber before my time. Since 1960, I have never carried a cup of coffee as a secretary. Even when I worked for a senior vice president."

"Did six years of Administrative Services change the staffing patterns?" I asked.

"The ratio of secretaries to managers was just about double when we started," Sophia answered. "Of course we began with a lot of cuts. Probably too drastic at the beginning.

"As I look back on it, I believe we tried to make too many changes at once. Everybody had to change, the secretaries, the bosses, the whole system. People had to adjust to a technical change and a social change. They had to learn the machine and they had to learn the team concept. As I think about it, I believe the first thing should have been the split of the boss/secretary relationship."

"Why?" I asked. "Why not just give the secretary a word processor, especially now that we have small computers. I never met a secretary who didn't like her own word processor."

Sophia agreed with the last observation. "I don't know anyone who would want to go back to a Selectric."

"Then why not put the word processor on the secretary's desk first?"

"Because the first would be the last," she answered. "If you brought your word processor in first, the secretaries would be more productive but the individual manager still wouldn't allow his secretary to move into a team concept and support others. She might finish two hours earlier but he would not admit that he didn't have the work for her. He would rather have his secretary do nothing 40 percent of the time, just so long as she was totally available outside his door.

"Besides, if you brought the word processors in first, you'd have to give them to everybody. You could not afford to do that and keep all those people on.

"No," Sophia insisted with unflinching logic, "if you're going to move to the team concept you have to change the social relationship first. You have to move to the work center first and bring the technology in after. Of course you wouldn't be able to cut your staff until after you had the word processors. But you cannot begin to move forward," she concluded with conviction, "till you split the one-to-one relationship."

My jaw dropped with admiration. All by herself Sophia Crandall had reformulated one of the toughest tenets of industrial automation. *First* you rationalize the job, change the physical layout, break the old social relationships, *then* you bring in the new machinery.

□   □   □

In 1980 I attended the Office Automation Conference in Houston and listened to automation managers describe their disappointments with the Office of the Future. Many found that despite large investments in word processing equipment, the cost to get out a single letter never went down.

The companies citing "success" were those that had been

willing to go all the way, breaking the one-to-one relationship first, then rationalizing the clerical job and monitoring both secretary and principal. In the end these successful companies had cut office payrolls more by getting rid of unnecessary secretaries and managers than by reducing the cost per letter.

The lesson they drew was that unless you can control the social office, the time savings from word processing will be pilfered by the boss/secretary duo and piddled away. But if you centralized and rationalized *first,* it almost didn't matter which word processing machines you chose.

But the pioneering automaters at Procter & Gamble were not prepared to think this severely, so they hadn't mobilized to smash monogamy at all costs. Furthermore, the top managers in engineering apparently didn't like to say, even to themselves, that middle managers were the primary targets. Early on, they had discussed and discarded more rigid management monitoring schemes as "just not right," one of their systems analysts told me. "And Procter is a company that likes to do just about what's right."

In the face of this vacillation there had been continual backsliding toward traditional monogamy. "If I had a question about the dictation I just walked straight to the man's office," an information processor told me. "I wasn't going to sit there typing nonsense."

Managers also defied the laws of word processing purdah (though usually more stealthily) by slipping in and out of the work centers to ask for changes. "If you're a friendly kind of a guy, you can always get things done," an engineer told me with a wink I could practically hear over the telephone. Others, like Tom Oppdahl, had learned to relate one-to-one via computer.

Meanwhile uncounted anonymous dissenters did their bit to undermine the tracking systems. Secretaries had been too busy to fill out production reports; managers had objected or, more characteristically, diddled helplessly about filling out

work orders; supervisors like Sophia Crandall had openly refused to measure lines of type.

Eventually, as I learned later, Administrative Services was
officially disbanded. Ivan was out. All Administrators and
Word Processors would now report directly to the heads of
the areas they served. Apparently no one in authority at P&G
had been ready to twist arms far enough to enforce a new
morality. So the system had rolled back toward monogamy.

Perhaps if someone as clear-headed as Sophia Crandall had
been the head of Administrative Services it would have
worked.

Actually it did work. It's true that Administrative Services
was disbanded as a separate hierarchy. But the work centers
still existed. Even where the women reverted to a one-to-one
approach (dividing the men, instead of the tasks, among
themselves), it was now more commonly one-to-four. Where
it had been one-to-four before, it was often one-to-ten or even
one-to-twenty. More important than the numbers on either
side of the ratio, the relationship that connected them had
been redefined.

Under a work center plan, a manager still receives secretarial
service but he no longer has a helper with unspecified duties.
Even if someone titled Secretary still sits outside his door,
she's no longer *his* secretary in the old sense.

The head of an eight-man technical team at a computer
company tried to explain this subtle change to me.

"If you ask the younger men on my team, they'll tell you
they have a secretary. And I guess they do. She types, she files,
she requisitions supplies. But—did you ever see that movie
Invasion of the Body Snatchers? Well that's not my real secretary:
that's a pod."

I winced to hear a secretary like Elizabeth Anderson called
a pod. Yet I know how much less of a full person she must
seem as she sits in a cluster processing rough drafts at 125
lines per half-hour for no one in particular.

For the sake of enumerating and regulating all office functions, Elizabeth's employers are willing to forgo the use of the initiative and common sense that she once brought to her work. Elizabeth types like a pod, allowing silly errors to go through because, as a Word Processing Specialist, she's not supposed to understand each dictator's correspondence. Like the Administrative Support Specialist who ferries work back and forth to the appropriate pools, Elizabeth is now restricted to aiding the managers in narrowly specified ways that don't require learning their business or using her judgment. Underlying the IBM plan is an assumption that the autonomous secretary and middle manager are enemies of the company. More is to be feared than gained by allowing them to function as full human beings.

When the Office of the Future is successfully installed, the physical bodies may be the same, the secretarial service may be the same (though that's rare), but something less tangible, the relationship, has been automated out. By now this nonrelationship secretarial system is so pervasive that younger managers may not notice anything peculiar about the atmosphere in which their phones are answered and their words are processed. Managers and secretaries who remember the old days can only look around and wonder to themselves, "Didn't the tomatoes used to taste different?"

□ □ □

By the mid-1980s executives had adapted to the IBM word processing system in many different ways. Traditional managers like the men I met at Procter & Gamble felt slighted, helpless or even lonely when their secretaries were moved away to word processing centers. They missed the personal services they had received through the one-to-one relationship. Often they adapted by trying to cajole the old kind of personal attention from the new communal support staff.

But younger managers tended to make a different adjustment. Instead of trying to wheedle their way around the work center, they learned how to get a letter out by themselves. In just about a decade the predominant managerial support system shifted from private secretary to communal secretary to no secretary at all.

For all but the top executives, the office relationship of the future will be neither monogamy nor polygamy, but celibacy. With a few electronic aids, the rising MBA can do it himself. Many young executives prefer it that way.

Larry Hoover

"You see this slim little thing?" my former boss reached into his jacket pocket and took out a device as thin as a cigarette case. "This little thing," he said, stroking the tape recorder, "is ready for me any time of the day or night. If I get a bright idea at 8 o'clock in the morning, 10 o'clock at night, I never have to feel I'm taking advantage. I never find it standing out at the coffee cart or talking on the phone."

In the years since I'd left the firm, Larry had been promoted to a two-window office on the twelfth floor. Back on the fourth floor, where he had had only one window, he had shared me with seven other sales reps. Now, at forty-four, he was the chief sales executive for the region. Yet there was no secretary sitting outside his door.

"Weren't you looking forward to a secretary of your own when you moved up here?" I asked.

"I don't miss it one bit," he answered. "Quite honestly, I don't want to deal with someone's kid home with the chicken pox or those school half-days. We have enough legitimate crises to deal with.

"No," he shook his head, dismissing any lingering nostalgia. "I slip this into one of my folders [with one smooth motion he slipped a minature tape into a slot, checked a box, filled in a date and dropped the folder onto his Out basket]. The folder will disappear and then reappear after lunch with a perfectly typed letter. And I won't have had to hear a word about who's getting married or how crowded the bank was. No, I do not miss having a secretary outside my door."

Les Cummings

"Among our thousand employees," Les Cummings told me, "we have exactly two secretaries. Actually one and a half. I don't keep my secretary occupied, so I release her for other work."

Mr. Cummings is the Executive Vice President of a medium-size firm on the American Stock Exchange. He's about forty, plays tennis and loves computers.

"With the economic modeling programs I've developed," he told me, "I can see from the top to the bottom of the company—past, present and future—just by pushing a few buttons on a keyboard."

Les was glad to give me some of his time because he's interested in literature. He means to write a book himself someday.

"With my PC and soon my laser printer, I can, myself, produce a document with higher quality in terms of content, formatting and appearance, in less time than I could with a secretary.

"A secretary is superfluous and, even worse, gets in the way.

"I can put my entire Rolodex on my computer; Rolodex makes a program. Let's say I'm in the middle of typing a memo, I realize I want to speak to Barbara. Since I have 'Sidekick,' I can exit from word processing and flip to my Rolodex. I simply press 'Barbara,' and your phone rings at home. I don't have to bother with my secretary, who might be on a coffee break.

"Right now, today, her only function for me is screening my calls. I'll never want to answer my own phone. By 1990, where you now have ten secretaries, you'll have two receptionists.

"For the manager who isn't afraid of it, the computer means greater and greater control over his or her life. It means the security of less and less dependency on other people.

"For those other people, it means unemployment of course." This thought, apparently new, slowed Mr. Cummings down. But he recovered his positive spirit and raced ahead with another idea.

"Why don't you write a book about the Death of the Secretary?

"The traditional secretary will soon be displayed in a glass case in the natural history museum, with her steno pad. By 1990 most managers won't want to use secretaries. In ten years the traditional secretary will be obsolete. . . . You want to take down the reasons?

"First, managers want to be independent.

"Two, education. There are fewer people coming out of school literate enough to be good secretaries. The better-trained woman can get a management job in her own right. So a truly good secretary is harder and harder to find anyway.

"Three, feminism has taken away the fun of having a secretary.

"Hey this could be a big seller!" he interrupted himself enthusiastically. "How many millions of secretaries are there? They're literate; they buy books. They see the computer coming into the office but what will it mean to their jobs? *The Death of the Secretary,* that's the book you should write."

□ □ □

Aside from typing and filing, traditional secretaries provided diplomatic and personal services that ranged from screening phone calls and scheduling appointments to sending anniversary cards and sewing on buttons. Like a trainer at ringside, the secretary's job included everything she could do to send the company's champion out ready to take on his opponents. Today only the top few executives have true secretaries. They may now be called Administrators or Assistants or Administrative Assistants.

Whatever the title, I always assumed that anyone who could have a real secretary would want one. Yet I believe that Larry and Les are sincere about their declarations of independence. They'd rather get a report out by themselves, with the help of a few machines, than be dependent on a secretary who might bother them with her own problems.

I realized that independence had become a high-tech sales feature when I heard J. Peter Doonan of Data General Corporation use the word in his talk on "Successfully Improving and Measuring Productivity Gains through Automation."

Mr. Doonan described the kinds of administrative support —typing, filing, calendar assistance, reminders and to-do lists —that executives could now get from their computers.

"In the past," he said, "we had a good spouse or a good secretary to do this for us. Today in the electronic office you can get this done with less confusion and more independence."

Replacing secretaries with machines might be considered a form of democratization, like using household appliances instead of servants. Perhaps the younger executive's discomfort around a secretary reflects a feminist-inspired embarrassment about being waited on by a woman, often an older woman.

But I hear an undertone of mysogyny in the determination to be independent. The one-to-one relationship bogs a man down in mundane, female irrelevancies.

Corporate and government executives make a great many decisions about my job, my family and my world. Increasingly they make these decisions with the aid of profiles, economic models and other abstractions.

I'd feel safer if decision makers, male or female, were less insulated from the problems of strep throat, school half-days and long bank lines. It's dangerous for powerful people to be independent of everything bumpy, irregular and human.

8

□ □ □ □ □ □ □

Electronic Surveillance

By sending his typing out to the pool, Larry Hoover gained a certain kind of independence from secretaries. But at the same time he was sending out information to those above him about the way he spent his time.

Les Cummings had gained even greater independence than Larry. With the personal computer on his desk he could get letters and reports out all by himself. This made him feel as proud as a four-year-old who can tie his own shoelaces. But what happens to Les Cummings's independence when his "personal" computer is linked or integrated into a company-wide network? Probably nothing in his case, since Cummings is the top executive to whom all data flows. But in most cases, once computers are linked, anyone who touches the keyboard is automatically reporting on himself.

Today's standard computer system, the system most likely to be installed in anyone's office, is just such a linked or integrated network.

Back when the giant mainframes dominated the earth, all the terminals in any office had to be be hooked into one massive computer brain. Everything was controlled centrally. But once the tiny, agile micros began to proliferate, it seemed there would soon be no reason for every employee to be plugged into a central computer.

Early in the micro era, enthusiastic young professionals often brought their own small computers into the office before the Electronic Data Processing Department found uses for them. Some departments managed to buy personal computers out of funds set aside for typewriters or office supplies. Many popular business programs like VisiCalc were first developed and debugged in the underground world of personal computing.

Personal computing allowed individual office workers, from secretaries to scientists, to shop for the particular machines and programs they needed. Soon a mix and match of computers dotted the office.

Even in companies where individuals already had personal computers, fierce interdepartmental battles were fought to depersonalize the personal machines. Employees were often forbidden to buy their own computers or to modify the programs they worked with. The goal was to get everyone back onto a system controlled from the center. The official justification for restoring central control was usually communication.

The problem from the management point of view was that personal computers communicated in the same democratic way that a telephone system carries messages. But management's goal wasn't simply communication, it was controlled communication in which superiors had access to files of their subordinates on a hierarchical basis. ("Hierarchical" is the technical name for programming that gives some people access to other people's files but not vice versa—"I can see yours, but you can't see mine.")

How could this restoration be achieved when the new personal computers were cheap, adroit, and well suited for most office needs? The answer was found in "integrated computing."

The large vendors including IBM, Xerox, Exxon, AT&T and Wang now promote networks rather than computers. A network may consist of the very same machines that the company sells as personal computers. But the computers forming a network are selected, installed and programmed centrally.

Integrated computing is not a technology, it's a control mechanism. Some employers install hierarchical networks because they genuinely want the capacity to monitor and access their employees' work. Others have specific networking needs. But many organizations seem to be buying networks as a matter of course these days. I thought it would be interesting to see what happens in an ordinary, benign office when an integrated network is installed.

□ □ □

In 1984 a governmental agency decided to install its first front-office computers. The intention was to help secretaries with their typing and to help executives with their statistical reports: word processing and number crunching, two things computers do well. In order to enhance interoffice communication, and perhaps just to be modern, the agency decided on an integrated network. The basic network they selected— "plain vanilla" as the salesman called it—wasn't intended to change anyone's location, status or autonomy. In fact, management intended to let people go on working, as much as possible, the way they had before.

As it happened, the word processing system came with programs to time and count keystrokes. That's now a standard feature, built-in. (Like canned food without salt, an office program that doesn't monitor is getting to be such a specialty item that you have to pay more in order *not* to get the added ingredient.) But no one at the agency was assigned to check anyone else's keystroke count. The terminals would simply be placed on each secretary's desk and in each executive's office.

For once, automation was in no way part of a plan to deskill, demote or displace people. On the contrary, the agency seems to have computerized in the same spirit that an employer once bought his secretary an electric typewriter, to give her a better tool or just to be modern. Exactly a year after the integrated network was installed, I visited the director of one of the four divisions.

Brad Coffee

Brad Coffee, a tall, graying man with strikingly good posture, welcomed me, seated me and invited me with an amiable gesture to "fire away."

I opened with a plain vanilla question.

"How do you like working with computers after your one year's experience?"

He smiled.

"I come here from twenty-five years in the Pentagon."

"Oh," I said nonplussed. "Then you've had a lot more than one year's experience with computers."

He nodded like one who's learned from battlefield experience.

"Let me say that there are two general uses for computers," he said, slipping into a background briefing mode. "The first is to collect and process information. A computer can put a great deal of data at your disposal and in that way it becomes a great source of power.

"You sit around a table at the senior level in the Department of Defense [Brad graciously invited participation from imaginary generals convened around his office table]; he tells you what he knows, the other tells you what he knows, a third contributes from his personal experience. Then *you* say, 'Gentlemen, I've got all the projections here for the next fifteen years.' You carry the day.

"True, they can say to themselves GIGO [Garbage In/Garbage Out!] But are they going to take on all those statistics projected out for the next fifteen years?

"I saw McNamara bring in his whiz kids, the systems analysts. They were the people that could manipulate data. They'd show you their printouts and say, 'We can achieve a destructive capacity of such and such for an expenditure of such and such with a system requiring ammunition and upkeep costs of this or that.'

"It was difficult, let me tell you, for the old soldiers to say, 'Well I *feel* that this is the kind of weapon I need to win the war.' McNamara and his computers won the day.

"So that's one use of computers. But that's not the level in this organization. The other use, what I have here [he pointed to the trim, ecru terminal that let out an occasional beep from a desk against the back wall], what that does for me—it's a pain in the neck.

"This E-mail [electronic mail], before, if people wanted to send me messages it came through the secretary. She responded with a note or set up a meeting. Now, the matter can be seven levels removed from what I should be considering, but it comes directly to me.

"For instance, let's take whatever just came in. [There had been a discreet beep as he spoke.] We'll see what it is."

Director Coffee moved from the couch to the computer where he called up the E-mail message that had just arrived.

The screen was laid out like a standard memo. The message said, 'Jean Dowling's brother Gil passed away last night after a long illness. . . .'

"Now who else did she send it to?" Coffee muttered as he pushed a couple of buttons. "I can get the distribution list to check."

Having satisfied himself he called up the next waiting memo. This one said, 'Just to remind you that no office supplies can be requisitioned without an authorized signature. An authorized signature is one of the following. . . ."

"I don't want to deal with this," Brad balked. "There's no reason I have to know about supplies. But now I have at least to see that the correct person on my staff got it. Let's see." He checked the distribution again. "They sent it to the X list and the Y list. So Sarah Radcliff's got it. She handles my supplies. So I don't have to bother with it."

With a sweepingly dismissive gesture he pressed a delete button. "That's the first thing I learned to do on the computer —get it off my machine."

"Why did they send a message about office supplies to you?" I asked.

He shrugged.

"Does this system compile a record of who communicates with whom?"

"I don't have access to it if they do," he answered. "I don't know what *they're* doing." He pointed directly up.

I had asked Brad Coffee that question because some organizations analyze patterns of E-mail. By applying statistical techniques like block modeling, they believe they can spot fast- or slow-track employees and identify disgruntled cliques.

"In a suspicious atmosphere, workers sometimes protect themselves by sending everything to everyone, thus creating statistical static." I mentioned.

"Protective junk mail," Brad got the idea immediately.

"Exactly," I said. "Not that this seems like that kind of place."

"Here it's just laziness," the director explained. "There are general distribution lists already in the computer for convenience. It's harder to write down the three or four people you really should send it to. So I'm overrun with electronic junk mail. It increases my work load. And I'm a lazy executive." He said that last, proudly.

"Let me summarize for you this way. The only two things a senior manager manages are people and information. In a real sense I do not manage [he gave examples of facilities that would identify his organization]. That goes on at a much lower level.

"I manage people and I manage information. The computer gives me better access to information; it gives me worse access to people.

"On the information side, I'll be able to turn to Ted and say, 'Ted, tell me the status on all the projects being discussed at the next board meeting. But I won't actually be turning to Ted. Ted put the information in, but I'll be getting it off the machine. (In fact, I'll get it in printed form because I'll want to scribble all over it and take it home in my briefcase.) But the point I want to make is, I will not get it from Ted in person, so I will be just that much further away from the people who gathered the information.

"Let me tell you, I am good at sizing up people, either one-to-one or in a group. If I can sit down with the source of the information even for five minutes—for a five-minute summary—then I know whether I'm getting good information, good trend analysis.

"I'm not as valuable to this organization sitting at that computer as I am talking to people or having them sit around my table in a crisis. I'm good at making decisions in a crisis. I love crises.

"I can use that [indicating the computer] to keep my finger on just what my staff is doing. But I don't want to. I hire someone and I like to let them run with the ball.

"Now I have access to a lot of information about my subordinates. But I don't want that."

"Can people from other divisions now get summary information off the computer about your division?" I asked. "Would you want someone above you to be able to look at his computer screen and say, 'I see that 20 percent of the contracts negotiated in June are still unsigned,' or '30 percent of the construction is behind schedule'?"

"I prefer him not to be able to do that." Brad pointed up again at the word *him*. There was only one person in the agency above Brad Coffee.

"He'd be getting unwashed, unscreened information. What may look like a problem may be easy to explain. He'll say, 'Look, this project has doubled in cost,' and I may say, 'So what?'

"It's important that he come to me and ask for the report so I can pull out the data and shape it. I don't say you have to change the data. But the data by itself may be very unhelpful. Those numbers may not mean much.

"Let me say this," Brad declared. "Any manager wants to be the determiner of what information goes out to evaluate his performance. That's the nature of the beast.

"If they can take summary information off the computer without coming to me first, then I will be sitting in a glass office. They may leave these walls up [he gestured at his solid office walls], but my position will be no different than out there. [He pointed to the open landscaped office where the department's lower-level staff worked without walls.] I do not want to work in a glass office. Any manager who tells you different is not telling you the truth."

A roundish man, the division's second in command, stopped by Brad's office. Everyone at the agency seemed so open that I asked him right there how the computers affected his privacy.

"I play Big Brother myself sometimes," he confessed, "looking at what the secretaries are typing. Like if I ask for a letter by the end of the day. I don't want to be looking over her shoulder to see if it's ready. So I look through her computer files. Or when I tell a senior assistant to write a letter himself, I don't ask to see it before it goes out. That's one way to develop your staff's self confidence. But I can look at the letter from my terminal to see if it meets my specifications. [The assistant can't look into his boss's file, however. The access only goes one way.]

"I'm only reading official letters," the round man defended himself. "I don't feel that's spying. I feel it's developing your staff's independence. Besides, they don't know that we look."

Ceal Paoli

"With computers they can always look," Ceal Paoli, a red-headed secretary, assured me. "And I hate for anyone to see something full of typos." She was a lively woman of around thirty-five, with fifteen years of office experience. "You can type so fast now, you fly with these new machines. But what it looks like before you correct it! And what a table looks like before you format it! My boss would get scared if he saw it on the screen. He'd think his secretary had started writing in hieroglyphics. (He thinks I'm crazy as it is.)

"So what I do, if I'm halfway through something, let's say I did a rough draft but I didn't have a chance to edit it or run the spell check—I used to be such a perfect speller before I got this thing—if I'd be embarrassed to have somebody see it half done, I change the document's title to something like XMASMEMO. Especially if it's for Mr. _____. If he's going through my files, he'll never find it. Not that I'm saying they go through your files, but. . . . When it's ready, I change it back to BdSchd8/2."

"But what if they need the board schedule [BdSchd] and they can't find it?" I asked.

"If they can't find it then they have to come to me and ask. That way I can neaten it up before I print it out.

"The other way I would always be making my unfinished work look finished, which would really be a waste of time. It's more efficient to format afterwards on a lot of these things."

"You know," I said to the secretary, "I talked to a high executive who told me that having his department's interim reports available continuously on the computer would be like working in a glass office."

"If I couldn't hide my unfinished files," the secretary answered, "I would be working at a glass desk. Would you want everyone to be able to see right into your drawers?"

□   □   □

Ceal Paoli was trying to protect the same private space that the division head found so important. Both of them were aware of someone "up there" who could see down into their files. Like Brad Coffee, the secretary wanted to be able to present her work when it was ready. If someone needed a draft she wanted them to come ask for it so she could explain or "neaten it up." Brad was similarly worried that the head of the organization might see his "unwashed" or "unscreened" data.

In response to an uncomfortable feeling of exposure, the secretary and the director had both devised methods to keep their walls and desk drawers opaque. The secretary complicated the file system so that only she could find things. Meanwhile the director created programs that could only be run from the division. No one wants his own work-in-progress to testify against him.

Both the secretary and the division director feel that their private space is threatened. They both refer to computers in general as the invader. From their perspective, it isn't easy to see that today's integrated network is just one way of linking terminals. It's also possible to program privacy into a computer network.

At the Plain Vanilla Agency it wasn't policy to spy. But the standard business computer package is an integrated network that makes spying easy and acceptable. This network transforms each computer screen into a two-way mirror. Employees respond by trying to cover them up.

Most of the secretaries at the agency were making good use of computers for word processing. Some, though not the majority, of their bosses were saving time with the number crunching features. But the secretaries and executives both took many extra steps each day to make detours around their two-way mirrors. They were trying to turn their integrated machines back into personal computers.

□   □   □

Electronic surveillance has been built into every system we've looked at so far. At the benevolent Plain Vanilla Agency, the monitoring capacity was hardly used, yet there was still a mildly uncomfortable feeling of being watched. Among stockbrokers and middle managers, monitoring entailed a subtle loss of autonomy and signaled a decline in prestige. For clerical workers whose keystrokes are counted by the minute or airline clerks whose "stats" are posted daily, electronic monitoring has been linked to pain, stress and serious disease.

Each of the white-collar labor-controlling devices we've so far encountered has been essentially an extension of nineteenth-century industrial management practices. Surveillance itself is not new. As a matter of fact it's as old as the pyramids. The pharaoh had hundreds of overseers to make sure the slaves kept working.

But electronic monitoring is a species unto itself. Electronic monitoring is cheap, efficient and total. Anyone who touches a keyboard can be monitored. Without an expensive, disruptive army of supervisors, the computer can monitor every worker every minute.

In several European countries electronic monitoring is regulated by law. But in the United States it's unrestricted and on the increase. Personally, I think we should outlaw computer surveillance. But before I argue the point, I'd like to present the most sympathetic use of electronic monitoring that I could find.

Norma Bowers: A Sensitive Spy

Norma Bowers is the highest-paid department head in a municipal agency. For many years the agency had been a dump for incompetent civil servants and political appointees. Beset by scandal and lawsuits, it was bankrupt and unable to deliver services when Norma was brought in as part of a "new broom" management team.

Norma said she'd be happy to see me on Sunday if I didn't mind talking while she cleaned out the garage. "Rain or shine, it's gonna get done this weekend."

Sunday it shined. Before I could ring the bell, Norma waved to me from the driveway. Even in baggy pants and paint-stained sneakers, Norma Bowers was clearly an effective executive. She was excellent at motivating the staff—her husband and three kids—and she showed calm decisiveness when it came to tossing out old paint cans and bedsprings. Old employees were more worrisome, though.

"Monday I have a hearing on a termination in the Accounting Department," she said gloomily. "Well, it's gotta be done."

"Rose was a political appointee," Norma explained, as she and her team hauled trash bags. "She'd been there forever. Her main pleasure was carrying poison bonbons between one clique and another, then sitting there to watch the trouble she caused."

I asked for an example.

"She would say something like, 'I don't see why Brenda is

getting to put codes on the vouchers when Stan never had to do that.'

"Do you hear the double whammy there? Stan was an older man, who finally retired after open-heart surgery. It was all I could do to keep him on till then. Brenda is a young black woman who wanted to learn as much as she could. To the older people, Rose says, 'Look at Brenda, *she's* getting to code' (as though I'm giving her special advancement). To Brenda she says, '*Stan* never had to code' (making Brenda feel resentful about the part of the job that would give her a little variety.)

"It's subtle, but if you were there you'd see. She's so good at it, so thorough, it's almost pathological.

"Well, I happened to have a consultant in, a young man I hired to get certain computer programs that my in-house staff couldn't provide—having to do with general ledgers, quite unrelated to personnel.

"So I said to him, 'Doug, I'd like to know how she gets time to cause all this animosity.'" Norma stopped stuffing trash bags for a moment. "It's so destructive. Have you ever really experienced it? People were spending so much time defending themselves against supposed insults. It was not a pleasant atmosphere.

"So I said, 'Doug, she's got so much time to gossip. Is she doing her real job?'

"Her title was terminal operator. Her purpose is to support any of the areas in the department. But she only had time to help Client Accounts. She was always too busy to help Payroll. (Now let me explain, there is a bit of racism here, too, because the places she was too busy to help were departments with blacks.)

"So I said, 'Doug, look, she says she doesn't have time to help out in Payroll but I see her reading the paper, I see her having a coffee break, I see her having a cigarette break. I wouldn't mind these things, but the gossip breaks . . .'

"At which point Doug said, 'You know, she's a terminal operator. If you want I can get up a program that will zero in on her output, count the number of entries and the number of lines.' " Norma stopped to explain. "A journal entry is at least two lines but can be fifty-two or even a hundred lines.

"So we did it. And all I had to do was run it at the end of the day. I could tell what she did, the amount, and when she did it.

"At the same time I asked her to keep a log. I told her plainly it was because she maintained that she didn't have time to help out in Payroll. Every day I took her log—'9:00– 10:30, journal entries; 11:00–12:30, client accounts'—and matched it with what she was actually doing according to the computer."

"Did you tell her she was being monitored electronically too?"

"No, I didn't tell her because . . . well, I was using this as a tool to decide whether it was appropriate for me to give her an official warning. I don't like to discipline my employees without cause. I had to find out whether my subjective feeling about the situation was true. I could never have watched her closely enough to get that information. I have twenty-five employees. I would never have had the time."

"So what did you find out?"

"I found out that it was taking her about four or five times as long to do each entry as it should have. I even did a series of them myself to see how long was reasonable."

"Did you time yourself in order to establish a rough quota?" I asked.

"No, I was definitely not intending to set a quota. I would never do that because once a person knows their own job and takes pride in their work, if they're really a good, interested employee, they will get the normal work out of the way fast to do what they perceive as the fun, which is to figure out

.how to do their work better. If I set a quota no one would figure out better ways."

"Did she perceive it as spying?"

"Absolutely. One day I finally said to her, 'Rose, I'm sorry but I feel you do have time to do this Payroll work.' And I showed her the computer figures. She had a fit. She did the Payroll work for a week's time under protest, then she took a three-month leave and reported me to the union. When I showed the union what I had, with the computer printouts, they didn't want to fight it."

"Didn't the union object to electronic monitoring?"

"No, the union did not object to the monitoring. The level was so unsophisticated. Besides I don't think they have any policy on it. And the other employees didn't object either. That woman caused so much distress. She thought she was above the same kind of requests that her colleagues were responsible for. That's what made them angry. I think they know I would not do that to them. I would never adopt that kind of monitoring as a standard practice."

"Could you?" I asked. "Are most of the jobs arranged that way?"

"Yes. There are a half dozen other jobs done on terminals, and they're all quantitative things that I could measure in the same way. And it didn't cost me anything. There was no materials cost. The program was simple and Doug was anxious to try his hand at that type of thing. And even if he had charged us for his time, it would have been negligible.

"But I still wouldn't do it. To start that kind of monitoring as a general policy would defeat exactly what I have been trying to do here in the last three years. And succeeding I think.

"I expect my people to do the best they can just as I do the best I can. And with few exceptions they do, even if one person's best isn't the same as another's.

"If I started instituting that kind of system the mechanism would then dictate completely what happens in my department. Nobody would use their own brains except to try and beat the system.

"The way I supervise, people do a good job in order to get something done, in order to go home feeling better about themselves. But Rose was taking advantage and making them feel worse about themselves. That's why I resorted to this tool, which, yes, you could definitely call 'spying.'

"I know big places monitor all the time. It's standard operating procedure. But I feel it's just a substitute for good supervision."

It was getting chilly. The sun was going down and the garage was just about cleared. Norma wanted time before dinner to prepare for the termination hearing. "I feel clear," she said as she walked me out, "that it's the best thing for the department. Still, it's too bad the economy prevents you from saying, 'You'd be better off working somewhere else,' and really having a 'somewhere else' to send them."

Less Sensitive Spies

I recently attended a conference on Computers and Privacy. The participants showed a citizen-like concern about their credit ratings, medical reports and FBI records. They wanted to limit the information being collected about them and stop its prolific downloading from database to database. This alert body of civil libertarians was even concerned with such esoteric invasions of privacy as interactive television. (This experimental system, which allowed viewers to vote or order products through their televisions, might, they feared, someday yield records of the household's responses.)

But when I described the already-routine monitoring and

keystroke counting in the office, no one seemed to think it was a privacy issue. Apparently the right to privacy only exists in private life—not at work.

Or perhaps the conference participants, mostly professionals, could only imagine electronic monitoring applied to factory workers or clerks.

At any rate, I got no response when I coupled privacy and electronic surveillance at work, except from a newspaper reporter who was worried about the security of his notes. Everyone agreed that a reporter's notes should be protected. But another speaker suggested that keystroke counting was not an invasion of privacy because the clerk or factory worker has no private material, no *content* to protect.

At this meeting I was unable to convey the distress caused by constant monitoring, even when there is no "content" but the motions of your hands, lips and eyes being tracked.

Now that electronic monitoring has been linked with serious illnesses, there's been some call to limit monitoring on medical grounds. However, the issue is almost never raised in terms of human rights or privacy.

All forms of supervision and surveillance have always been permissible in a factory. The assumption is that the boss owns 100 percent of your worktime. Whatever your hands produce on his time is his property.

This is theoretically true with white-collar jobs as well. Scientific discoveries made on company time belong to the company. Using the firm's time and disk space to collect recipes or revise your resume is time theft.

Nonetheless there's always been a countervailing sense that it's wrong to go through an executive's file cabinet or listen in on his phone. But this weak and not very clear ethic is eroding with electronic monitoring.

Many new phone systems routinely track and time all calls, incoming, outgoing and between extensions. One reason, of course, is to see who's running up the phone bill. But the resulting printouts also allow management to see who's on the phone to whom, how often and for how long.

The common telephone dictation systems that link tape machines to typing pools also monitor executives. These systems yield performance records (volume, time and type of work) not only for the typist but for the "dictator." Dictaphone's *Mastermind* and Lanier's *Supervision IV* are two of the many dictation systems with executive monitoring features. Their basic surveillance purpose is indicated by their names. Tower Systems International advertised the following features of an E-mail monitoring program actually named Surveillance:

- Reporting on all electronic mail messages sent and received
- Reporting on all electronic mail messages sent but not yet opened
- Reporting on all operator sign-on's and sign-off's
- Reporting a list of all attempted security violations, including information on the operator, the location and the time that the attempt took place

Some office doors are now opened by I.D. cards instead of keys. But every time an employee inserts his card to open the outer door, his office door, the supply room or even the bathroom, he also makes a record of the time he came in or went out.

Increasingly, salesmen and executives are asked to put their schedules onto calendar forms in their management information systems. So far the only resistance I've observed is passive. Suddenly, no one can type. If pressed, salesmen keep two calendars, one on the machine and one in their jacket pocket, as routinely as they always kept two expense accounts.

An executive would still be shocked, I think, if his superiors claimed the right to go through his desk and check his appointment book. But riffling through screens seems to be emerging as acceptable business etiquette.

The universal assumption is that the boss has a right to look at whatever you're doing. After all, your job is to do your job. So why do you need privacy?

These were rules of the game in the era when the supervisor could creep up from behind and the workers could counter by warning each other "Shhh, he's coming." In those days it was an almost even match.

Before electronic supervision, human supervisors were stationed throughout factories and offices in such a way that they duplicated the entire production process in outline. This shadow or silhouette work force was costly and cumbersome. To achieve complete supervision the company would have had to hire a full-time foreman for every worker.

But electronic monitoring doesn't interfere with the workflow. Statistics are collected unobtrusively, seemingly as a by-product of the work.

I understand why Norma Bowers used an electronic monitoring program to get rid of Rose. If I ran her agency, I too would want the woman out. With such a simple, silent and "clean" way to collect the information, why should Norma skulk around, peering from behind desks?

Norma Bowers is an unusually ethical woman. She was the only manager I met who equated electronic monitoring with spying—even when she did it herself. Furthermore, Norma stopped. She understood that monitored workers were unlikely to experiment and improve office procedures. To her, human ingenuity was a hopeful rather than a frightening trait. She didn't want to stifle it. She respected people more than she wished to control them.

But very few bosses will voluntarily give up this powerful control tool. A U.S. Department of Labor publication estimated that in 1984 nearly two-thirds of the people who worked at video display terminals were monitored by their employers.[1] In less than ten years, electronic surveillance has leaped from the factory into the office in a form that's frighteningly effective. Even Charlie Chaplin's *Modern Times* factory, with its corn-eating machine and its camera in the bathroom, didn't approach total surveillance. In our own "moderner" times, monitoring is not only total but it's fearfuly cheap and easy. Once a worker is connected to the keyboard, he times himself.

I don't think we'll ever persuade management to give up electronic monitoring. I think we should outlaw it instead. Or at least ban *individual* monitoring, and restrict electronic monitoring to the collection of aggregate statistics. How we can enforce this ban—who will bell the cat—I can't say. But we can begin by recognizing this increasingly routine bit of programming as a serious invasion of privacy.

9

□ □ □ □ □ □ □

Piecework Professionals

Studies show that customers become frustrated enough to leave a supermarket when the checkout lines are longer than seven people. With the help of computerized scanning systems, large supermarkets can predict that they'll need three checkers after 2 o'clock on Tuesday afternoons but five on Thursdays to keep the checkout lines hovering at around seven. In most parts of the country, housewives are available to work these odd shifts.

With the aid of its computers, an airline can predict in the morning that it will need 433 reservation agents between 4:30 and 5 that afternoon. Fewer may be needed for the same half hour the next day.

There's little advantage to such precision if an employer doesn't have a flexible labor force to fill in the slots. In many areas, McDonald's is running out of minimum-wage teenagers to fill these hours. So the company is recruiting retirees in the hope that they'll be more flexible about their time.

The tendency to slot in part-timers and temps isn't restricted to low-paid or low-skilled work. News writers at ABC, NBC and CBS were told that the companies want the right to fire full-time workers and hire temps (perhaps the very same individuals) without health benefits or job security.

We've seen how individual employees, from burger flippers to brokers, become more interchangeable as their jobs are routinized. With computers, employers can predict their fluctuating need for these workers by the week, by the day, or even by the half hour.

With or without computers, a growing number of companies have calculated that disposable workers are the most convenient. At the very time that economists are citing the efficiency of "lifetime" Japanese employees, American businesses are rapidly turning their labor force into temps. Discarding old ideas about the value of loyalty and continuity, many American companies now hire typists, technicians, janitors, bookkeepers, artists, editors, programmers, engineers and even executives by the project, by the hour or by the piece.

In the nineteenth century the phrase "factory hand" suggested an interchangeable part or a tool to be used as needed. A hand is not treated the same way as a whole person. So far there's no equivalent white-collar phrase like "hourly brain" or "piecework pencil" to describe the fast-growing class of consultants, freelancers and executive temps. But there is a new ethic arising both toward them and among them.

□   □   □

After his "early retirement" from Procter & Gamble, Tom Oppdahl (see Chapter 7) was hired by an engineering job shop that did some work for P&G. At Procter Tom had designed thermal units for factories around the world. If his new shop should get the contract on a Procter & Gamble boiler or sprinkler system, will Tom have become a high-priced consultant to his former employer or a new kind of LO? (LO, meaning Low Overhead—is the Procter & Gamble term for an office temp.)

The leasing of employees as consultants, temps, adjuncts and casual workers means a flexible work force with low overhead. During a recession, a slight downturn, or just a slow half hour (as we've seen at airline reservation offices), unnecessary employees can be sent home. If it's efficient to hire clerical temps, it could be even more efficient to hire professional and managerial temps, since the salaries and perks of professionals and managers on staff use up well over half of the average office budget.

Why should Procter & Gamble employ a staff of full-time engineers to meet their periodic design needs? Now, if they need Tom Oppdahl, P&G can rent him either through a job shop or as an independent consultant. No insurance, no sick leave, no long-term obligations.

Brain workers are responding to these new leasing systems with entrepreneurial strategies that allow the brightest or most fortunately situated to keep ahead of the game. Some people are making a lot of money as brains for hire. Furthermore, some of them enjoy the mobility and independence. But others find themselves working as adjunct teachers, freelance editors, business consultants and independent programmers whether they like it or not.

I find it painful to listen to young McDonald's workers who are prepared to drift from one part-time, minimum-wage job to another all their lives. Their response to being so transitory is often a sullen, defensive indifference. But I sense that most would like to belong to a team if they could.

I find it distressing in a different way to talk to the many elite workers, some earning very good money, who are evolving a new morality to deal with their status as piecework professionals.

Lenore King

I told a friend of mine about Tom Oppdahl. Maybe I should say an acquaintance. Until three years ago, Lenore King had been a freelance magazine writer, specializing in fitness and displaced homemakers. We sometimes met at parties, where we compared notes on health insurance for freelancers.

Shortly after she bought her first word processor, Lenore approached the computer company with a proposal to rewrite their users' manual. We met recently on a movie line, and she brought me up to date. For the last two-and-a-half years she's been employed steadily on a freelance basis, writing manuals.

Last year Lenore earned somewhere between $50,000 and $65,000. (That's as close as I could get in a higher/lower, hotter/colder guessing game. She was anxious to tell me that she was now making real money, but she couldn't bring herself to utter the magic number aloud. This may be the only taboo left in modern society.)

When we finished with Lenore's income, she asked if I was still "into workers." So I told her about my trip to Cincinnati, about Tom Oppdahl and the other fifty-five-year-old unemployed engineers and executives with college kids and mortgages.

Ignoring the hearts and flowers, Lenore asked me whether Oppdahl had gotten a piece of the action when he signed on with the engineering job shop.

I hadn't thought to ask about his new employment contract. It hadn't occurred to me that you can negotiate subsidiary rights or royalties on engineering jobs.

Lenore explained to me that neither Tom's Procter contacts nor his knowledge of computer-aided design would remain salable for very long. Two years at the most, she estimated. Retooling would be expensive.

Lenore was facing these problems herself. Computer documentation was becoming standard. Users needed less help.

She wasn't sure in what area to retool. She mentioned something like Interactive Orientation Manuals (I'm not sure I got that right). But whatever it was, this time she was going to branch into something that she could copyright in her own name. As a freelancer with a topical specialty, she had to have money coming in the next time she needed to retool.

As to Tom, Lenore thought he sounded like a "sap" to have worked all those years for nothing but a salary and a pension (even if he'd gotten the whole pension). The only slightly mitigating thing she could see was that Tom might be able to use his P&G contacts to get big jobs for his new firm. That would put him in a position to bargain for a piece of the action, if he had the sense to.

Arthur Levin

I mentioned Tom Oppdahl to another acquaintance, one who had boldly seized a piece of the action in his own field. Arthur Levin had worked as a systems designer, automating switchboards for a large company. I remember years ago when Arthur told me proudly how he'd worked out a formula to tie a supervisor's bonus to the average number of times the phones rang in his area before they were answered. He thought I'd appreciate the fact that he was monitoring the supervisor instead of the worker.

Five years ago Arthur had the idea for a system that his company wasn't ready to develop. It wasn't the first time they'd held him back. So he spoke to an old friend from Wharton who was then with a prestigious management consulting firm. The friend agreed that it was the right time for Arthur's system. Together they created an independent company that customizes and services the switchboard system that's become standard in the industry. Arthur's consulting firm now does for several companies what he would have done in-house before for one employer. His former firm is one of his clients.

Although we didn't play salary guessing games, I gather that Arthur is very successful. His income comes from so many different sources—consulting, royalties, investments—that his magic number may be truly impossible to say.

Arthur is more charitable then Lenore. When he heard about Oppdahl and the hundreds of unemployed engineers, he suggested that Tom might have asked Procter & Gamble to join him in establishing a consulting firm that would lease out the under-used engineers. He envisaged it as a kind of internal spin-off to retail Procter's experience in plant construction (P&G plants would get the engineers at a discount). Under Arthur's imagined plan, Tom would be salaried but the individual engineers would probably be hired on a per-project basis. In a way Procter may have tried it when they sent Oppdahl to California.

I suggested that Tom and the other engineers may have been too hurt by Procter & Gamble to set up a joint venture. They felt that a promise had been broken. I believe it would be difficult for a man like Tom Oppdahl to act as the head of what amounts to a temporary employment agency for his fellow engineers.

Arthur replied regretfully that Tom probably couldn't do much for himself or anyone else if those were really his sentiments. Arthur's own computer programs had helped corporations to time mental work, predict volume and measure productivity. Why shouldn't the companies use this information to streamline their professional staffs? If Tom took efficiency personally, he couldn't ever have functioned very well as a manager of other engineers.

Stuart Briznakowsky

"He's got to *leverage* himself!" Stuart Briznakowsky told me. Stu is a skinny, intense man whom I've known for years "from around." As a freelance programmer, Stuart is often introduced to corporate clients through more businesslike consultants who present him as the *enfant terrible* who'll solve their knottiest programming problems if he's just left alone in the computer room.

Stuart says that today's knotty problems are simpler than in the old days when he rode the giant mainframes. But he still wears a tee-shirt, torn jeans and cowboy boots on a first interview just to keep up the image. He also claims to bring along some toy, like a paddleball or pick-up sticks to be absorbed in while new clients talk to him. Stu pretends to his friends to be faking eccentricity, but, in fact, he's a freelancer because he could never have fit in as an employee.

Stuart Briznakowsky survives by keeping ahead of the field, and that was essentially his advice to Tom Oppdahl. He thought Tom should pick his consulting jobs not according to how much they'd pay but according to how much he'd learn. Oppdahl should scour the country for design disasters. "The guy's gotta learn to leverage his mental assets."

□   □   □

I'm not sure, but I think Arthur also used the word "leverage" or "leveraging." It must be the "in" word.

In his book *The Gold-Collar Worker,* Robert E. Kelley of SRI International describes the attitudes of a type of neocapitalist brain worker with nothing to invest or leverage but his mental assets[1]:

> They are coming to view themselves as individual businesses with assets to be utilized. Each person is, in other words, his or her own entrepreneur, responsible for investing his or her

own portfolio of talents, skills, and abilities to provide maximum returns with minimum risk.

Kelly advises managers to get the most out of their brain workers by accommodating to this new entrepreneurialism, encouraging rather than discouraging internal spin-offs and outside consultantships. Gold-collar workers, he feels, have the right to leverage themselves.

From what I saw at Procter & Gamble, the most common form of leveraging was plain old moonlighting. It was difficult to interview P&G engineers and managers, not only because they were worried about their jobs, but because almost all of them were busy working second jobs or developing consulting businesses to vend computer skills, business advice, engineering or whatever else they'd learned at Procter & Gamble. Some were busy babysitting, too, because their wives were selling real estate on the weekends.

You can call this entrepreneurialism or insecurity.

During the first industrial revolution entrepreneurial opportunities seemed to be everywhere. Manufacturers argued that unions were unnecessary and should be outlawed because the individual factory worker was an entrepreneur, well placed to trade his valuable labor for wages. Only a man with no initiative would want a sinecure—a guaranteed weekly wage.

Some skilled workers, especially those who made the machines that automated other people's work, did well as independent contractors. In the same way, freelance programmers earned a lot of money early in the computer era. More important to most of them, they had a lot of freedom at the keyboard. (In the sixties even IBM had to tolerate long-haired hippies in the computer room.) But programmers quickly programmed not only other people but themselves into a highly routinized—so many lines of program per hour—medium-paying job.

Though a few well-paid hourly craftsmen were needed to

build machines at the beginning of the industrial revolution, it's clear in retrospect that hourly wages meant a step down in status, security and pay (though pay was eventually raised through union organization) for most manual workers.

The same decline is already apparent in many white-collar fields. Adjunct professors, the pieceworkers of academe, earn from $900 to $3,500 for teaching a university course. At first, "guest" lecturers were paid "honoraria" to teach special subjects like creative writing. Administrators insisted that these guests would never replace regular professors. But by now adjuncts routinely teach English 1A and Introduction to Sociology. Full-time jobs with normal salaries and benefits are less common at universities than they used to be.

The semesterly migration of medievalists and art historians is becoming as predictable as the seasonal movement of farm workers. (Eventually many adjuncts realize that their taxi licenses are more valuable than their Ph.Ds.) Will we soon see a similar bicoastal trek between Route 128 and Silicon Valley? And what will happen to all the computer consultants when and if their systems are finally up and working?

Is a particular individual better off as an employee or as an independent consultant?

On a dollars-and-cents level the answer will depend, at least for a while, on business fluctuations in each industry. But on a psychological level the direction is clearly toward increased insecurity. And people are making the psychological adjustments to deal with it.

As divorce becomes more common, married people, both men and women, begin to realize that they can only count securely on the assets in their own names. You own half a house, the records you bought, and a pension for the years you yourself worked. But some of us adjust as slowly as Tom Oppdahl.

I'm still shocked by the way young people move in together for the school term or while they're both assigned to Chicago.

234 □ *The Electronic Sweatshop*

"If it lasts, O.K. If not, I only sublet my apartment for a year." I used to feel that this kind of talk was just bravado. Underneath they must have the same hopes for permanence that I do.

I forget that their generation was raised in the shifting households that my generation created. They adapted appropriately to a stream of Daddy's girlfriends and Mommy's boyfriends.

But I have to admit that, as much as I worry about the new callousness, I'd also worry about my daughter if she said, "Put the house in my husband's name: what's his is mine."

Young McDonald's workers prepare themselves psychologically for a lifetime of shifting, minimum-wage jobs. Only the most naive express loyalty to their store or their manager. Many will quit without notice to take a job for 10¢ more an hour or just to go away for the weekend. These workers are responding appropriately to a manning system designed to turn them over almost as fast as the burgers.

It hurts to be around kids with no illusions. But sometimes it hurts even more to hear one of them say, "My manager likes me," or "I know I did a good job today."

My independent-consultant friends thought Tom Oppdahl was a sap to invest so much of himself in a Procter & Gamble job. Tom's wife and daughter were vaguely embarrassed by his company loyalty. Mrs. Oppdahl felt it was ill placed because, in this particular case, her husband's superiors never appreciated him. Their daughter, Dana, was offended by company loyalty in general. She was almost angry at what she saw as her father's pathetic desire to be liked by an institution. Dana herself works as an independent contractor. She designs brochures and stationery for firms that would otherwise have the work done by in-house commercial artists.

An employer generally makes a greater investment in a salaried than in an hourly worker. When a staff artist is injured, the employer pays his medical bills, his department signs a get-well card and some fellow workers phone and visit. When a freelance artist gets hit by a bus, you find a new one. The card is optional, and fewer people are likely to visit even if the freelancer worked on the premises. Somehow, the company's limited financial responsibility affects everyone's personal commitment.

As piecework professionalism becomes more common, a smaller group within the company comes to regard itself as the permanent core whose jobs are to be protected. At one time the entire office staff constituted that core. Factory hands may have been hired by the day or by the hour, but even Ebenezer Scrooge took on the responsibility to pay his clerk, Bob Cratchit, full time.

During the fifties the back office or the operations departments became part of the factory. By then most of Cratchit's work was done by women at typewriters or keypunch machines. These clerical jobs were often moved out of the headquarters to "campuses"—white-collar industrial parks. In this setting, part-timers and temps became the rule rather than the exception.

Today's increase in hourly work for professionals is one indication that the front office is finally becoming industrialized also.

A narrowing circle of senior managers regards itself as the corporate core—the ones who strap on golden parachutes or pass out the poison pills to others during a takeover siege. Sadly for American industry, this permanent core often excludes the people who have the most to do with the product. It's not unusual for design to be done freelance and for the entire manufacturing operation to be contracted out to foreign factories.

In some cases, clerical production work can also be contracted out to foreign factories. So far American data-entry work is most often exported to English-speaking countries like Ireland, India or Barbados. But data originating in Texas has been efficiently keyboarded in China, at salaries of roughly $7 a week. The hard goods manufactured in offshore factories have to be transported in ships or planes. But the data processed in overseas clerical sweatshops can be viewed at the company headquarters as quickly as data processed on the premises.

The stripped-down core of an American corporation is a financial and marketing, but not a production, unit. Outside this core stand the rings of professionals, technicians, middle managers and their support staffs who are no longer part of the immediate family. They may still do skilled work, but they're now part of the factory/back-office crew, whose size fluctuates according to the week's or even the day's orders.

How should a man like Tom Oppdahl adjust to the new morality? Will he be better off when he learns to have no more loyalty to the company than the company has to him? Will we all learn to operate as efficient freelancers in a world of serial monogamy and seasonal employment?

Will today's consultants and freelancers continue to regard men like Tom Oppdahl as saps who sold their birthrights and royalties for a mess of benefits, or will they eventually envy the group just a few years older than Oppdahl as the last generation that was able to retire with a paid-off mortgage and a company pension?

IO

□ □ □ □ □ □ □

Command and Control

We used to have armed soldiers.
Now we have manned weapons.
FRANK SMITH

Since the Second World War, the basic technologies used to automate offices and factories—these include lasers, computers, robots and organizational techniques like systems analysis —have been developed first for the military. One of their explicit functions has been, in military terms, to enhance "command and control."

As command and control are tightened or centralized in the civilian world, increasingly prestigious jobs are reorganized so that employees have less privacy, make fewer decisions and perform according to procedures that make them easier to train and easier to replace. This loss of autonomy and the loss of importance is equally painful at all levels.

A griddleman at McDonald's laments, "You don't have to know how to cook, you don't have to know how to think. There's a procedure for everything and you just follow the procedures." A store manager complains that he, too, makes no decisions: "There is no such thing as a McDonald's manager. The computer runs the store."

A few steps higher on the occupational ladder, middle managers are monitored electronically and stockbrokers "choose" investments on the basis of expert systems. Finally, at the top, or perhaps just coming full circle, a military commander grumbles that he doesn't get to pick his own bombing targets.

What is actually happening when battlefield decisions are made from computerized command centers?

Some analysts suggest that the computers themselves are now making the decisions. I don't believe that's true. After all, someone programs the computer. But who? And how did things get arranged in this extraordinarily centralized manner? In this final chapter we talk to some military men who were powerful enough, or close enough to power, to help us understand the drive to centralize control.

Admiral Thomas H. Moorer

In 1973, while testifying before the Senate Armed Services Committee about the secret bombing of Cambodia, Admiral Thomas H. Moorer (then Chairman of the Joint Chiefs of Staff) became so enmeshed by data from military computers that he swore, "It's unfortunate that we had to become slaves to those damned things."

Twelve years later I asked the retired admiral what he had meant. How had he, the Chief of Naval Operations during the Vietnam War, become a slave to his own computers?

"I made that statement in relation to our bombing in Cambodia," he answered. "You see, it was a political issue. Mr. Johnson, in his wisdom, had said [the admiral unconsciously broadened his own slight drawl as he became Lyndon Johnson], '*We seek no wider war.*' And since Mr. Johnson had chosen to make that statement, the bombing of Cambodia was held as an 'escalation' of the war.

"Now the number of bombs dropped was put into a computer for the reason that the flow had to be tracked in order to replace expended ammunition and bombs. It's very much like your supermarket computer," the admiral explained, "where they move the tomato juice over that thing. [He made the motion of a supermarket clerk moving the bar-coded can over a scanner.] When you've sold a certain amount a flag goes up and says, 'Order two more crates of tomato juice.' It's just logistics.

"But our computers supplied information which led into diverse questions before the Congress. . . .

"Now this computer printout did not identify the targets. It just said Target *A,* Target *B,* Target *C.* For the reason, as I said, that if the ammunition supply dropped below a certain level we had to send for more. But the Congress wanted to know what was Target *A* and Target *B* and Target *C.* They accused us of keeping a secret. As if the grocery store was keeping a secret of who was eating its food. They insisted on knowing who was eating our ammunition. 'Where were you dropping this tonnage?' We were only saying Man A was eating it, Man B was eating it, Man C was eating it.

"We did not say more because we did not want to make this printout classified, or else it couldn't have been used at embarkation points and other places. The people handling the food do not need to know who eats it.

"But they accused us of keeping the information secret. They also accused us of falsifying the records, which we did not.*

---

* The subject of the Senate hearing was how the military and the President had managed to keep the 1969 bombing in Cambodia secret from the Congress. The evidence of a concerted effort was just a little more complicated than the Admiral bothered to go into with me.

"The problem is not the computers," Admiral Moorer emphasized. "A computer lends itself marvelously to logistics. Logistics," he explained courteously, "is simply support. It includes the people, the tonnage, the transportation, everything required to carry out the operation.

"In the old days we had to do just what you're doing." He gestured toward my old-fashioned pad and pencil. "For every individual killed in a division you had to draw a line through him and then go back and count up the number of lines. It would take you a very long time to know how many men you had left.

"The computer keeps the tally continuously and up-to-date. You've got to give the devil its due. But suddenly our record-keeping system generates a lot of information that lets a lot of people ask me how I conduct my business."

Admiral Moorer was disturbed at the possibility that I might be blaming the computer itself.

"The computer itself is not the problem. With a war games computer like the one we have at the Naval College at Newport, Rhode Island—I started that myself in the midfifties—with that computer you can do all kinds of problems that involve not only military command but performance data, substituting one weapon for another, the results if you had more of this or less of that. A commander can come to Newport with his entire staff and go through all kinds of scenarios trying to read the other guys' minds. It's an outstanding training tool as long as you realize that the scenario does not substitute for the man on the spot. . . .

"If someone believes he can give orders from a desk in Washington, based on computer information, well, that's not a problem of the computer, it's a problem of delegating authority."

Admiral Moorer repeated many times and in many ways that the problem of overcentralizing command is political, not technical.

"It happens with or without computers. In Vietnam, [Secretary of Defense Robert] McNamara was selecting the targets. . . .

"But you've got to separate the computer from the tendency of the executive or the boss or whoever to substitute himself for the man in the field. . . . Yes, the computer printout tempts them to think they have all the information they need to tell their juniors how to do it. They can read into those figures what they like. They can call up and say, 'I looked at the figures this morning and I can see there's something wrong with the way you're handling Tabasco sauce.' . . . Hitler was always trying to handle these details. He was always debating with his generals over the logistics of supporting his troops in Russia.

"But let us not blame the computers. . . . In World War II there was a strategy of unconditional surrender. We were given that general objective and it was our duty to carry it out.

"But in Vietnam we had no real objective established. So it devolved into a political fight in the U.S.—as reported by the press. The result was micromanagement from Washington, made possible technically by the computers. So what should have been decisions based on the activity in Vietnam became decisions based on the activity in Washington."

I suggested to Admiral Moorer that what he saw in the military was very much like what I was observing in industry where financial officers dominate the corporation. Little respect is paid to those who directly supervise production. (Even less to those who actually work on the line—but that's an older story.)

I had interviewed senior executives in central offices who delighted in playing their own form of computerized war games based on economic models of the corporation. The statistics they juggled were sometimes accurate and sometimes as dubious as Vietnam body-counts. But they were always abstractions. Still, these top executives began to feel omniscient because they could peer right down to the bottom of the company through their inverted statistical periscopes. As a result, more and more decisions were made further and further away from the "battlefield" of production. Meanwhile, those with the experience and visceral knowledge were shunted aside and initiative on their part was discouraged.

Admiral Moorer immediately saw the analogy. He obviously identified himself with the middle manager, the line commander who was being turned into a mere messenger boy.

"The detail with which McNamara and President Johnson, particularly, got involved in the Vietnam War impeded the development of the junior officers, because they quickly found out that they could not do anything without asking Washington. It got to the point in my case—I was in the service for thirty years and I was being told what to do by people who never fired a shot."

Had he been allowed to make his own decisions during the Vietnam War, Admiral Moorer has indicated that he would have landed troops in North Vietnam and bombed Haiphong harbor from the very beginning. Moorer was the chief hawk given special questioning (with General Westmoreland) by the Congress about every new weapon and every extension of the bombing. You can see why "micromanagement from Washington" would be annoying to a man who wanted to be let alone to win the war.

"Getting back to your question at the beginning," said the admiral, "the problem with those computers was that they generated so much information that everyone wanted to get into the act. That information was not classified; it could not be kept from the Congress. But Congress was tackling it like Mike Wallace. Like adversarial reporting. This was a political fight—which is nothing new.

"But the computer is not the cause of the problem. A computer can present a commander with a great deal of information in a timely and condensed form so he can have the factors that have to be considered before him at all times in making a decision."

Admiral Thomas H. Moorer is not afraid of power. As the first man to command both the Pacific and Atlantic Fleets of the United States, as NATO's Supreme Allied Commander in the Atlantic and finally as the Chairman of the Joint Chiefs of Staff, he gladly used any technology that could put more information and more decision-making power in his hands. His problem in Vietnam was not that he had computers but that he had bosses. Those civilian bosses could use "his" computers to keep tabs on him.

I guessed that Admiral Moorer wouldn't worry much about the overcentralization of information or authority when the resulting power was used to carry out his own policies.

To test that guess I asked about the most centralized form of war, the one where the game-playing technocrats dominate. "Are you worried," I asked, "by the preeminence given to the nuclear strategists these days?"

The Admiral caught my drift and countered.

"The papers give you the impression that the President's got two buttons by his bed. You press one and the Filipino boy brings you a cup of coffee. Press the other and it fires all the missiles. But there is no button. There are many checks and balances."

I nodded, not really reassured.

I have such an automatic sympathy with the craftsman, the worker, the man who knows his job, that I'd almost forgotten my differences with Admiral Moorer. Now I looked around his office at the James Forrestal bookends and the walls covered with pictures of ships and planes.

"That's the first nuclear aircraft carrier," Admiral Moorer explained.

I got up to examine an expansive aerial photo of the U.S.S.

Enterprise. The sailors on the deck with their white caps were spelling out $E = MC^2$.

"We sent this ship around the world twenty-five times without refueling," he said proudly. "And that's the kind of energy we could be using right now if it weren't for the Jane Fondas sitting down everywhere."

Suddenly I felt treacherous. What would Admiral Moorer think if he knew I had written a skit for the antiwar show that Jane Fonda brought to army bases in Asia during the Vietnam War?

Admiral Moorer's consuming objective is to show strength to the Russians. Since the Vietnam War he had mobilized opposition to every "show of weakness" from SALT and SALT II to the return of the Panama Canal. He even joined General Francisco Franco to review troops in Madrid at the Generalissimo's thirty-second Victory Day parade.

Before he retired as head of the Joint Chiefs of Staff, Moorer became the center of a scandal as the recipient of many "eyes only" documents taken from Henry Kissinger. He also received unauthorized FBI documents on internal enemies like me.

I should be grateful then for the strong U.S. tradition of civilian control over the military that checked some of Moorer's policies.

Yet I wasn't misleading Admiral Moorer when I nodded in sympathy as he told me about the Johnsons and the McNamaras and the other civilians with their computer printouts who tried to tell him how to run his war.

I enjoyed talking to Moorer because at least he was clear and specific. He compared the logistics computer to an ordinary supermarket scanner because he really wanted me to understand.

It was the opposite with civilian technocrats at the Department of Defense and the Defense Advanced Research Projects

Agency who talked in code about C^2 (Command and Control) or C^3I (Command, Control, Communications and Intelligence). Sometimes they even raised it one more power to C^4 (Command, Control, Communications, and Computers). ("Since the invasion of Grenada," a military source informed me, "we call it C^5. That's Command, Control, Communications, Computers and Confusion." As has been widely reported, the military communications systems worked so poorly that commanders in Grenada had to call each other on pay phones.) The only information these military experts were trying to convey to me through their jargon was that modern war is too technical for anyone but them to run.

I enjoyed talking to the outspoken admiral because he didn't obfuscate the question of power. He understood that if you control the computer it's a tool, if it controls you it's a weapon. I have heard dozens of corporate consultants explain middle-management resistance to computers as "fear of typing," or "resistance to anything new." They never suggest that responses are based on corporate geography: which way the data flows. If a management information system brings information to the managers, they usually learn to use it quickly. If it collects information about them, they tend to resist. At least Admiral Moorer understood that the question is political, not technical. Whether in the corporate world or the military, it all depends on one's position in the chain of command.

"Were there any computers in Vietnam that could pick the targets for you?" I asked Admiral Moorer.

"Oh no, no, no, no, no." he answered. "The way the targets were picked in Vietnam was so stupid that even a computer couldn't understand it. The art of computerizing the decision-making process wasn't developed when the Vietnam War ended. No, they weren't trying to run the whole war with a computer then. But don't kid yourself. They'll try today to do it."

Frank Smith

The Cheap Hawks are a loosely organized group of military reformers who consider themselves as patriotic as Admiral Moorer. But they object consistently to the expensive systems that in their opinion make weapons more important than men.

One of the Cheap Hawk heroes, Colonel ("Mad") John Boyd is credited with having turned off Robert McNamara's line of electronic sensors along the Ho Chi Minh Trail. Among its other problems, it confused large apes with small Communists.

Because they oppose boondoggles that waste defense funds, the Cheap Hawks sometimes appear to line up with liberals in exposing Pentagon extravagance. But they are not liberals. The Cheap Hawk position on military technology is, roughly, "Just give me a rifle that works."

□   □   □

"Our military doesn't respect its killers," Frank Smith concluded regretfully. Then, trying to soften his words, "Well, that's the combat soldier's job, to kill. But the great killer colonels of Vietnam were never promoted. They were forced out after the war."

Frank, forty-one years old, had served in Vietnam, but the hand grenades decorating his desk came from three wars: a Mark 2 pineapple (World War II), a Mark 26 (late Korea, early Vietnam) and a Mark 67 (late Vietnam).

As a helicopter pilot with the 9th Infantry Division, Smith earned 1400 combat hours in Vietnam.

"The missions I preferred were flying in the troops. I was told to pick up sixty infantry at their base camp P.Z. [Pick-up Zone] and land them on the bad guys in an L.Z. [Landing Zone]. But how I got there, the actual tactics of inserting these people in the L.Z., was up to me.

"The missions I hated were called 'command and control.' We'd go to one of the command headquarters and pick up a bird [full colonel] or a division commander—he might be a two-star general. We'd pick him up, fly to where his unit was in battle, and then we'd cut donuts. That's fly in circles at about 1500 feet to keep a constant point on the ground in view.

"This commander in the back seat had four radios. He's in contact with everyone. Now, in Vietnam, particularly in South Vietnam, a helicopter was safe at 1500 feet. The V.C. [Viet Cong] had no weapon that could reach you. So there was this lieutenant colonel or general orbiting 1500 feet in the air, cutting donuts and giving orders by radio to the men on the ground. The lower officers, the platoon leaders were doing nothing but passing along messages.

"One time in a sweep operation I actually heard a general say, 'See the fourth man on the left. He should move forward four feet.'

"Now one of the historical strengths of the American military, and this is going back to the Revolution, is that we're good at individual initiative.

"You're given a broad goal—'We're gonna take that strip of woods'—and you adjust the details. The guy on the ground makes the most specific orders. 'Bill, I want you to take your fire team and establish a base of safety so we can maneuver.' That is, " Frank explained to me, "give us protective fire.

"But when Bill gets there he says, 'Hey it's full of V.C. I can't establish the base here.' He has to observe and react.

"If you look at it as a career path, the sergeant in charge of a platoon of forty, fifty guys, a couple of years down the road he'll be in charge of four platoons or, as a lieutenant colonel, four companies. But the fucking colonel cutting donuts has been looping over his company commanders and platoon leaders and giving orders directly to individuals.

"It may seem efficient at the moment, but the company

commander and the platoon leaders did not get to exercise leadership.

"What if they kill off the senior officers? It'll be like the Russian army, where they continue to follow the last order they got from a dead officer. In a way, we're doing the equivalent of what Stalin did; we're killing off a whole generation of leadership. In 1995 our generals will be those lieutenants and captains who were used as messengers in Vietnam.

"Why I personally hated these command-and-control missions was that the bird in the back seat was also telling *me* what to do and he may not have known fuck-all about helicopters.

"Now, suppose it's a brigade involved in the action. You could have three battalion commanders fucking around in the helicopters, plus the division artillery commander, and the brigade commander and the division commander, who is usually a two-star general and has a one-star general as his assistant. (If he gets killed the one-star takes over.) In a big operation, he might have two assistants in the air, each in his own helicopter. It looks like Kennedy Airport at 9 A.M.

"If that battalion leader is now a general, his command experience in Vietnam tells him that he can control the most minute elements of his force.

"They say that by the end of World War II Hitler was literally moving platoons around on a board. Well, he had lost his marbles by then. But that's what our commanders were doing in Vietnam. The technology made it feasible, so they did it.

"In Vietnam it was just radios. Now they press for computers and high-speed computers that will help them control even more.

"So what you see," Frank explained, "is a shift of command to the top. It's the board of directors telling the man on the assembly line how to make fenders. They should have been thinking about making small cars.

"O.K., maybe making cars is a repetitious task that you can reduce to a routine," he shifted gears. "Maybe you can say you're producing efficiently if you get so many cars off the line a minute. But there's a richness of combat that cannot be reduced to the numbers.

"In Vietnam they tried to turn everything into numbers, because that's what they could put into their computers.

"At first the big number was body-count, enemy killed. The number crunchers thought they could judge how the war was going by body-count. But killing the enemy doesn't mean you're winning the war. Especially not in Vietnam, where we could wipe out some of their units four times in a year and they'd flesh them out again with new conscripts. Breaking the enemy's spirit is how you win a war. And you can't get a number that will tell you when you're doing that.

"After a while they stopped talking body-count and we went for sorties. The number of sorties you flew. So our pilots would go off five times a day with two bombs. Then the word would come down from Washington, "No more sorties. This week the big number is tonnage." So now you flew only two sorties (especially over North Vietnam, where they could hit you) but with bombs strapped on everywhere. Since tonnage was the big number you had to drop all those bombs somewhere, even if it was on an outhouse.

"The number crunchers were happy. They were looking at the numbers and they thought they were looking at the actual war.

"You call the P.I.O. [Public Information Office] at the Pentagon," Frank advised me. "I'm sure they'll be happy to tell you about all their new computers that will let them control the whole show from Washington.

"What we Cheap Hawks are saying about the technology is *make it simple and make it work.* What they're doing is putting the technology at the center and reducing the man to a plug-in element on the assembly line.

"We used to have armed soldiers. Now we have manned weapons.

"But the people that win put man at the center."

Rear Admiral Eugene Carroll

"I frequently lied to the computer," explained Rear Admiral Eugene Carroll, the former commander of an aircraft carrier and now the Deputy Director of the Center for Defense Information in Washington, D.C.[1]

"One night, during the Vietnam War, one of our planes accidentally bombed China. He was confused and out of control and trying to keep from crashing. So he attacked the first target that shot at him. When he got back we pieced together where he'd been and realized he must have bombed in China.

"But if I told the computer that we bombed a target in China it would automatically generate an OPREP 3, that's an Operation Report—I believe it was a 3 then. It's a flash report of major significance. Then the bells would ring and the lights would flash and the system would go bananas.

"It was my human judgment not to put this piece of information into the computer."

"Did anything happen about the bombing?" I asked. "What did the Chinese do?"

"Nothing. Maybe someone there realized it was just bad luck. Maybe they thought if they complained we'd do it again.

"This impersonal flow of information up and down through automatic systems was grotesque in Vietnam.

"The JCS [Joint Chiefs of Staff] target list included hundreds of targets without any military significance whatsoever.

"If you never attacked a particular target before, you had to go to Washington to ask for permission. But if it had been attacked, you could attack it again and again. The computers would tally the tonnage dropped as if it actually meant something. It was a bookkeeper's war.

"Everyone from sergeant to general was caught up in an information flow so impersonal that it was easy to lose your bearings entirely.

"Let me give you an example on the nuclear side. Let's say you're a member of a team in a missile silo in Nebraska or Wyoming. You're trained to receive and respond to signals from higher levels. These signals start coming in—Alpha, Romeo, Foxtrot—in groups of five or six letters. You look in a code book. It says fire your missiles. There's two people with keys who must turn them at the proper time and the missile goes.

"But there's little a man gets to know about the world and the wisdom of firing that missile from the bottom of a silo."

"But what would happen to military discipline," I asked with consternation, "if the man at the bottom of the silo—at the bottom of the chain of command—made his own decision each time about not firing a missile?" It was strange for me to be defending the chain of command to a commander, but I suddenly saw it from the command-and-control point of view. "Wouldn't that be dangerous?" I asked.

The admiral shrugged. "Who knows how many times we've been saved," he asked, "by men who decided not to follow a computerized command?"

□ □ □

As the commander of an aircraft carrier, Admiral Carroll didn't report the bombing of China because the system's flash response, its OPREP 3, would have been automatic. He couldn't lean over to the computer and say, "Look, let me first tell you what happened, then we'll see the best way to handle it."

As a result, Navy headquarters in Norfolk, Va., got less

instead of more information through their computers. An information system can become so mechanical that humans simply stop talking to it.

One way around this problem is to make the airplane, instead of its human pilot, do the reporting. Today it might be harder to conceal the accidental bombing of China because monitoring equipment on the plane could be linked directly to a central computer. No human need input the flight report.

Through false alarms and tests at nuclear installations, the military learned that a high percentage of the men assigned to fire nuclear weapons simply don't fire them when given the order. (In *Parade Magazine,* August 14, 1983, Jack Anderson reported on the failure to follow missile-launching procedures at two Air Force bases during a false alarm.) Apparently, they don't believe an impersonal communication of this kind.

Perhaps human soldiers will require intensive drilling and conditioning before they can be trusted to automatically obey the electronic links in a chain of command.

The other possibility for military authorities is to take all the human links out of the chain. After all, humans are the unreliable elements. Only the human links willfully substitute their own judgment for orders. Indeed, circumventing human judgment at lower levels is a basic direction of Pentagon research on expert systems.

As Admiral Moorer reminded me, "The art of computerizing the decision-making process wasn't developed when the Vietnam War ended. No, they weren't trying to run the whole war with a computer then. But don't kid yourself. They'll try today to do it."

Dr. Craig Fields

DARPA (the Defense Advanced Research Projects Agency) is the central research organization of the Department of Defense. It was established in 1958 in response to Sputnik. Its official mission is "to fund speculative or high risk research" in order "to maintain U.S. technological superiority."

DARPA's current emphasis, under the Pentagon's $600 million Strategic Computer Initiative (not to be confused with the later Strategic Defense Initiative—"Star Wars"), is on developing "intelligent" computers with humanlike capacities to see, hear, respond to spoken language and make expert decisions.

□   □   □

A replica of Dr. Craig Fields' head stood on the lamp table in his office at DARPA. The sculptor had caught every line and blemish of the deputy's thin face. Feature for feature, it was a realistic work. Yet something I couldn't put my finger on gave it a flat, affectless look.

It had been difficult to get an interview at DARPA. Finally, with the help of my Congressman, I'd been promised half an hour with Dr. Fields, the deputy director of engineering. He showed me into his office exactly on time. The atmosphere didn't encourage chit-chat. Yet I couldn't help asking about the precise likeness on the lamp table. Dr. Fields took my query as a compliment and explained that the artwork had been produced by six different sensors at an artificial intelligence project site.

Though its purpose is military, DARPA funded the basic research for almost all the computer and laser technologies now used in industry. Through its support for artificial intelligence research, DARPA contributed to the development of the expert systems that I saw juggling financial data and picking investments at Shearson and Merrill Lynch.

It seemed to me that expert systems could just as easily juggle statistics on body-count, tonnage, sorties, enemy weapons captured, villages pacified and so on. If the rules of attack could be extracted from the generals and admirals, then perhaps an expert system could actually pick the bombing targets. I was thinking about Admiral Moorer and wondering if an admiral or a general in our next conventional war might find himself with little more to do than a McDonald's manager. So I began the formal interview by asking Dr. Fields what functions expert systems might take over for the military in the future.

"You'll have to specify more exactly what particular period of the future you are interested in," said the precise young deputy. "The history of predicting where A.I. will be is one of overenthusiasm."

I asked for both far-fetched and near-fetched speculations, if he wouldn't mind.

"If you go back fifteen years, artificial intelligence wasn't good for anything yet. If you look into the far distant future, I don't see why it won't be good for everything. It will show the same intelligence and the same creativity as people. At its present stage of development it can do a little."

I asked what expert systems were now being developed.

"Hundreds and hundreds. Though only a few are in daily use. It's a technology that lets you extract rules, policies and guidelines from the experts and lets the system draw conclusions. The difficulty is extracting the guidelines."

I pressed for an example of a functioning expert system.

"Let me first tell you where you can't use expert systems." He enumerated: "*One*. You can't use expert systems where there aren't any experts, if a human can't do it, like predicting the downfall of governments or the stock prices. *Two*. If a person is incapable of articulating how he does it, like the fine artist. *Three*. You can't develop an expert system if you have experts who are articulate but they're too busy to spend the time with you; if they won't give the hours it takes to educate the system.

"Extracting the rules of thumb is the difficulty. . . . You might want to note that the current direction is to automate the job of *making* the expert system so we won't need the knowledge engineer. The experts themselves will be able to program the system. . . . But the difficulty, as I indicated, is extracting the guidelines from the expert."

(I imagined how difficult it would be to extract the guidelines on admiralship from Admiral Moorer.)

I asked Dr. Fields once more for an example of an expert system in use in the military today.

"They're beginning to be used for jobs that require high speed with routine decisions."

"Like?"

"Auto pilots can now do the same things that pilots do on routine flights. When they were first introduced lots of people said, 'I'll never let *that* pilot my plane.' But now they do. With all artificial intelligence systems, people are at first threatened. . . . They will not be used—not yet—for things requiring insight, brilliance. . . . Decisions can move up the line, clearly true. But currently there are no higher decisions made by expert systems."

So I asked what lower decisions they now make.

"To take a dull case, you can let it go through data and alert you to danger, for instance an alert to an air threat."

"Can it tell you with which weapon to respond to the threat?" I asked.

"Today's expert systems can say, 'The best thing to do is X.' But will anyone agree? That, you might say, is a question of race relations—the race relations between computers and people. Do they trust it? Will they do what it says?"

"Should we?" I asked. I was intrigued by Dr. Fields' race relations analogy. It was interesting, too, how strongly he identified with the computer "race."

The deputy responded by enumerating the advantages of computers over people.

"When the computer makes decisions under stressful circumstances it does no worse than when it isn't stressed. It can look at much more data than people can—perhaps. I say perhaps. It can combine the experience of five, six or seven experts, using many rules of thumb—experts who can't all be present.

"But the fundamental point is that the only thing in the world getting cheaper and faster is computers. People aren't getting cheaper and faster. So if I have to bet on anything, I'll bet on computers."

The Deputy informed me that my half hour was up.

□ □ □

Dr. Craig Fields has faith in artificial intelligence. "If you look into the far distant future, I don't see why it won't be good for everything. It will show the same intelligence and the same creativity as people."

Certainly humans can re-create human intelligence. My husband and I did it when we had a baby. But DARPA is ready to spend millions to reproduce human intelligence artificially. Perhaps the important question is not whether they can do it but why. Or, to ask the question in reverse, why not use people?

Dr. Fields gave me a practical reason. He said that if he had to bet, he'd bet on computers over people because they were the only thing in the world getting cheaper and faster. But who decided to invest the vast sums that may eventually make expert systems cheaper than experts?

Because of the huge Pentagon budget and the American aversion to economic planning, DARPA is, in effect, our only national R&D establishment. Through its research grants, the military can set the tone and goals for civilian computer research. But industry has its influence, in turn, on the Defense Department.

Dwight D. Eisenhower coined the phrase "military/industrial complex" to describe two strands so entwined that he couldn't say who was calling the shots. If a general who became President of the United States couldn't untangle the military/industrial complex, neither can I.

Regardless of who's setting the tone, military and corporate decision makers seem to share a technological aesthetic. Both groups have a taste for strong, simple lines of command and control.

In his book *Forces of Production*,[2] David Noble suggests that since World War II, U.S. industries, working closely with the military, have developed the most centralized and expensive forms of certain technologies, while suppressing more democratic variations even when they might have been more efficient.

The example he studies in detail is numerical control. To summarize this brilliantly written history too briefly, American designers, influenced by Defense Department contracts, discarded the earlier versions of numerical control in which machine tools (tools for cutting metal parts) were programmed on the shop floor by the machine operator. Instead, industry developed a form of numerical control in which the programming for an entire factory is done by a small number of technicians in a central office. In this version the machinist merely tends the computerized tool.

As industrial analysts point out, such highly centralized systems tend to be expensive and rigid. The Japanese generally use simpler forms of computer technology that leave more thinking on the shop floor. Because American manufacturers produced numerical control systems suitable for military tasks, they were too expensive, too hard to program and too unreliable for the small and medium-size shops that dominate the metalworking industry. (The few shops that bought them often went bankrupt either trying to pay them off or trying to make them work.) When the Japanese started to sell simpler numerical control systems, they were able to take the market away from U.S. manufacturers despite protectionist attempts to keep them out.

There's a second reason why less centralized systems may be more efficient. Human beings can spot and correct problems quickly. No programmer can forsee everything. If humans retain some autonomy, they can make the little adjustments along the way that allow the best-laid plans of mice and managers to work as intended.

The Cheap Hawks extol this kind of efficiency when they make a legend of Colonel "Mad" John Boyd for turning off McNamara's electronic band. McNamara couldn't forsee that his sensors would flash for every passing ape. Admiral Carroll used the same kind of personal judgment when he failed to report the bombing of China.

The folklore of World War II is rich with stories about lowly privates who used their common sense to subvert military orders and thereby save the day. Office folklore is full of unthanked secretaries who bend the rules and juggle the files to keep the papers flowing.

One of my favorite secretary-saves-the-day stories came from Joseph Weizenbaum of MIT, ELIZA's creator. He told it as a parable.

"A student came to me and asked if he could drop Physics 4 and take Physics 5. First, I made sure that he had the prerequisites, then, as his advisor, I talked to him and decided that it would be the right thing in his particular case. Finally I signed the slip.

"But the student came back to me the next day and said, 'The computer won't let me do it.'

"So I went to the office and spoke to the woman there. I said, 'Isn't it true that he meets the prerequisites?' She said, 'Yes.' 'And isn't it true that I signed my approval?' She said, 'Yes. Yes, but the computer will not permit that change.'

"She seemed like a reasonable woman so I asked, 'What can we do about it? She said, 'Tell him to drop Physics 4 and sign up for Gym. Then let him drop Gym and sign up for Physics

5.' You see she had experimented with the program long enough to work out these ways around it."

Weizenbaum insists that no computer expert at MIT could fix that program without inviting other unforeseen and possibly more wide-scale problems. "It's like a brain surgeon. You know which area of the brain controls what, but you don't know what will happen when you touch it." To Weizenbaum the moral of the tale is that no program is ever totally predictable. (That's why he opposes military and other life and-death decision systems that are too fast for human intervention.)

I doubt that DARPA folklore features secretaries who kick the computer to make it work. Their expert systems to drive tanks, pilot planes and pick bombing targets deliberately circumvent the Gal Fridays, G.I. Joes and Admiral Moorers who might otherwise put their two cents in. (I wonder how much they spent on the expert system that allowed them to produce that weird white statue without an artist. Well, at least the results were predictable. You never know what an artist will come up with.)

To some planners it's the people, rather than the programs that are frighteningly unpredictable. To them, workers who can change things on the spot suggest menace, not security. Intelligent machines are reliable. Intelligent human beings are dangerous.

Right after World War II, Charles E. Wilson, the President of General Electric and Vice Chairman of the War Production Board said, "The problems of the United States can be captiously summed up in two words, 'Russia' abroad, 'labor' at home."

I used to have a dentist who said, "An empty mouth is a healthy mouth." To him, teeth got in the way. For some managers an empty factory is a healthy factory, an empty office is neat, efficient and predictable. Since the office can't be totally empty yet, they believe, at least let it not be filled with people who have the power to mess up the official plans.

Decision-making programs don't make decisions. The people who control them make the decisions. Artificial intelligence doesn't substitute computer intelligence for human intelligence: it substitutes some people's intelligence for others'. In the applications we're looking at, decision making is moved higher up on the chain of command and further away from visceral experience.

Many military reformers, both hawkish and dovish, oppose this high-strung expensive and centralized technology in the name of efficiency. It's no good in conventional war, they argue, because it impedes quick decisions in the field. Most of these critics happen to be located in the field.

The artificial intelligensia are located at military command centers and, by coincidence, this is where they think it's most efficient to place decision-making power.

Ultimately the arguments aren't based on efficiency. In the end it's a matter of faith and trust—or distrust. Centralizers are fearful of what ordinary people may do to their systems. Decentralizers are fearful of what those systems may do to us.

If you trust people then you'll want to leave as many decisions as possible with the man on the spot, partly because he's a man, partly because he's on the spot.

If you think labor is the enemy, or soldiers or secretaries or everybody besides yourself, then you will aim for strongly centralized command and control. If people are the problem, then an empty mouth is a healthy mouth.

Conclusion

□ □ □ □ □ □ □ □

It Could Be Different
(But It Probably Won't Be)

The underlying premise of modern automation is a profound distrust of thinking human beings. More than any particular technology, this unanalyzed prejudice against people determines the way work is organized.

In the modern factory, parts move continuously along an assembly line that human beings feed and tend as necessary. Everything seems bent on production. You may feel sympathy for the machine-paced humans along the line, but objecting to their condition is like objecting to the benefits of mass production. At this late date in the industrial age, it's almost impossible to walk through a functioning factory and separate the labor-saving from the labor-controlling devices. It all seems purposeful and of a piece.

Soon, when you walk into the fully automated office, it will seem equally ordained and complete. To object to the pace, the monitoring or the tiny scope of your own job will sound like a complaint against computers in general. Which is almost like objecting to electricity.

But there's a difference between an electric blanket and an electric chair.

Computers may be used in many ways. Like the sewing machine, the computer is just a tool. A sewing machine can be used by one person to make an entire dress. It can also be used in a sweatshop to sew zippers or right cuffs so fast and with such small, repetitious motions that the result is eye strain, neck ache and damage to the wrists.

During the first industrial revolution, manual workers like weavers, iron molders and sewing machine operators were systematically de-skilled, separated from decision making and frequently displaced or discarded. It was a horrible hundred years, justified in the name of progress. In place of "progress" a similar abstraction, "the economy," is used today to justify sacrifices by working people. Through a peculiar inverse anthropomorphism, "the economy" can somehow be doing well while the majority of people are doing poorly.

Eventually some of the superfluous suffering of the first industrial revolution was limited by labor unions and legislation restricting child labor, long hours and the more obvious physical hazards. But the basic organization of industry was never questioned. No union was in a position to say, "We want the sewing machine but not the sweatshop." By the time they looked, it was too late to see that an entirely different kind of efficiency might have been possible.

At this point in the history of white-collar automation, we can still discern some of the irrational, antihuman choices being made. A few years from now it will be difficult to see that there might have been other ways to use computers.

Hierarchical automation is arranged on the assumption that most people are lazy, stupid or hostile. All over the world, technology is controlled undemocratically by people who scorn, fear or simply want to use their fellow human beings.

But it seems clear to me that people want and need to work. The joy we feel in planning and carrying out a task is probably biological. Any system that expends so much money and energy on limiting instead of using human creativity has got to be inefficient. Yet the individuals now making the basic decisions about white-collar automation assume that the best way to run things is to further centralize control—with themselves in command.

Computer programs can be changed. There are many ways to combine the efficiency of computers with the skills and talents of human beings. Frankly, though, I doubt that our workplaces will change simply because we start dropping pro-people ideas into the suggestion box. The pull in the other direction is extremely powerful. Still, if we insist forcefully enough, perhaps it's not too late to say, "We want the computer but not the electronic sweatshop."

□ □ □ □ □ □ □ □

NOTES,
BIBLIOGRAPHY,
INDEX

Notes

□ □ □ □ □ □ □ □

CHAPTER 1

1. These statistics come from John F. Love, *McDonald's Behind the Golden Arches* (New York: Bantam, 1986). Additional background information in this chapter comes from Ray Kroc and Robert Anderson, *Grinding It Out* (Chicago: Contemporary Books, 1977), and Max Boas and Steve Chain, *Big Mac* (New York: Dutton, 1976).

2. Ray Kroc and Robert Anderson, *Grinding It Out* (Chicago: Contemporary Books, 1977), p. 176.

CHAPTER 3

1. Ida Hoos, *Systems Analysis in Public Policy* (Berkeley, Los Angeles, London: University of California Press, 1972, revised 1983), presents incisive and witty descriptions of the sometimes bizarre results when the systems method is applied to public problems like solid-waste disposal.

CHAPTER 4

1. Joseph Weizenbaum, *Computer Power and Human Reason: From Judgment to Calculation* (San Francisco: W. H. Freeman and Company, 1976). All quotations in the following section of this chapter come from Weizenbaum's book.
2. Quoted by Weizenbaum, from Carl Sagan, *Natural History,* vol. LXXXIV, no. 1 (Jan. 1975), p. 10.
3. Quoted by Weizenbaum, from K. M. Colby, J. B. Watt and J. P. Gilbert, "A Computer Method of Psychotherapy: Preliminary Communication," *The Journal of Nervous and Mental Disease,* vol. 142, no. 2 (1966), pp. 148–152.

CHAPTER 5

1. Arthur Miller, *Death of a Salesman,* Act II, copyright 1949 by Arthur Miller. Reprinted in *The Play: A Critical Anthology,* Eric Bentley, ed. (Englewood Cliffs, N.J.: Prentice-Hall, Inc., 1951), p. 688.

CHAPTER 7

1. *Business Week,* 6/30/75
2. Conversation between "Mary L_____" and the author, 1985.
3. "New Software Genre Planned: Major Corporations Fund 'White Collar' Productivity Development Project," *InfoWorld,* July 15, 1985.
4. These quotes are taken from the splendid summary of Taylor's principles found on pages 113–121 of Harry Braverman, *Labor and Monopoly Capital: The Degradation of Work in the Twentieth Century* (New York: Monthly Review Press, 1975).
5. I described some back-office jobs I held just before and during the introduction of computers in *All the Livelong Day: The Meaning and Demeaning of Routine Work* (New York: Penguin, 1977).
6. Harry Braverman, op. cit.
7. Datapro Research Corporation, "Evolving Office of the Future," *Office Automation Solutions* workbook (Delran, N.J.: Datapro, June 1978).
8. From a personal interview with Helms in 1980.

CHAPTER 8

1. *Women and Office Automation: Issues for the Decade Ahead.* U.S. Department of Labor, Office of the Secretary, Women's Bureau, 1985. The number of computer operators who are electronically monitored is a difficult piece of information to collect. I suspect that the two-thirds figure is high. I cite this statistic, not to insist on a particular percentage, but only to indicate that electronic surveillance is not a 2 percent aberration but a mainstream practice.

CHAPTER 9

1. Robert E. Kelley, *The Gold-Collar Worker: Managing Brainpower in Business* (Reading, Mass.: Addison-Wesley, 1985).

CHAPTER 10

1. The organization's purposes are to: "Support an effective but not excessive military program; eliminate waste in military spending; reduce military influence on U.S. domestic and foreign policy; avert nuclear war." Their bulletin, *The Defense Monitor,* is a well-written source of information on military policy.
2. David Noble, *Forces of Production: A Social History of Machine Tool Automation* (New York: Knopf, 1984).

Bibliography

□ □ □ □ □ □ □ □

There are thousands of books by people who love computers and a smaller but growing number of books concerned with hazards to computer workers. Unfortunately, the computer people and the people people don't usually talk to each other. In writing this book I've been inspired by the works of a few unusual experts who know and respect both human beings and their technology.

Harry Braverman's *Labor and Monopoly Capital: The Degradation of Work in the Twentieth Century* (New York: Monthly Review Press, 1975) is infused with a love of skill and craftsmanship. Harry Braverman worked as a machinist and in the early sixties designed one of the first programs to computerize orders, inventory and royalty payments in the publishing industry. He wrote about the degradation of labor in factories and offices not because he scorned ordinary work but because it meant so much to him.

Mike Cooley, *Architect or Bee?* Slough, England: Hand and Brain Publications, 1980. Reprinted Boston: South End Press, 1982. This collection of speeches and articles by a former Lucas Aerospace Engineer is poorly organized. Start on page 84. Here Cooley tells what happened when the employees at a declining factory tried to design new products that could be manufactured with the existing plant and workforce. As a result of consulting directly with shop floor workers, Lucas engineers became aware that their own engineering had been limited by the assumption that the workers' input should be as limited as possible. Freed from this unconscious premise, they quickly began to evolve not only new products and tools but entirely new manufacturing and programming principles.

Race Against Time: Automation of the Office, An Analysis of Trends in Office Automation and the Impact on the Office Workers. Cleveland: Working Women, 1980. This remarkably prescient report was prepared by Judy Gregory for Working Women (also known as "9 to 5"), at a time when office automation seemed a jumble of contradictory trends, claims and statistics. By a miracle of clarity Ms. Gregory was able to balance the projections of computer industry spokesmen with first-hand accounts from clerical workers to produce an accurate picture of the way office automation would develop. The report is still available and still relevant. It was in Judy Gregory's pamphlet that I first saw the phrase "The office of the future is juxtaposed with the factory of the past."

Ida Hoos, *Systems Analysis and Public Policy*. Berkeley, Los Angeles, London: University of California Press, 1972. Revised 1983. This is a witty and erudite description of the way systems analysis is used as a substitute for thinking. The examples come from public agencies that deal with services ranging from education and transportation to welfare, defense and garbage disposal. Unlike some officials at the agencies she studied, Ida Hoos is unintimidated by printout artists who juggle 25,000 bits of data that turn out to contain not one single fact. Mrs. Hoos is a traditionally educated humanist who draws from many years of experience with NASA and the Space Sciences Laboratory of the University of California.

David Noble, *Forces of Production*. New York: Knopf, 1984 and David Noble, *America By Design*. New York: Oxford University Press, 1979. David Noble demonstrates that the content of today's technology is determined not by natural paths of scientific inquiry or inevitable forces of progress but by those who hire and fire or fund the operation.

Joseph Weizenbaum, *Computer Power and Human Reason: From Judgment to Calculation.* San Francisco: W. H. Freeman and Company, 1976. Chapters 2 and 3 of this book are supposed to teach us how computers work. I suggest that you read the introduction about ELIZA and then skip to Chapter 4. The bulk of the book is an impassioned defense of human intelligence by a man who is credited with developing artificial intelligence but insists that there is no such thing.

Andrew Clement, "Electronic Management: The New Technology of Workplace Surveillance," *Session 84 Proceedings.* Canadian Information Processing Society, Toronto, Canada, 1984. In this and unpublished papers, Andrew Clement combines computer expertise with office research—both of which he shared with me. He teaches Computer Science at York University in North York, Ontario.

Barbara Baron and Pat McDermott gave me the benefit of their unpublished research. Among other things, Ms. Baron introduced me to the concept of the exception worker and Ms. McDermott pointed out the help yourself phenomenon in service automation. Barbara Abrash of the Institute for Research in History helped shape my ideas during the months in 1980 when we tried to produce a documentary about office automation.

Index

□ □ □ □ □ □ □ □ □

actuaries, expert systems for, 155

adjunct professors, 233

Air Canada, 51–60, 66, 70

  resistance to change at, 59–60

airline reservation agents, 41–70

  clients put on hold by, 48, 56–57

  electronic surveillance of, 45, 46–48, 51–60, 69, 215

  exception workers and, 59, 105

  information systems for, 68–69

  initiative and flexibility of, 54, 57, 60, 64–66, 69

  listening in on, 45, 47, 48–50, 52, 55, 62–64

  self-booking machines as replacements for, 57, 61

  standardized conversations of, 41–42, 45–49, 57–66

  uniformity of, 60–61, 65

  unions of, 51–52, 55, 58, 59–60

  wages of, 44, 45, 50, 59

  work schedules of, 50–51, 62, 225

American Airlines, 11, 12, 42–51, 54, 126, 166

American Airlines (*cont.*)
  computer screens at, 68–69
  managers at, 61–70
  reservation agents at, 42,
    43–51
Anderson, Jack, 252
Applied Expert Systems Inc.
  (APEX), 122
artificial intelligence, 116,
  119, 260
  cost efficiency of, 167–68
  military research on, 253–
  256
  see also expert systems:
    financial expert systems
AT&T, 166, 207
Auto Assess, Inc., 156–58
automatic pilots, 119, 255
automation, 109
  control as goal of, 11, 113,
    159, 167, 169–69, 178
  of conversation, 42
  of decision making, 120–
    121, 168
  elimination of drudge work
    as goal of, 104–5
  exception workers and,
    105–6, 110
  help yourself approach in,
    57, 61, 90, 101, 103, 157
  of human services, 74–159
  industrial, 74, 109, 165,
    168
  mechanization stage in, 74
  of offices, 163–204
  rationalization stage in, 74–
    75, 109
  of social workers, 74–76,

    84, 90, 100–101, 102,
    103, 106–14, 115–16
automobile production, 109,
  168

bank loan officers, expert
  systems for, 155
block modeling, 210
Blue Cross/Blue Shield, 113
bombing targets, picking of,
  245, 250–51, 254
Boyd, ("Mad") John, 246,
  258
Braverman, Harry, 171
brokerage firms:
  asset gathering as goal of,
    129
  clients' ties to stockbrokers
    vs., 128–29, 130, 134,
    135, 137, 139, 141–42,
    146, 153, 154
  expert systems and, 128–54
  stockbrokers pressured by,
    136–37, 143
  stockbrokers turned into
    financial planners by,
    129–30, 131
  transferring assets out of,
    137, 138–39
  see also Merrill Lynch;
    Shearson Lehman
    Brothers; stockbrokers

CAD (computer-aided
  design), 184, 228
calendar forms, 222
Cambodia, secret bombing of,
  238–39

Canadian Postal Workers Union, 113

Carroll, Eugene, 250–52, 258

centralization:
airline reservation agents and, 66
in command and control, 237–60
of decision making, 11, 156, 166, 168, 241–42
inefficiency of, 257–58, 260
personal computers and, 206–7
in U.S. industries, 257

chain of command, 251, 252

change, expert systems and, 126

Chaplin, Charlie, 224

Cheap Hawks, 246–50, 258

checkout lines, 225

China, 48
accidental bombing of, 250, 251–52, 258

Choate, Natalie, 121–24, 125

clerks:
in fifties, 169–70, 235
foreign workers and, 235–236
social workers downgraded to, 74, 75–76
in Victorian era, 169

clothing, mass-production of, 157, 158

CMAs (Cash Management Accounts), 129, 136–37

CollegeBuilder, 134, 147, 149–52

command and control, in the U.S. military, 119, 237–260
corporate decision making compared to, 241–42
expert systems and, 252–256, 259, 260
jargon of, 245
leadership development hindered by, 242, 247–248
and micromanagement from Washington, 240–43
nuclear strategy and, 243, 251, 252
in Vietnam War, 238–39, 241, 242, 243, 245, 247–249, 250–52

computer-aided design (CAD), 184, 228

computer consultants, 229–231, 232, 233

Computer Power and Human Reason (Weizenbaum), 116

computers:
advantages of, over people, 255–56
as decision makers, 238
hierarchical networks and, 206–7, 212–14
integrated computing and, 207–15
introduced into front office, 171, 207
mainframe, 206, 231
multiple numerical ratings made possible by, 146–147

computers (*cont.*)
  personal, 206–7
  see also specific topics
Computers and Privacy
    Conference, 220
Congress, U.S., 238, 239, 242
consultants, *see* freelancers and
    consultants
Consumer Union, 156
control:
  as goal of automation, 11,
    113, 159, 167, 168–69,
    178
  integrated computing as
    mechanism for, 207
  personal computers and,
    206–7
conversation, 115
  ELIZA as parody of, 116–
    119, 120, 156
  standardization of, 41–42,
    45–49, 57–66
cost efficiency, automation
    and, 166–68
Creative Socio-Medics Corp.,
    156

DARPA (Defense Advanced
    Research Projects
    Agency), 12, 244–45,
    252–56, 259
databases, personal
    information in, 220
Data General Corporation,
    203
decision making:
  automation of, 120–21,
    168

centralization of, 11, 156,
    166, 168, 241–42
  by computers, 238
Defense Advanced Research
    Projects Agency
    (DARPA), 12, 244–45,
    252–56, 259
Defense Department, U.S.,
    106, 114, 208–9, 249,
    252, 253, 257
  computer research at, 244–
    245, 252–56, 259
DeLucia, Gene, 106–9, 110
Dictaphone, 222
divorce, 233
Donahue, Dan, 139–40
Doonan, J. Peter, 203

Eisenhower, Dwight D., 256
electronic mail (E-mail), 209–
    211, 222
electronic surveillance, 205–
    224
  of airline reservation agents,
    45, 46–48, 51–60, 69,
    215
  to discipline workers, 216–
    220, 223
  human supervision vs.,
    218–20, 223
  of managers, 66–68, 69–
    70, 205–24, 238
  methods to prevent, 213–
    215
  of phone systems, 221–
    222
  privacy issue and, 214,
    220–24

regulated in Europe, 215
of secretaries, 212–15; *see
   also* keystroke counts
of social workers, 84, 107,
   108, 111–13
of stockbrokers, 143–44,
   146–47, 215
stress-related illnesses and,
   113, 215, 221
unions and, 113, 219
ELIZA, 116–19, 120, 156
artificial intelligence notion
   and, 119
example of conversation
   with, 117–18
human therapists vs., 118–
   119
responses to, 118–19
E-mail (electronic mail), 209–
   211, 222
employee benefits, 234–35
engineers, measuring
   productivity of, 164–
   165
entrepreneurialism, of
   freelancers and
   consultants, 227–32
estate planning, expert systems
   for, 121–25, 126, 127
exception workers:
   in airline reservations, 59,
      105
   service automation and,
      105–6, 110
expert systems, 116–59, 166,
   252
   building of, 120–21, 133–
      134, 254–55

change and diversity
   discouraged by, 126
circumstances when
   infeasible, 254
cost efficiency of, 167–68
ELIZA, 116–19, 120,
   156
financial, 121–54, 156,
   238, 253; *see also* financial
   expert systems
human learning vs., 125–26
in industrial settings, 119–
   120
intuition and, 121, 122–23
as means to control workers,
   159, 168
for medical diagnosis, 120
for methadone maintenance
   clinics, 156–58
military, 119, 166, 252–56,
   259, 260
for probation officers, 155
unpredictability of, 259
updating of, 126
for Workers' Compensation
   judges, 155
Exxon, 207

feminism, 195, 202, 203
Fields, Craig, 252–56
financial expert systems, 121–
   154, 156, 238, 253
   building of, 120–21, 133–
      134
   CollegeBuilder, 134, 147,
      149–52
   for estate planning, 121–
      125, 126, 127

financial expert systems (*cont.*)
  and losses due to
    inexperience, 152
  at Merrill Lynch, 11, 130,
    133–34, 136, 147–52
  Shearson's PRO, 130–33,
    147, 156
  for stockbrokers, 128–54
  stockbrokers' resistance to,
    130–34, 153
  stockbrokers' status and,
    129–30, 131
  stockbrokers who use, 147–
    153
Fonda, Jane, 244
food stamps, 89–90
Forces of Production (Noble),
  257
Ford, Henry, 109
Franco, Francisco, 244
freelancers and consultants,
  226–36
  adjunct professors, 233
  and advantages of flexible
    labor force, 225–26
  computer, consultants,
    229–31, 232, 233
  cores of U.S. corporations
    and, 235–36
  leveraging by, 231–32
  psychological adjustments
    made by, 233–35
  retooling by, 229
  and routinization of jobs,
    226
  wage workers in first
    industrial revolution
    compared to, 232–33

Gamble, James, 182
General Motors, 60, 168
Gilbreth, Frank, 120
Gold-Collar Worker, The
  (Kelley), 231–32
Great Britain, "work to rule"
  job actions in, 102
Grenada invasion, 245
Grinding It Out (Kroc), 21
GTE, 164–65

Hamburger Central, 18, 30,
  31
Helms, Hans, 178
Henderson, Bruce, 122, 124–
  125
hierarchical programming,
  206–7, 212–14
Hitler, Adolf, 241, 248
Ho Chi Minh Trail, 246
HomeBuilder, 134
Honda, 168
human contact, minimized by
  automation, 115, 157
human services:
  automation of, 74–159
  psychological, 116–19,
    120, 156–58
  see also social workers;
    stockbrokers

IBM, 182, 189, 190, 199,
  207, 232
  middle management as
    target of, 178
  office of future as
    envisioned by, 163, 176–
    177, 183, 199

industrial revolution, 165, 166, 169, 262
  transition to wage workers in, 232–33
industry:
  automation in, 74, 109, 165, 168
  centralization in, 257
  expert systems in, 119–20
  numerical control systems in, 257
  supervision and surveillance in, 221
information:
  managers' access to, 209–13
  military, 239, 240, 242
information systems, 211–12
  for airline reservation agents, 68–69
  for social workers, 82, 84
  for stockbrokers, 133
InfoWorld, 163
initiative:
  of airline reservation agents, 54, 57, 60, 64–66, 69
  of McDonald's workers, 19–20, 27, 35–37, 38
  of word processors, 174, 199
integrated computing, 207–15
  as control mechanism, 207
  E-mail and, 209–11
  spying on subordinates with, 211–15
  word processing in, 207–8, 212–15
intuition, expert systems and, 121, 122–23

Japan:
  "lifetime" employees in, 226
  numerical control systems in, 257
Johnson, Lyndon B., 238–39, 242, 244
Journal of Nervous and Mental Disease, The, 118

Kelley, Robert E., 231–32
keystroke counts, 10, 167, 170, 174, 189–90, 194, 207–8, 215, 221
Kissinger, Henry, 244
Kroc, Ray, 21, 36–37

Labor and Monopoly Capital (Braverman), 171
Labor Department, U.S., 223
language, learning of, 125–26
Lanier, 222
Laughlin, William F., 163
learning process, 125–26
leveraging, by brain workers, 231–32
living together, 233–34

McDonald's 12, 17–41, 60, 115, 126, 166
  burger production at, 17–20, 36, 41, 237
  cashiers at, 23–29, 35–36, 38
  cash register races at, 30–31
  computerized cash registers at, 28, 30
  computerized management at, 31, 36–37, 39

McDonald's (*cont.*)
  crew labor productivity at,
      31–32, 33, 34–35
  french fry production at, 11,
      20–23
  initiative and creativity at,
      19–20, 27, 35–37, 38
  managers at, 29–39, 237–
      238
  media hotline of, 38–39
  overtime taboo at, 34
  scheduling of workers at,
      22, 23, 25–26, 31–33,
      34, 36, 225
  standardization by, 41
  training of labor force at,
      22–23, 26, 40
  turnover of workers at, 19,
      28–29, 32, 33, 40, 227,
      234
  unpaid time at, 22, 25–26,
      34
  wages paid by, 25, 26, 30,
      40
McNamara, Robert, 209, 241,
      242, 244, 246, 258
mainframe computers, 206,
      231
managers:
  computers resisted by,
      245
  costs of, 175
  electronic surveillance of,
      66–68, 69–70, 205–24,
      238
  functions of, 175
  information access of, 209–
      213

middle, as target of office
    automation, 178, 197
  numerical ratings for, 163–
      165, 175–76
  without secretaries, 200–
      202
  secretaries' relationships
      with, 173, 175–78, 179,
      185–97, 198–99, 202–4
  travel arrangements for,
      185, 187
Martino, Louis, 21
Massachusetts Department of
    Social Services (DSS), 75,
    90–91, 94, 103–6
Massachusetts Public
    Assistance Control
    System (MPACS), 106–
    109, 110–11, 113, 114
Massachusetts Welfare
    Department, 75, 76–103,
    104, 106–14, 115–16
  point system in, 78–84, 86,
      88, 89, 92, 93, 99–100,
      101, 102, 104, 106, 109
  social workers in, 76–98,
      103, 110–14
  supervisors in, 83, 98–102
  systems group in, 106–9
Mastermind, 222
McOpCo (McDonald's
    Operating Company),
    29
mechanization, 74
Medicaid, 157
medical diagnosis, expert
    systems for, 120
Merrill Lynch, 12, 127, 133–

137, 143, 144, 153, 158, 253

CMAs at, 129, 136–37

computerized aids for brokers at, 11, 130, 133–134, 136, 147–52

salaried brokers at, 139–40

stockbrokers turned into financial planners by, 129–30, 131

Merrill Lynch Advanced Office Systems (ML/AOS), 133–34

methadone maintenance clinics, expert systems for, 156–58

micro computers, 206–7

military, 237–60

chain of command in, 251, 252

civilian bosses and, 243, 244

computerized war games and, 240

expert systems for, 119, 166, 252–56, 259, 260

logistical concerns of, 239–240, 241

reformers in, 246–50, 258, 260

see also command and control

military/industrial complex, 256–57

Modern Times, 224

monitoring, *see* electronic surveillance

moonlighting, 232

Moorer, Thomas H., 238–45, 246, 252, 254, 255, 259

Mother Jones, 179

MPACS (Massachusetts Public Assistance Control System), 106–9, 110–11, 113, 114

National Bureau of Standards, 168

Naval College (Newport), 240

news writers, temps as, 226

Noble, David, 257

nuclear strategy, 243, 251, 252

numerical control systems, 257

numerical ratings:

of airline reservation agents, 45, 46–48, 51–60, 63–64

keystroke counts, 10, 167, 170, 174, 189–90, 194, 207–8, 215, 221

of managers, 163–65, 175–176

multiple, made possible by computers, 146–47

of social workers, 78–84, 86, 88, 89, 92, 93, 99–100, 101, 102, 104, 106, 109

of stockbrokers, 143–44, 146–47

Objective Matrix (OM), 164

Office Automation Conference, 196–97

offices:
  automation of, 163–204
  back, organized on factory model, 169–71
  electronic surveillance in, 205–24
  front, computers introduced into, 171, 207
  measuring efficiency of, 167
  in nineteenth century, 169–170
  see also, managers; secretaries; word processing
OM (Objective Matrix), 164

Paine Webber, 143
Parade Magazine, 252
part-timers, 226, 235
PASER, 51, 54, 55
PathFinder, 130, 134, 136, 147, 148–49, 156
Pentagon, *see* Defense Department, U.S.
personal computers, 206–7
Personal Review Outline, *see* PRO
piece-work systems, 79
pilots, automatic, 119, 255
PlanPower, 121–25, 126, 127
  building of, 122–23
  use of, 123–25
Principles of Scientific Management, The (Taylor), 165
privacy rights:
  in private life, 220, 221
  at work, 214, 220–24

PRO (Personal Review Outline), 130–133, 147, 156
  designing of, 131
  selling to sales force, 130–133
probation officers, expert systems for, 155
Procter, William, 182
Procter & Gamble (P&G), 12, 179–98, 226–27, 229, 230, 232, 234
  accelerated attrition at, 184–85
  history of, 182–83
  word processing experiment of, 179–82, 186–98
Procter & Gamble Administrative Services, 179–81, 185–98
  accountability in, 189
  assertiveness training in, 193
  boss-secretary relationship broken by, 179, 186, 191–93, 195–96
  circumventing of system in, 187–89, 197
  correction process in, 186–187, 193
  disbanding of, 198
  efficiency of, 189–90
  friendships and, 187–88
  production reports of, 194–195, 197–98
  supervisors in, 180–81, 190–96
  travel arrangements and, 187

productivity:
  creativity and, 164–65
  measuring of, 163–65; *see also* electronic surveillance; numerical ratings
Productivity Map, 163–65
programmers, 232
  measuring productivity of, 164
programming, hierarchical, 206–7, 212–14
Prudential-Bache, 129, 143
PSYCH SCANS, 156–58

quotas, 218–19
  for social workers, 79, 83, 93, 98, 108

rationalization, 74–75, 109
retirees, as flexible labor force, 225
retooling, by freelancers and consultants, 229
Rogerian therapists, ELIZA and, 116–19, 120, 156

Sagan, Carl, 118
Saturn plant (General Motors), 168
scanning systems, 225
secretaries, 172–204
  bosses' relationships with, 173, 175–78, 179, 185–197, 198–99, 202–4
  doing without, 200–202
  electronic surveillance of, 212–15; *see also* keystroke counts
  male-female dynamics and, 192, 193, 203–4
  nonmonetary rewards for, 192
  personal services performed by, 191, 202–3
  reduced to receptionists, 202
  reduced to word processors, 172–74, 176–82
  replaced by machines, 200–4
  save-the-day stories about, 258–59
  see also word processing
self-booking machines, 57, 61
Senate Armed Services Committee, 238, 239
Shearson Lehman Brothers, 127, 138–39, 143, 153, 253
  PRO of, 130–33, 147, 156
  stockbrokers turned into financial planners by, 129–30, 131
Shop Management (Taylor), 165
short-order cooks, 41
Simpson, John, 168
Smythe, Paul, 166
social workers, 73–114, 155
  automation of, 74–76, 84, 90, 100–101, 102, 103, 106–14, 115–16
  bureaucratic procedures fought by, 86–90
  communication skills of, 93–97

social workers (*cont.*)
 discretion of, 102, 103, 108
 downgraded to clerks, 74,
  75–76
 electronic surveillance of,
  84, 107, 108, 111–13
 exception workers and,
  105–6
 food stamp calculations and,
  89–90
 house calls made by, 94–95
 information systems for, 82,
  84
 job titles of, 75, 115–16
 point system for, 78–84,
  86, 88, 89, 92, 93, 99–
  100, 101, 102, 104, 106,
  109
 productivity standards for,
  in future, 107–8
 quotas for, 79, 83, 93, 98,
  108
 rationalization process and,
  74–75, 109
 supervisors of, 83, 98–102
 time-and-motion studies on,
  75, 76, 78
 unions of, 99, 100, 101,
  102, 107, 111, 112
 wages of, 78, 104
 work style of, in past, 73
Stalin, Joseph, 248
standardization:
 of conversation, 41–42,
  45–49, 57–66
 by McDonald's, 41
 of management jobs, 69–70
 of office work, 169

STAR, 51–52, 54, 56, 57
stockbrokers, 128–54, 238
 analysts and research reports
  for, 143
 clients' ties to firms vs.,
  128–29, 130, 134, 135,
  137, 139, 141–42, 146,
  153, 154
 computerized monitoring
  of, 143–44, 146–47,
  215
 earnings of, 139
 expert systems resisted by,
  130–34, 153
 firms' pressure on, 136–37,
  143
 as independent professionals
  vs. employees, 128
 information systems for,
  133
 losses and, 152
 private programs developed
  by, 135, 145
 salaried, 139–40, 145, 153
 as trusted advisors to clients,
  142–43, 144–45, 147
 turned into financial
  planners, 129–30, 131
 who use expert systems,
  147–53
 work methods of, 140–41
Strategic Computer Initiative,
  253
stress-related illnesses, 113,
  180, 215, 221
supermarkets, checkout lines
  in, 225
Supervision IV, 222

Surveillance, 222
Sweden, automation of
welfare workers in, 113
systems, analysis, 106, 108–
109, 209, 237

Taylor, Frederick, 120, 165,
166, 167
telephone systems, 221–22
television, interactive, 220
temps, 226, 235
therapy, ELIZA and, 116–19,
120, 156
time-and-motion studies, 74,
120
on office work, 170
on social workers, 75, 76,
78
Tower Systems International,
222
Toyota, 168
travel arrangements, 185, 187
Travelers Insurance Company,
122

uniformity:
of airline reservation agents
responses, 60–61, 65
in financial services, 130,
144
unions:
of airline reservation agents,
51–52, 55, 58, 59–60
electronic surveillance and,
113, 219
in first industrial revolution,
232, 233, 262

of social workers, 99, 100,
101, 102, 107, 111,
112
"work to rule" job actions
of, 102

Vietnam War, 244, 246–49
accidental bombing of
China in, 250, 251–52,
258
body-counts in, 249
command and control in,
238–39, 241, 242, 243,
245, 247–49, 250–52
number crunching in, 249,
251
picking of targets in, 245,
250–51
secret bombing of
Cambodia in, 238–39
VisiCalc, 206

Wallace, Mike, 242
Wang, 182, 189, 207
war games, 240
Weizenbaum, Joseph, 116–
119, 258
Westmoreland, William C.,
242
Wilson, Charles E., 259
word processing, 167, 171,
172–74
bosses split from secretaries
by, 176–78, 179, 186,
191–93, 195–97
in integrated computing,
207–8, 212–15

word processing (*cont.*)
  keystroke counts and, 167,
    174, 189–90, 194, 207–
    208, 215, 221
  P&G's experiment with,
    179–82, 186–98
Workers' Compensation
    judges, expert systems for,
    155

"work to rule" job actions,
    102
World War II, 241, 248,
    258
writers, freelance, 226, 228–
    229

Xerox, 178, 207